To Michelle on her engagement:
Best wishes for your
future with Zach

2011

Love from Granjam

THE OLD FARMER'S GARDEN-FRESH COOKBOOK ALMANAC

Fresh-from-the-garden flavor all year long!

Copyright © 2011 by Yankee Publishing Inc. All rights reserved. No part of this publication may be reproduced or transmitted in any form or by any means, electronic or mechanical, including photocopy, recording, or any other information storage and retrieval system, without the written permission of the publisher.

The Old Farmer's Almanac Books

Publisher: Sherin Pierce

Editor: Janice Stillman
Project manager: Heidi Stonehill
Art director: Margo Letourneau
Copy editor: Jack Burnett
Editorial staff: Mare-Anne Jarvela, Sarah Perreault, Amy Nieskens
Interns: Molly Buccini, Greg Danner, Sara Schultz
Indexer: Samantha A. Miller

compiled by Heidi Stonehill

V.P., New Media and Production: Paul Belliveau
Production directors: Susan Gross, David Ziarnowski
Production artists: Lucille Rines, Rachel Kipka, Janet Grant

Web site: Almanac.com
Web editor: Catherine Boeckmann; **Web designer:** Lou Eastman
Web design associate: Amy Bidder; **Online marketing manager:** David Weisberg
Programming: Reinvented, Inc.

Photography:
Full-page food photography: Becky Luigart-Stayner
Food stylist: Ana Kelly
Prop stylist: Jan Gautro

Illustrations, cover and inside: Kim Kurki

photo, previous two pages: Karen Bussolini

For additional information about this and other publications from The Old Farmer's Almanac, visit **Almanac.com** or call **1-800-ALMANAC**.

distributed in the book trade by Houghton Mifflin Harcourt

Yankee Publishing Inc., P.O. Box 520,
1121 Main Street, Dublin, New Hampshire 03444

Thank you for buying this cookbook! Thanks, too, to everyone who had a hand in it, including printers, distributors, and sales and delivery people.

ISBN/EAN: 978-1-57198-541-5

first edition

Printed in the United States of America

A Guarantee of Goodness Every Day...

To create delicious meals, you need great recipes at your fingertips, and *The Old Farmer's Almanac Garden-Fresh Cookbook* serves up a heaping helping.

To get great taste, you need fresh, nutritious ingredients—vegetables, fruit, and herbs at the peak of flavor—and whether you buy these at a local market or grow your own, the advice on these pages will help you to bring home a ripe and wholesome harvest.

It's all here in this colorful edition:

- nearly 350 recipes, both new and classic selections, that celebrate the season's bounty

- timesaving tips and helpful hints on how to successfully grow vegetables, kitchen herbs, edible flowers, and berries

- recommendations on ripeness, whether you pick off the vine or purchase at the farmers' market or grocery

- how-to help on making healthy choices and preparing nourishing dishes

- plus, handy charts on storing fresh and prepared foods, measuring fresh vs. cooked produce, changing pan sizes, substituting common ingredients, and more!

Growing, cooking, and sharing the goodness of the farm and garden has been the mission of *The Old Farmer's Almanac* since 1792. With the *Garden-Fresh Cookbook,* we endeavor to continue this tradition for new generations. We hope that you enjoy many pleasurable hours sifting through the pages of this collection and turning garden-fresh ingredients into kitchen-delicious menus, meals, and treats for family and friends. We welcome your comments at **Almanac.com/Feedback.**

The Editors of *The Old Farmer's Almanac*

Contents

FOREWORD 5

CHAPTER 1: Breakfast & Brunch 8

CHAPTER 2: Appetizers, Dips, & Spreads 25

CHAPTER 3: Soups 38

CHAPTER 4: Salads 69

CHAPTER 5: Vegetable Dishes 100

CHAPTER 6: Canning & Preserving 149

CHAPTER 7: Poultry 173

CHAPTER 8: Meats 191

CHAPTER 9: Fish & Seafood 203

CHAPTER 10: Pasta & Rice 215

CHAPTER 11: Sauces & Condiments 230

Vermont Butternut Squash Soup, page 47

White Bean and Tuna Salad, page 77

CHAPTER 12: Breads **244**

CHAPTER 13: Desserts **261**

CHAPTER 14: Beverages **296**

SPECIAL SECTIONS:

    A Kitchen Herb Garden **36**

    A Beginner's Vegetable Garden **98**

    An Edible Flower Garden.................................. **242**

    A Berry Garden... **294**

Reference **304**

Sources.. **320**

Index... **321**

Strawberry Crunch Muffins, page 248

Cranberry Pears, page 271

CHAPTER 1

Breakfast & Brunch

Granola With Sunflower Seeds 9

Scandinavian Asparagus Soufflé With

    Creamy Butter Sauce 10

Scrambled Eggs With Creamed Spinach 11

Chile Cheese Casserole 11

Pepper Eggs and Tortillas 12

Crabmeat Omelet 12

Crostada 13

Mexican Quiche 14

Chicken Quiche 14

Broccoli Quiche 16

Basic Crepes 16

Shrimp and Asparagus Crepes 17

Fancy Crepes With Berries in Grand

    Marnier Syrup 19

Apple Crepes à la Mode 20

Fruit Salad 20

Watermelon Basket With Honey Lime

    Dressing 21

Fruit Salad With Pineapple Sage 22

Apple Fritters 22

Blueberry Pancakes 23

Parsnip Griddle Cakes 24

All happiness depends on a leisurely breakfast.

–John Gunther, American journalist (1901–70)

Granola With Sunflower Seeds

½ **cup canola oil**

½ **cup honey or molasses**

½ **cup flaxseed**

6 **cups rolled oats**

1 **cup coarsely chopped pecans**

¾ **cup hulled, unsalted sunflower seeds**

¾ **cup wheat germ**

Preheat the oven to 350°F. In a large saucepan over low heat, combine the oil and honey and stir until warm. Turn off the heat. One by one, stirring to coat each thoroughly, add the flaxseed, oats, pecans, and sunflower seeds. Spread the mixture onto an ungreased, rimmed cookie sheet (two, if necessary) and bake for 15 minutes. Mix in the wheat germ and bake for an additional 15 to 20 minutes, or until lightly browned, stirring every 5 minutes or so. Remove from the oven and let the granola cool on the cookie sheets. Store in an airtight canister in the refrigerator for up to 6 months. **Makes 9 cups.**

How to Harvest: Sunflower Seeds

■ **Sunflower seeds are ready to harvest when they are plump and the back of the flower head is brown and dry. Cut the flower head off the stalk, taking about 1 foot of stalk. Rub the seeds over a plate or box; they should fall off easily. Store them in a sealed container.**

Scandinavian Asparagus Soufflé With Creamy Butter Sauce

SOUFFLÉ:

1 pound asparagus, trimmed
5 tablespoons butter
½ cup all-purpose flour
1¾ cups milk, scalded
4 large eggs, separated
salt and pepper, to taste
heaping ½ teaspoon baking powder

SAUCE:

½ cup (1 stick) butter
a few drops of fresh lemon juice
parsley, for garnish

For soufflé: Preheat the oven to 400°F. Grease a 2- or 3-quart soufflé dish. Cook the asparagus in boiling, salted water for 4 to 6 minutes, or until just tender. Drain, then chop the stalks into 1-inch pieces. In a saucepan over low heat, melt the butter and add the flour, stirring to blend. Gradually stir in the milk and cook gently, stirring, until thickened. Cook for an additional 2 to 3 minutes, stirring constantly. Remove the saucepan from the heat. In a medium bowl, beat the egg yolks. Pour them into the saucepan, stirring to blend. Add the asparagus, season with salt and pepper, and stir to coat the asparagus. Set aside to cool for 15 to 20 minutes. In a large bowl, beat the egg whites until foamy, add the baking powder, and beat until stiff. Gently fold a portion of the whites into the asparagus mixture. Add the asparagus mixture to the remaining whites, folding gently to combine. Pour into the prepared soufflé dish. Bake for 45 to 60 minutes.

For sauce: Warm a small bowl by pouring boiling water into it and letting the water sit for 15 to 20 seconds. Then empty and dry, reserving a spoonful of water. In the bowl, immediately beat the butter with a couple of drops of warm water until the butter is creamy white. Beat in the lemon juice. Put the butter sauce into a small crock or bowl and garnish with parsley.

Serve the soufflé hot, with the butter sauce on the side. **Makes 6 servings.**

In the Kitchen: Asparagus

■ Before cooking asparagus, cut or break off about an inch of the tough stalk. Use a potato peeler to peel thick stalks; thin stalks do not need to be peeled.

Scrambled Eggs With Creamed Spinach

8 tablespoons (1 stick) unsalted butter, divided
¼ pound spinach, stemmed and shredded
1 tablespoon heavy cream
12 eggs
salt and pepper, to taste

Melt a tablespoon of butter in a large saucepan. Add the spinach and cook over low heat for 3 to 5 minutes, or until the spinach is wilted and the liquid evaporates. Stir in the cream and cook for 1 to 2 minutes, or until the cream thickens slightly. Cover the saucepan and set aside. Prepare a hot water bath by filling a 13x9-inch roasting pan with water. Bring the water to a simmer on the stove top. Beat the eggs in a bowl. Season with salt and pepper. In a separate saucepan, melt the remaining butter. Set the saucepan in the water bath. Pour the eggs into the saucepan and cook gently. As the eggs thicken on the bottom and sides, stir and scrape the saucepan constantly with a wooden spoon. Continue until the eggs are thick but still moist, about 15 minutes. Add more salt and pepper, if desired. Spoon the eggs onto warm plates and add a dollop of the spinach mixture to each portion. **Makes 4 servings.**

How to Harvest: Spinach

■ For best results, harvest spinach on the day that you plan to use it. For a longer harvest, select only the outside leaves and let those in the center of the plant mature.

Chile Cheese Casserole

4 large chiles, or 1 can (7 ounces) whole green chiles
2 cups grated longhorn or sharp cheddar cheese, divided
2 eggs, separated
salt and pepper, to taste

Preheat the oven to 350°F. Grease a 1½-quart casserole or four single-serve, ovenproof dishes. Remove and discard the seeds from the chiles. Stuff each chile with grated cheese, reserving about ½ cup. Place the chiles in the casserole and cover with the remaining cheese. Beat the egg yolks and season with salt and pepper. Beat the egg whites in a separate bowl until stiff and fold them into the yolks. Spread the egg mixture over the cheese. Bake for 30 minutes, or until the eggs set. **Makes 4 servings.**

Pepper Eggs and Tortillas

5 extra-large eggs

salt and pepper, to taste

2 tablespoons corn oil

½ small onion, minced

1 clove garlic, minced

1 cayenne pepper, stemmed, seeded,
  and minced, or ⅛ teaspoon
  cayenne pepper

2 small corn tortillas, cut in half and
  then crosswise into ½-inch strips

⅔ cup grated sharp cheddar cheese

2 tablespoons chopped fresh cilantro, divided

salsa *(see recipe, page 239)*

In a small bowl, beat the eggs and season with salt and pepper. In a skillet over medium heat, warm the oil, add the onion, then sauté until soft. Add the garlic and cayenne pepper and cook, stirring, for 2 to 3 minutes. Add the tortilla strips, stirring until they absorb the oil and soften. Add the eggs, stirring constantly until they start to set. Add the cheese and 1 tablespoon of cilantro. Continue cooking, stirring constantly, until desired doneness is reached. Sprinkle with the remaining cilantro and serve with salsa. **Makes 2 to 3 servings.**

Fun Food Fact: Cilantro

■ **Cilantro seeds have been found in ancient Egyptian tombs, suggesting that it has been grown for more than 3,000 years.**

Crabmeat Omelet

FILLING:

2 tablespoons crabmeat

2 to 3 drops fresh lemon juice

EGG MIXTURE:

3 eggs

1 teaspoon milk

salt and pepper, to taste

1 tablespoon chopped fresh cilantro

1 tablespoon chopped fresh parsley

1 tablespoon butter

For filling: In a small bowl, combine the crabmeat and lemon juice. Mix to blend and set aside.

For egg mixture: In a separate bowl, combine the eggs with the milk and beat until foamy. Add the salt and pepper and beat to blend. Add the cilantro and parsley and stir.

In a skillet over medium heat, melt the butter. When the foaming subsides, pour the egg mixture into the skillet. As the eggs set, use a spatula to lift the firm portions and allow the liquid egg to make contact with the skillet and cook. Continue to free the edges of the omelet, tilting the skillet until the omelet can slide. Place the filling on one half of the omelet, then fold the other half over on top of it. Cook until the inside of the omelet is firm, about 1 to 2 minutes. Turn onto a serving dish. **Makes 2 servings.**

Crostada

8 ounces salami or other Italian
    sandwich meat, thinly sliced and
    cut into strips
½ cup sliced black olives
¾ cup peeled, seeded, and chopped
    Italian plum tomatoes
1 tablespoon chopped fresh parsley
1 teaspoon all-purpose flour
salt and pepper, to taste
pinch of dried oregano
½ cup grated Romano or Parmesan
    cheese
½ cup grated fontina cheese
3 eggs
1½ cups cream
1 unbaked 9-inch piecrust *(see recipe,
    page 272)*

Preheat the oven to 375°F. In a large bowl, combine the first nine ingredients and stir to blend. In a separate bowl, beat the eggs and cream together. Pour the egg mixture into the large bowl and stir to blend. Pour into the piecrust and bake for 25 to 30 minutes, or until a toothpick inserted into the center comes out clean. Let stand for 10 minutes before serving. **Makes 6 to 8 servings.**

In the Kitchen: Parsley

■ Parsley comes in curly and Italian, or
    flatleaf *(right)*, types. They can be used
    interchangeably in recipes, although
    some cooks prefer the slightly sweeter
    taste of the Italian type.

Mexican Quiche

½ cup grated cheddar cheese

1 unbaked 9-inch piecrust
   (see recipe, page 272)

1 tablespoon vegetable oil

1 small onion, chopped

1 small green bell pepper, chopped

2 cloves garlic, minced

1 small tomato, diced

7 black olives, pitted and sliced

½ cup corn

2 teaspoons chili powder

1 teaspoon cumin

½ teaspoon dried oregano

salt and pepper, to taste

6 eggs

1 pint whipping cream

sour cream and picante sauce,
   for garnish

Preheat the oven to 350°F. Sprinkle the cheese onto the piecrust. In a skillet, heat the oil and sauté the onion, green pepper, garlic, tomato, olives, and corn until tender. Add the chili powder, cumin, oregano, and salt and pepper and stir to blend. Spread the vegetables over the cheese in the piecrust. In a separate bowl, beat the eggs until frothy, add the cream and beat to blend. Pour the egg mixture over the vegetables. Bake for 1 hour and 10 minutes, or until the eggs are firm in the center. Let stand for 10 minutes. Garnish with dollops of sour cream mixed with picante sauce. **Makes 6 to 8 servings.**

Chicken Quiche

1 unbaked 9-inch piecrust *(see recipe, page 272)*

1½ cups diced cooked chicken

1 tablespoon minced celery

2 shallots, minced

4 eggs

2 cups whipping cream

dash of hot sauce

salt and pepper, to taste

½ cup grated Gruyère or Swiss cheese

Preheat the oven to 450°F. Bake the piecrust for 5 minutes—and no longer, or the crust will shrink. Remove from the oven and set aside to cool. In a bowl, combine the chicken, celery, and shallots. Spread the mixture onto the crust. In the same bowl, beat together the eggs, cream, hot sauce, and salt and pepper. Pour the egg mixture over the chicken. Sprinkle the cheese on top and bake for 10 minutes. Reduce the heat to 350°F and bake for 20 minutes more, or until a toothpick inserted into the center comes out clean. Let stand for 10 minutes before serving. **Makes 6 to 8 servings.**

Mexican Quiche
(recipe at left)

How to Harvest: Broccoli

■ Broccoli heads are ready to harvest when the head is firm and full-size and the florets have swelled but have not yet opened and turned yellow. On a cool morning, cut the stalk 5 to 7 inches below the head. The plant will produce many edible tender shoots for several weeks.

Broccoli Quiche

1¼ cups chopped broccoli

3 eggs

¾ cup light cream or milk

⅛ teaspoon salt

1½ cups shredded Monterey Jack cheese

1 cup sautéed sliced mushrooms

1 unbaked 9-inch piecrust (see recipe, page 272)

paprika

Preheat the oven to 350°F. Bring a small pot of water to a boil and cook the broccoli for 5 minutes. Drain the broccoli, plunge it into ice water to stop the cooking process, then drain again well. In a bowl, beat the eggs, cream, and salt. Stir in the broccoli, cheese, and mushrooms. Pour into the piecrust. Sprinkle with paprika. Bake for 50 to 60 minutes, or until a toothpick inserted into the center comes out clean. Let stand for 10 minutes before serving. **Makes 6 servings.**

Basic Crepes

For herb crepes, add ½ teaspoon of dried herbs to the batter during blending.

3 eggs

3 cups milk

3 tablespoons melted butter, plus some for pan

¾ cup all-purpose flour

½ teaspoon salt

In a medium bowl, combine the eggs, milk, and butter and beat until smooth. Add the flour and salt and stir to blend. Cover the bowl with a plate and refrigerate the batter for 1 hour. Warm an omelet pan, crepe pan, or small skillet over medium-high heat until a sprinkling of water sizzles when dropped onto its surface. Brush the pan lightly with melted butter. Pour in just enough chilled batter to cover the bottom of the pan. Slowly swirl the pan to distribute the batter evenly around the edges. Cook until the crepe is lightly browned on the bottom and the top is dry. Turn the crepe over and cook the other side for 20 to 30 seconds, or until lightly browned. Stack the crepes between sheets of wax paper and cover with a clean dish towel until ready to fill and serve. **Makes 12 to 16 crepes.**

Shrimp and Asparagus Crepes

½ **pound asparagus, trimmed and cut into 1-inch pieces**

1 pound raw medium shrimp

6 tablespoons (¾ stick) butter

1 bunch scallions, chopped

6 tablespoons all-purpose flour

3 cups cold milk

½ **teaspoon salt**

½ **teaspoon coarsely ground black pepper**

1 teaspoon chopped fresh dill

¾ **cup shredded Parmesan cheese, divided**

8 crepes *(see recipe, left)*

Preheat the oven to 350°F. Lightly grease a 13x9-inch baking dish. Place the asparagus in a steamer basket over boiling water. Cover and steam for 6 minutes, or until the asparagus is crisp-tender. Plunge the asparagus into ice water to stop the cooking process, drain, and set aside. In a large saucepan, bring 1 quart of water to a boil. Add the shrimp and cook for 3 to 5 minutes, or just until they turn pink. Drain and rinse with cold water. Peel the shrimp, devein, and set aside. In a heavy saucepan over medium heat, melt the butter. Add the scallions and cook for 2 minutes, stirring constantly. Whisk in the flour and cook for 1 minute, whisking constantly. Gradually add the milk, whisking constantly, until the mixture is thickened and bubbly. Add the salt, pepper, dill, and ½ cup of the Parmesan cheese, whisking to combine. When the cheese has melted, remove from the heat and reserve 1 cup of sauce. Add the shrimp and asparagus to the remaining sauce and stir to coat. Spoon about ¼ cup of the shrimp and asparagus mixture down the center of each crepe. Roll up the crepes and place them seam side down in the prepared baking dish. Spoon the reserved sauce over the crepes and sprinkle with the remaining ¼ cup of Parmesan cheese. Bake for 20 minutes, or until thoroughly heated. **Makes 4 servings.**

In the Garden: Asparagus

■ Asparagus, a perennial, can produce for 15 to 25 years. Start a bed in a well-drained site in full sun. In the fall, amend the soil with rich organic matter. In spring, plant 1-year-old asparagus crowns 12 to 18 inches apart in 6-inch-deep trenches. Cover the crowns with 2 inches of soil and repeat the cover every 2 weeks, until the trench is filled. Fertilize the bed each year.

Fancy Crepes With Berries in Grand Marnier Syrup

(recipe at right)

Fancy Crepes With Berries in Grand Marnier Syrup

FRUIT FILLING *(make 3 hours ahead of serving):*

1 pint strawberries, hulled and cut in half

½ pint blackberries

½ pint blueberries

½ pint raspberries

1 cup sugar

1 tablespoon fresh lemon juice

¼ cup fresh orange juice

½ cup Grand Marnier or other orange liqueur

CREPES *(make at least 1 hour ahead):*

¾ cup all-purpose flour

1 tablespoon sugar

¼ teaspoon salt

2 eggs

1 cup milk

2 tablespoons vegetable oil

1 tablespoon Grand Marnier or other orange liqueur

2 tablespoons butter

WHIPPED CREAM *(make 1 hour ahead):*

2 cups heavy cream

3 tablespoons confectioners' sugar

½ teaspoon vanilla extract

For fruit filling: Combine the berries in a large bowl and set aside. In a small saucepan, bring the sugar and 1 cup of water to a boil. Stir in the lemon juice, orange juice, and Grand Marnier. Remove the pan from the heat and set aside for 5 minutes to cool. Pour the syrup over the berries, then store in the refrigerator.

For crepes: In a blender or food processor, combine all of the ingredients except the butter and blend until smooth, stopping occasionally to scrape down the sides of the container. Cover and chill the batter (for at least 1 hour; it will keep up to 3 days). In a 6-inch skillet or crepe pan over medium heat, melt the butter. Add 3 tablespoons of batter and quickly tilt the skillet in all directions until the batter covers the bottom. Cook for 1 minute, or until the crepe shakes loose easily from the skillet. With a spatula, flip the crepe and cook it for about 30 seconds on the other side. Repeat the procedure with the remaining batter, adding more butter if necessary. Stack the crepes between sheets of wax paper and cover with a clean dish towel until ready to serve, or store in a heavy-duty plastic bag for up to 3 days in the refrigerator or up to 4 months in the freezer.

For whipped cream: Beat the cream until it is foamy. Gradually add the sugar and vanilla, beating until soft peaks form, then set aside.

Gently warm the berries over low heat. Spoon about ⅓ cup of whipped cream into the center of each crepe. Roll up the crepes and arrange them on individual serving plates. Top with the warmed berries. **Makes 12 servings.**

Apple Crepes à la Mode

2 tablespoons butter

3 cups chopped apples

⅓ cup chopped raisins

½ cup chopped almonds

⅓ cup brown sugar

½ tablespoon cinnamon

6 crepes *(see recipe, page 16)*

vanilla ice cream and 6 mint leaves,
    for garnish

In a large skillet over medium heat, melt the butter. Add the apples, raisins, and almonds and cook for 5 minutes, or until the apples are tender, stirring frequently. Add the brown sugar and cinnamon, stir, and cook for 2 minutes. Remove the skillet from the heat. Spoon a portion of filling into the centers of the crepes. Roll up the crepes and serve seam side down. Garnish each with a scoop of ice cream and mint leaf. **Makes 6 servings.**

Fruit Salad

The lemon-sugar (or -honey) mixture will prevent the fruit from browning for a few hours.

juice of 1 large lemon

¼ cup sugar or mild honey

2 apples, cored and cut into pieces

2 large oranges, peeled, cut into pieces,
    and seeded, with pith removed

1 large or 2 small pears, cored and
    cut into pieces

1 banana, halved lengthwise and
    thickly sliced

2 kiwifruit, peeled and cut into chunks

2 cups melon balls (watermelon,
    cantaloupe, or other melon)

2 peaches, nectarines, or plums,
    pitted and cut into pieces

1 cup berries (blueberries, raspberries,
    or any combination)

1 cup seedless red or green grapes, halved if desired

fresh orange juice (optional)

In a large bowl, whisk together the lemon juice and sugar. Add the fruit, one kind at a time, tossing gently after each addition and striving for a colorful mixture. If it seems too dry, add a splash of fresh orange juice. **Makes 8 to 10 servings.**

Watermelon Basket Cutting Tips

■ Use a very sharp knife to carve out the shape of a basket handle, then carve the body of the basket. Scoop out the flesh. If you feel artistic, cut the basket edge in a zigzag fashion.

■ For a simple watermelon bowl, cut off the top third of the watermelon and scoop out the flesh. If necessary to get the melon to stand upright, cut a thin slice from the bottom.

Watermelon Basket With Honey Lime Dressing

SALAD:

1 large watermelon

1 cantaloupe

1 honeydew melon

1 pineapple

2 peaches or nectarines

2 cups blueberries, strawberries, or
    raspberries

DRESSING:

2 tablespoons fresh lime juice

3 tablespoons honey

½ cup white wine or ginger ale

fresh mint leaves, for garnish

For salad: (See "Watermelon Basket Cutting Tips," above.) Use a melon ball cutter to remove the pink flesh of the watermelon. If desired, remove the seeds from the melon balls, then put the balls into a large bowl. Drain the resulting watermelon rind shell, or "basket." Halve the cantaloupe and honeydew melons, cut balls from them, and put their fruit into the large bowl. Remove the rind and core from the pineapple and cut its flesh into bite-size pieces. Add the pineapple to the bowl. Cover the bowl of fruit and chill both it and the basket. Just before serving, peel and slice the peaches and prepare the berries (hull the strawberries). Drain the melon balls and the pineapple chunks. Combine all of the fruit in a large bowl.

For dressing: In a small bowl, combine the lime juice, honey, and white wine. Stir until thoroughly combined.

Pour the dressing over the fruit and stir to coat. Spoon or pour the fruit and dressing into the watermelon basket. Garnish with mint leaves. **Makes 10 to 12 servings.**

Fun Food Fact: Watermelon

■ A watermelon is 92 percent water.

Fruit Salad With Pineapple Sage

This dish is delightful for Sunday brunch. The pineapple sage blossoms add a festive fleck of color and flavor. If desired, leave out the orange liqueur.

2 kiwifruit, peeled

2 cups pineapple chunks

2 bananas

1 orange, peeled and separated into
   segments

½ cup orange juice

½ cup Grand Marnier or other orange liqueur (optional)

2 tablespoons sugar

¼ cup pineapple sage flowers

Cut the fruit into bite-size chunks and place in a large bowl, along with any juice that is generated. Add the remaining ingredients and mix gently to coat. Cover and refrigerate until ready to serve. **Makes 6 to 8 servings.**

For more ideas on how to use edible flowers in recipes, see pages 242–243.

How to Choose Fruit

■ **Use ripe but firm fruit in a salad. Start with a few fruit that are always available and add a mixture of whatever is in season.**

Apple Fritters

6 Cortland apples

2 eggs

2 tablespoons sugar

½ teaspoon salt

2⅔ cups all-purpose flour

4 teaspoons baking powder

1½ cups milk

vegetable oil, for deep-frying

¼ cup sugar and 1 teaspoon cinnamon,
   combined

Peel and core the apples, then cut each apple into eight pieces. In a large bowl, mix the eggs, sugar, salt, flour, baking powder, and milk to the consistency of a thick pancake batter. In a deep fryer or cast-iron skillet, heat enough oil for frying to a depth of 2 inches. Use tongs to dip the apples in the batter to coat them. When the oil is hot (about 375°F), place apples in the fryer a few at a time (so that the oil stays hot), cook until golden-brown, then drain. Put the cinnamon sugar into a paper bag; drop the fritters into it. Shake the bag to coat the fritters. Serve warm. **Makes 4 dozen fritters.**

Blueberry Pancakes

1½ cups all-purpose flour

2 tablespoons sugar

1 teaspoon baking powder

½ teaspoon baking soda

1 large egg

1 cup, plus 2 to 6 tablespoons
   buttermilk

2 tablespoons butter, melted and
   cooled

¼ teaspoon ground mace

½ teaspoon grated lemon zest

vegetable oil or 1 strip uncooked
   bacon

1 cup blueberries

In a large bowl, combine the flour, sugar, baking powder, and baking soda and whisk to blend evenly. In a small bowl, beat the egg, 1 cup of buttermilk, and melted butter. Make a well in the dry ingredients. Pour the egg mixture into the well. Add the mace and lemon zest and stir to blend with quick, light movements (do not beat). The batter will be lumpy. Cover and refrigerate for 10 minutes. Gently stir in 2 or more tablespoons of buttermilk until the batter develops the consistency of thick heavy cream.

Warm a griddle over medium-high heat until a sprinkling of water sizzles when dropped onto its surface. Brush the surface with vegetable oil or rub with a strip of bacon. Pour ¼ cup of batter onto the griddle per pancake. Sprinkle a handful of blueberries evenly over the surface of the pancake. Cook until the underside of the pancake is browned and half of the bubbles on the surface are broken. Turn the pancake and cook the other side. Repeat with the remaining batter and berries. **Makes 8 to 10 pancakes.**

In the Garden: Blueberries

■ Blueberries grow best in acidic soil, with a pH of 4 to 5. If a soil test indicates a need for acidification, add sulfur according to directions. Work it in about 4 inches deep and at least 3 months before planting. After planting the bushes, mulch with pine needles.

Parsnip Griddle Cakes

6 cooked parsnips

1 egg, well beaten

¾ teaspoon salt

1 tablespoon melted butter

2 tablespoons all-purpose flour

vegetable oil

In a medium bowl, mash the parsnips with a fork. Add the egg and beat until light. Season with the salt and butter, then fold in the flour. Warm a griddle over medium-high heat until a sprinkling of water sizzles when dropped onto its surface. Brush the surface with vegetable oil. Drop the batter by spoonfuls onto the hot griddle. Cook until lightly browned, turn over the cakes, and brown the other sides. **Makes 6 to 8 cakes.**

In the Kitchen: Maple Syrup

- Real maple syrup usually becomes darker and stronger in flavor as the season progresses. Color and flavor determine the syrup's grade; the name of each grade may vary by region.

- The lightest syrup (sometimes called Grade A Light Amber or Fancy Grade) is produced early in the season and has the most delicate flavor. It is good for making maple candy or as an ice cream or pancake topping.

- Medium grade syrup (such as Grade A Medium Amber and Grade A Dark Amber) is often used on pancakes and occasionally in cooking.

- The darkest syrup (sometimes called Grade B or Cooking Syrup) has a strong molasses flavor and is especially useful for baking.

CHAPTER 2

Appetizers, Dips, & Spreads

Basil Torta 26

Cheesy Stuffed Potato Skins With Broccoli 27

Marjoram Mushrooms 28

Roasted Garlic Bulbs 29

Hummus. 29

Nasturtium and Shrimp Salad Appetizer 30

Avocado and Bacon Spread. 32

Caponata With English Muffin Melbas 33

Eggplant Dip. 34

Garden Dip. 34

Black Bean Dip. 35

Layered Bean and Tomato Dip 35

Where salt is good, so is basil.
–Italian saying

Basil Torta

Rich, elegant, and easy.

1 pound robiola cheese*

1 pound mascarpone cheese*

2 generous handfuls fresh basil leaves, plus some for garnish

¼ cup (½ stick) unsalted butter, softened

⅓ cup olive oil

¾ cup grated Asiago or Parmesan cheese

2 cloves garlic

½ cup pine nuts or walnuts

¼ teaspoon salt

Cook's Glossary: Torta

■ In Italian, *torta* means tart, pie, or cake. Both sweet and savory tortas are favorites in Italy, where they typically take the form of a meat or cheese filling inside a pastry shell.

Put the robiola and mascarpone cheeses into separate bowls. Allow them to sit at room temperature until soft enough to spread easily, about 1 hour. Cut two 18-inch squares of cheesecloth and lay them one on top of the other inside a loaf pan or round mold pan. Moisten with water and let the corners hang out over the sides. In a blender or food processor, combine the basil, butter, olive oil, Asiago cheese, and garlic to make a paste (pesto). Add the nuts and salt and process to a coarse texture. Beat the robiola and mascarpone cheeses until they achieve the consistency of cream cheese. Spread one-third of the mascarpone in the lined pan or mold. Spread on it a thin layer of pesto and top with a layer of robiola. Repeat until you have six layers of cheese alternating with five layers of pesto. Bring up the corners of the cheesecloth and lay them over the surface of the cheese. Press down firmly to set the layers. Refrigerate for 1½ to 2 hours.

When the cheese feels firm to the touch, invert it onto a serving platter and remove the cheesecloth. If you don't plan to serve the torta immediately, lay plastic wrap directly on the surface of the cheese and return it to the refrigerator. (The indentations left by the cheesecloth are considered an integral part of a torta; however, if you prefer a smooth surface, you can remove the lines by smoothing them out with a knife or metal spatula heated in boiling water.) Garnish with fresh basil. **Makes 16 servings.**

*You can substitute for robiola and mascarpone cheese with equal parts (1 pound each) of cream cheese and unsalted butter. Allow them to soften, then blend them together thoroughly.

In the Garden: Basil

- Bush basil, which grows 6 to 12 inches tall, is more compact than other types. The leaves are smaller and milder in flavor than sweet basil leaves.

Save 'n' Store

- Fresh basil leaves, loosely wrapped in damp paper towels and placed in a plastic bag, will keep 4 to 7 days in the refrigerator. Or, put basil stems with leaves into a glass of water, cover with a plastic bag, and then store in the refrigerator.

Cheesy Stuffed Potato Skins With Broccoli

6 medium baking potatoes

4 slices bacon

1 small onion, diced

½ head broccoli, cut into 1-inch pieces

⅓ cup warm milk

freshly ground black pepper, to taste

1 cup shredded pepper jack cheese

1 cup shredded sharp cheddar cheese, divided

2 tablespoons butter, melted

Preheat the oven to 400°F. Scrub the potatoes, then wrap in foil and bake for about 1 hour, or until tender. While they are baking, fry the bacon in a skillet over medium heat until crisp, then remove to drain. Add the onion to the skillet with the bacon drippings and sauté until golden brown. Put the onions into a large bowl. Steam the broccoli for 3 to 5 minutes or until crisp-tender, then chop finely. Remove the potatoes from the oven, take off the foil, and cool slightly. Cut the potatoes in half lengthwise. Scoop out the pulp and place one-half of it into the bowl with the onion. Save the rest for another meal. Add the milk and pepper and mash. Mix in the pepper jack cheese and ½ cup of the cheddar cheese. Add the broccoli and stir to combine. Crumble the bacon. Add the bacon to the potatoes and stir to combine. Brush the potato skins with melted butter and place on a cookie sheet. Spoon the potato-cheese mixture into the potato skins. Bake at 400°F for about 10 minutes to warm. Remove the sheet from the oven. Set the oven to broil. Sprinkle with the remaining cheddar cheese. Place the cookie sheet in the oven and broil for 4 to 7 minutes, or until the cheese is melted. **Makes 12 servings.**

Cheese Bits

■ When a recipe calls for shredded, crumbled, or grated cheese, use these guidelines for purchasing cheese by weight:

4 ounces regular cheese = 1 cup shredded

4 ounces blue or feta cheese = 1 cup crumbled

3 ounces hard-grating cheese = 1 cup grated

Marjoram Mushrooms

12 large white button mushrooms

3 tablespoons olive oil

1 clove garlic, minced

⅓ cup chopped fresh parsley

2 tablespoons chopped fresh marjoram or 2 teaspoons dried marjoram

⅓ cup dry bread crumbs

¼ cup Parmesan cheese

salt and pepper, to taste

½ cup dry white wine

Preheat the oven to 350°F. Lightly butter an 11x7-inch baking dish. Wipe the mushrooms with a damp cloth. Separate the mushroom caps from the stems and set the caps aside. Mince the stems. In a small saucepan over medium heat, warm the olive oil, then sauté the stems with the garlic for about 3 minutes. Remove the saucepan from the heat and stir in the parsley, marjoram, bread crumbs, and cheese. Season with salt and pepper. Mound a spoonful of stuffing into each mushroom cap. Arrange the mushrooms in the prepared baking dish, pour in the wine, and bake for 10 minutes. Turn the oven to broil and place the pan 2 inches from the heat for 1 to 2 minutes, or until the mushroom tops are golden brown. **Makes 4 servings.**

In the Garden: Mushrooms

■ Mushroom kits make fungi fun—and safe. Kits vary in complexity and may be for indoor or outdoor use. The easiest to grow are white button mushrooms, but kits for morel, oyster, portabella, shiitake, and many more fungi are available.

Roasted Garlic Bulbs

Slow roasting turns garlic cloves into a soft, creamy paste with a mild, nutty flavor.

2 heads garlic
1 tablespoon olive oil
5 sprigs thyme
salt and pepper, to taste
French bread

Preheat the oven to 300°F. Remove the outer layers of garlic skin. Slice about ½ inch off the tops of the heads to expose the cloves. Put the heads, cut side up, in an ovenproof dish or wrap in heavy-duty foil. Drizzle the oil over the garlic, add the thyme sprigs, and season with salt and pepper (before wrapping in foil, if used). Cover and bake for about 30 minutes, or until very tender. Remove from the oven. Squeeze the garlic heads at the base and spread the paste onto the French bread. **Makes 2 servings.**

Hummus

1 can (15½ ounces) chickpeas
   (garbanzo beans), drained and
   rinsed
¼ cup olive oil
½ cup tahini or natural peanut butter
juice of 1 lemon
2 cloves garlic, diced
2 to 3 scallions, sliced
½ cup chopped fresh parsley
salt, to taste

Combine all of the ingredients except the parsley and salt in a blender or food processor. Blend until smooth and creamy. Spoon the spread into a serving dish and stir in the parsley. Season with salt. (You can blend in the parsley in the food processor, but it will turn the hummus green.) **Makes 2 cups.**

How to Sprout Chickpeas

■ Chickpea sprouts add crunch to salads. To grow them, soak dry chickpeas in cool water for 12 to 24 hours. Drain in a colander and leave them there. Rinse the seeds with cool water two to three times a day until they sprout, in 1 to 2 days.

The appetite is sharpened by the first bites.

–Jose Rizal, Philippine dramatist (1861–96)

Nasturtium and Shrimp Salad Appetizer

This is delicious when served with bread or crackers.

2 teaspoons fresh lemon juice

¼ cup olive oil

salt and pepper, to taste

1 cup peeled, deveined, cooked shrimp, coarsely chopped

2 tablespoons chopped scallions

1 small tomato, coarsely chopped

½ avocado, pitted, peeled, and cubed

2 tablespoons chopped fresh nasturtium leaves

lettuce leaves

nasturtium blossoms, for garnish

Pour the lemon juice into a small bowl. Whisk in the olive oil and season with salt and pepper. Add the shrimp and scallions and toss lightly. Let stand for 15 minutes to let the flavors blend. Add the tomato, avocado, and nasturtium leaves. Mound the mixture on lettuce leaves and garnish with the nasturtium blossoms. **Makes 4 servings.**

In the Garden: Nasturtiums

- Nasturtium is an easy-to-cultivate annual flower that can grow to be 18 inches tall. Some vine varieties can reach up to 6 feet in one season. Start seeds indoors, ½- to ¾-inch deep, or sow outdoors when the soil is warm.

–J M Birchall

For more ideas on how to use edible flowers in recipes, see pages 242–243.

Nasturtium and Shrimp Salad Appetizer

(recipe at left)

Avocado and Bacon Spread

2 ripe avocados, pitted, peeled, and
  cubed

2 medium shallots, finely chopped

2 tablespoons fresh lemon juice

¼ teaspoon salt

freshly ground black pepper, to taste

½ teaspoon Worcestershire sauce

½ pound sliced bacon

6 slices whole wheat bread

3 tablespoons butter, slightly softened

In a shallow bowl, combine the avocados, shallots, lemon juice, salt, pepper, and Worcestershire sauce by mashing them with a fork to create a rough purée (using a blender or food processor would liquefy them). Transfer the mixture to a plastic container. Lay a piece of plastic wrap directly on the surface of the mixture, smoothing out any air bubbles with your fingertips. Refrigerate for 2 hours to allow the flavors to meld. Fry the bacon in a large skillet over medium heat until crisp, then remove and drain. Crumble the bacon into bits.

Toast the bread, then lightly butter one side of each slice before cutting into four triangles. (Remove the crusts if you wish; reserve as salad croutons.) Arrange the bread, buttered side up, on a serving tray. Just before serving, blend the avocado mixture and bacon bits together and spoon into a small bowl to set in the middle of the toast points. **Makes 6 servings.**

In the Garden: Avocados

■ Avocado trees can be grown from pits taken from fruit at the grocery store, but they may not bear fruit before at least 8 years have passed, and even then the avocados may not be good for eating. For best results, buy a grafted tree from a nursery that can produce edible fruit in as few as 3 years.

Fun Food Fact: Eggplant

■ **In Europe, eggplant is also called aubergine.**

Caponata With English Muffin Melbas

ENGLISH MUFFIN MELBAS:
English muffins

CAPONATA:
3 or 4 small eggplants (about 1½ pounds, total)
¼ cup olive oil
2 large red bell peppers, cut into chunks
1 large onion, cut into chunks
2 stalks celery, diagonally sliced
2 cloves garlic, minced
7 plum tomatoes, peeled (see tip, page 65), or 1 can (16 ounces) Italian-style plum tomatoes, drained
2 tablespoons red-wine vinegar
1 tablespoon sugar
1 tablespoon capers, nonpareil variety, drained and rinsed
10 pitted black Greek or Italian olives, coarsely chopped
½ teaspoon salt
freshly ground black pepper, to taste

For English muffin melbas: Preheat the oven to 350°F. Cut each English muffin into four or five very thin slices. (Most English muffins sold in supermarkets are halved and thus difficult to work with for this, so look for a brand that is not already split.) Arrange the muffin slices on a cookie sheet and bake for 10 to 15 minutes, or until the slices are crisp and lightly browned.

For caponata: Wash the eggplants and blot dry. Trim off the ends but do not peel, then cut into ¾-inch cubes. (Small, young eggplants don't contain any bitter juices, so there's no need to salt and drain the cubes.) Heat the oil in a 12-inch skillet over medium heat. Add the red peppers, onion, celery, and garlic. Toss the vegetables to coat with the oil and stir until the onion is tender. Add the eggplant cubes, stir, and cook for 5 minutes, or until they are soft. Remove the pan from the heat and add the tomatoes by pressing them with a wooden pestle or spoon through a coarse sieve. Discard the seeds and bits of tomato left in the sieve. Add the vinegar, sugar, capers, olives, salt, and pepper. Stir to combine, then place over medium heat. Cook uncovered for 10 to 15 minutes, stirring occasionally. When most of the liquid has evaporated and the vegetables are tender, transfer the caponata to a serving dish and surround with English muffin melbas. Serve hot or at room temperature. **Makes 8 servings.**

Eggplant Dip

1 medium eggplant

1 clove garlic, crushed

¼ cup olive oil

⅔ cup feta cheese, crumbled

¼ cup fresh lemon juice (or more,
   to taste)

1 teaspoon salt

¼ teaspoon freshly ground black
   pepper

2 tablespoons plain yogurt

black olives and fresh parsley, for garnish

Preheat the oven to 400°F. Lightly grease a baking dish, then bake the whole eggplant until it is soft and the skin crumbles (about 40 minutes). Peel it, cool it, slice it in half lengthwise, remove the seeds, and dice the flesh. Place the eggplant flesh, garlic, and oil in a blender or food processor and mix to a smooth paste. Add the cheese, lemon juice, salt, and pepper and process until smooth. Stir in the yogurt. Turn the mixture into a bowl, garnish with olives and parsley, and serve with raw vegetables. **Makes about 2 cups.**

Garden Dip

3 tablespoons vegetable oil

1 small onion, chopped

½ cup chopped green bell pepper

1 cup chopped eggplant

½ cup peeled, chopped, fresh tomatoes
   (see tip, page 65)

1 cup cooked dried beans

juice from ½ lemon

salt and pepper, to taste

In a large frying pan over medium heat, warm the oil. Add the onion and green pepper and sauté until just tender. Add the eggplant, tomatoes, and beans and stir. Heat on medium-low until juice forms. Reduce the heat to low, cover, and cook for 15 minutes, or until the vegetables are tender and the juices have blended. Add the lemon juice and stir. Drain the liquid if the mixture becomes soupy. Season with salt and pepper. Serve with pita bread. **Makes about 3½ cups.**

In the Garden: Tomatoes

■ Tomatoes grown in pots and raised
   beds mature faster because the soil
   heats up more quickly there than in
   ground-level gardens.

Black Bean Dip

2 tablespoons vegetable shortening
1 medium onion, finely chopped
1 clove garlic, minced
1 chipotle pepper, seeded
1 cup cooked black beans
⅛ teaspoon freshly ground black
    pepper
2 tablespoons Worcestershire sauce
1 tablespoon sugar
salt, to taste
milk, for consistency (optional)

In a skillet over medium heat, melt the shortening. Add the onion and garlic and sauté until soft. Transfer these and the remaining ingredients, except the milk, to a blender or food processor and purée until smooth. Put the mixture into a saucepan over low heat and simmer for 20 to 25 minutes, stirring occasionally so that it does not scorch. Stir in milk until the purée has the consistency of a dip. Serve hot or cold with crackers or corn chips. **Makes about 2 cups.**

Layered Bean and Tomato Dip

3 tomatoes, seeded and chopped
¼ cup chopped onion
2 tablespoons chopped jalapeños
1 clove garlic, minced
1 teaspoon red-wine vinegar
1½ cups cooked pinto beans, or 1 can
    (12 ounces) pinto beans, drained
1 tablespoon chili powder
⅔ cup cottage cheese
¾ cup shredded iceberg lettuce
2 ounces sharp cheddar cheese, grated
10 small pitted black olives, sliced

In a small bowl, combine the tomatoes, onion, jalapeños, garlic, and vinegar to make a salsa, then set aside. In a blender or food processor, purée the pinto beans with the chili powder; set aside. Clean out the blender, then process the cottage cheese until it is smooth and creamy. Spread the pinto beans on a dinner plate. Spread the cottage cheese on top of the beans, then layer half of the salsa, then the shredded lettuce, and then the remaining salsa. Top with grated cheese and olive slices. Serve with tortilla chips. **Makes 2½ cups.**

A KITCHEN
Herb Garden

Oh, better no doubt is a dinner of herbs,
When season'd with love.

—Edward Bulwer-Lytton,
English writer (1803–73)

A kitchen herb garden can be simple or ornamental, blended with decorative flowers or combined with other edibles. Herbs will thrive in pots on the patio, in raised beds, and in plots—even on a sunny windowsill. The following herbs have a range of culinary uses:

BASIL, an annual, grows 1 to 2 feet tall in moist soil. Encourage bushy growth by pinching off flower buds. Pick the leaves often, from the top. Use them with pasta, vegetable dishes, soups, salads, and oils or vinegars.

CHIVE, a perennial, grows 12 to 24 inches tall in moist soil. Harvest the hollow, grasslike leaves in the spring by snipping them close to the ground; they will soon grow back. Chives enliven rice, cheese dishes, eggs, vegetable dishes, dressings, sauces, and dips.

CILANTRO/CORIANDER, an annual, grows 6 to 30 inches tall in light soil and full sun to partial shade. Pick the leaves (cilantro) sparingly when the plant stands 4 to 6 inches tall. Pick the aromatic seeds (coriander) when they ripen. Use leaves and flowers raw in salads and cold vegetable dishes, and the seeds in pastries, custards, confections, and meat dishes.

DILL, an annual or biennial, grows 2 to 3 feet tall. Harvest the leaves when the flowers begin to open; collect the seed heads when they are dry and brown. Use the leaves with soups, seafood, salads, green beans, potato dishes, cheese, and sauces, and the seeds for pickles.

> ## Ground Rules
> - **Unless otherwise noted, herbs grow best in rich soil and full sun.**

basil   *chives*   *cilantro*   *dill*   *mint*

Fresh vs. Dried

- Most herbs keep their flavor when properly dried, and often the taste is concentrated. When cooking, you may be able to exchange fresh for dried, or vice versa. As a general rule:

FOR DRIED, use one-third of the fresh amount.

FOR FRESH, use three times the dried amount. For example, 1 tablespoon of a fresh herb, minced and packed, equals about 1 teaspoon of dried.

- **Plant sage near rosemary, cabbage, and carrots but away from cucumbers. The herb deters cabbage moths and carrot flies.**

MINT, a perennial, grows 1 to 3 feet tall in moist soil and partial shade. (Mints can be invasive. To prevent spreading, plant them in pots.) Harvest young sprigs and leaves frequently for a bushy plant. Use fresh or dry leaves and stems with roast lamb or fish and in salads, jellies, or teas.

OREGANO, a tender perennial, grows 1 to 2 feet tall and tolerates poor soil. Harvest leaves when young and use in any tomato dish. Try it also with beans, mushroom dishes, potatoes, and summer squashes, or in a marinade for lamb or game.

PARSLEY, a biennial, grows 12 to 30 inches tall in partial shade. Leaves can be curly or flat, depending on the variety. Cut or pinch the leaves as needed. Use fresh in soups, salads, and sauces or as garnish for anything.

ROSEMARY, a tender perennial, grows 4 to 6 feet tall in neutral to slightly acidic soil. Gather leaves and sprigs as needed for use with vegetables or in lamb, poultry,

and tomato dishes; breads and custards; and soups and stews.

SAGE, a perennial, grows 1 to 3 feet tall in well-drained soil. Pick the leaves as needed for use in soups, salads, stuffings, cheese dishes, and pickles. Its strong flavor makes it excellent for salt-free cooking.

THYME, a perennial, grows 12 to 18 inches tall in well-drained soil and full sun to partial shade. Harvest the tops of the plants when they are in full leaf. Use the leaves, fresh or dried, in casseroles, stews, soups, and ragouts, and with fish, potatoes, green vegetables, and eggs.

Pamper These Perennials

- "Tender" perennial herbs will not survive cold temperatures. Where frost occurs, they need special winter protection or should be treated as annuals.

oregano *parsley* *rosemary* *sage* *thyme*

For information on how to dry herbs, see page 316.

Soups

CHAPTER 3

Apple Artichoke Soup 39

Apple Curry Soup 40

Cold Strawberry Soup 41

Cranberry Soup 41

Chilled Blueberry Soup 42

Arugula, Egg, and Lemon Soup 42

Lamb and Bean Soup 44

Black Bean Soup With Grapefruit 45

Vermont Butternut Squash Soup 47

Chinese Cabbage Soup 48

Peel-a-Pound Cabbage Soup 48

Cucumber Chervil Soup 49

Portuguese Bean Soup 50

Broccoli Soup 50

Cream of Fiddleheads Soup 51

Hearty Kale, Bean, and Zucchini Soup 51

Classic Gazpacho 52

Lentil and Brown Rice Soup 54

Main Dish Minestrone 55

Moussaka Soup 56

Cream of Onion Soup 57

Perfect Pumpkin Soup 58

Curried Pattypan Soup 58

Potato Chowder 59

Autumn Garden Soup 61

Root Soup 62

Spinach, Basil, and Walnut Soup 63

Spinach and Chicken Soup 64

Sorrel Soup With Rosemary 64

Fresh Tomato Soup 65

Winter Vegetable Beef Stew 66

White Turnip Soup 67

Vichyssoise (Potato Soup) 67

Zucchini Potato Soup 68

Turkey and Potato Chowder 68

I live on good soup, not on fine words.

–Molière, French playwright (1622–73)

Apple Artichoke Soup

2 tablespoons butter

2 tablespoons finely minced onion or
    scallions

¼ cup peeled, cored, and minced
    yellow apple

2 tablespoons all-purpose flour

8 cooked artichoke hearts, or 1 can
    (8½ ounces) artichoke hearts
    in water, drained and divided

2 cups chicken broth

1 tablespoon fresh parsley

1 cup light cream

salt and pepper, to taste

In a stockpot over low heat, melt the butter. Add the onion and apple and sauté for 2 minutes, or until soft. Sprinkle the flour into the stockpot, stir to blend, and cook for 2 minutes, stirring constantly. Set aside two artichoke hearts for garnish. Add the chicken broth, remaining artichokes, and parsley to the soup. Simmer for 10 minutes, then set aside for 10 minutes to cool. In a blender or food processor, purée the mixture until smooth, in batches. Return the soup to the stockpot. Just before serving, add the cream, stir to incorporate, and season with salt and pepper. Warm the soup over low heat but do not let it boil. Coarsely chop the reserved artichokes and float them on the soup. **Makes 6 servings.**

MAKE AHEAD: *This soup can be prepared up to the purée stage, covered, and refrigerated for 2 days or frozen in an airtight container for 3 months.*

SOUPS

How to Remove an Artichoke Heart

■ Cut off the stem close to the base of the vegetable. Remove the leaves, or bracts, starting with the outer layer. The leafless fuzzy center is called the choke. Using a spoon, scrape out the fuzz (immature, inedible florets). Cut off any remaining tough parts surrounding the heart.

Homemade Curry Powder

2 tablespoons coriander seeds

2 tablespoons cumin seeds

1 tablespoon mustard seeds

1 tablespoon black peppercorns

1 tablespoon fennel seed

1 tablespoon whole cloves

1 tablespoon ground turmeric

1 tablespoon ground cardamom

2 tablespoons ground cinnamon

2 tablespoons ground cayenne

■ Preheat the oven to 200°F. Place the whole spices on a baking sheet and roast them for 15 minutes, or until the spices are fragrant. Remove from the oven and let cool. Pour the spices into a bowl and grind well. Stir in the ground spices. Store the mixture in an airtight jar. Makes about 1 cup.

Apple Curry Soup

1 tablespoon butter

2 large apples, cored and diced

2 medium onions, diced

1 teaspoon all-purpose flour

½ teaspoon curry powder

2 cups chicken broth

¼ teaspoon salt

¼ teaspoon cayenne pepper

1 cup dry white wine

½ cup diced cooked chicken

In a saucepan over medium heat, melt the butter. Add the apples and onions and sauté until soft. Sprinkle the flour and curry into the pan, stir to blend, and continue cooking for about 3 minutes. Add the remaining ingredients except the chicken, and simmer for 15 minutes. Set aside for 10 minutes to cool. In a blender or food processor, purée the mixture until smooth, in batches. Return the soup to the saucepan and warm on low heat until ready to serve. Add the chicken, stir, and heat until warmed through. **Makes 4 servings.**

Cook's Glossary: "Clear Soup" Terms

■ STOCK is made by simmering bones (or shells) and vegetables in water.

■ BROTH is made by simmering meat and vegetables in water.

■ BOUILLON is similar to stock and broth but is reconstituted from a dehydrated form (usually a cube).

■ CONSOMMÉ is a clear soup made from strained meat or vegetable stock and is served hot or cold (as a jelly).

Fun Food Fact: Strawberries

■ Strawberries take their name from the custom of mulching them with straw to preserve them from rot.

Cold Strawberry Soup

Cool and refreshing, this soup is a winner during strawberry season.

2 quarts strawberries, hulled
1 cup sugar
¼ cup fresh lemon juice
grated zest of 1 lemon
2 cups Rhine wine

Purée the strawberries in a blender or food processor and set aside. In a large saucepan over medium heat, bring the sugar and 2 cups of water to a boil and cook for 10 minutes to make sugar syrup. Cool. Add the berries to the syrup. Stir in the lemon juice and zest. Chill in the refrigerator. Just before serving, stir in the wine. **Makes 8 to 10 servings.**

Cranberry Soup

4 cups cold water
1 cup sugar
1 cinnamon stick (2 to 3 inches long)
dash nutmeg
4 cups cranberries, picked over
1 cup rosé wine
1 cup sour cream

In a saucepan over medium-high heat, combine the water, sugar, cinnamon stick, and nutmeg and bring to a boil. Add the cranberries and return to a boil. Reduce the heat and simmer covered, stirring occasionally, for about 15 minutes. Using a fork, mash some of the berries against the side of the pan. Remove the cinnamon stick. Stir in the wine and simmer for 5 minutes. Serve warm or refrigerate until cold, about 4 hours. Top each serving with a dollop of sour cream. **Makes 6 servings.**

Chilled Blueberry Soup

1 tablespoon cornstarch

2 cups cold water, divided

2½ cups blueberries

3 tablespoons sugar

1½ cups marsala wine

½ cup sour cream or yogurt

In a small bowl, dissolve the cornstarch in ¼ cup of the cold water. In a saucepan over low heat, warm the blueberries, cornstarch, remaining water, sugar, and wine. Cook for 15 minutes, or until the blueberries are soft. Set aside for 10 minutes to cool. Process the blueberry mixture in a blender or food processor until all of the ingredients are incorporated and smooth. Chill in the refrigerator. Before serving, add the sour cream and stir. Serve in chilled bowls. **Makes 6 servings.**

Arugula, Egg, and Lemon Soup

For a milder flavor, stir in sliced spinach instead of arugula.

3 cups chicken broth

3 eggs

juice of 1 to 2 lemons, to taste

½ cup thinly sliced arugula leaves

1 to 2 teaspoons chopped fresh chives
 (optional)

1 cup cooked brown or white rice
 (optional)

In a saucepan, bring the chicken broth to a boil over medium heat, then set aside. In a medium bowl, beat the eggs, then add the lemon juice gradually. Add the broth to the eggs, beating constantly with a whisk. Return the soup to the saucepan and cook over low heat for several minutes, stirring until thickened. Do not let it boil. Just before serving, stir in the arugula and cook over medium heat for 30 seconds, or until the leaves wilt. Add the chives and rice, if desired. **Makes 4 servings.**

In the Garden: Arugula

■ Arugula, also known as rocket or roquette, is a salad green native to the Mediterranean. Seeds germinate quickly, even in cold soil, so in spring, sow in full sun as soon as the soil can be worked. Harvest may be in as little as 3½ weeks.

Chilled Blueberry Soup

(recipe at left)

How to Soak Beans

The two common ways to prepare dried beans for cooking are the traditional and quick-soak methods:

- Into a stockpot, put 2½ to 3 cups of water for each cup of beans. Make sure that the water completely covers the beans. Soak the beans overnight. (The beans will absorb most of the water.)

- Put the dried beans into a stockpot and add enough water so that the level is 2 to 3 inches above the beans. Bring the water to a boil. Cook for 5 minutes, remove the pan from the heat, and set the beans aside for 1 to 2 hours. Drain and rinse.

Lamb and Bean Soup

1 package (16 ounces) dried navy beans
2 tablespoons vegetable oil
2 lamb shanks
2 large carrots, sliced
1 stalk celery, sliced
1 large onion, diced
1 clove garlic, minced
2½ cups green beans, trimmed and cut into 1-inch pieces
salt and pepper, to taste
2 cubes beef bouillon or 2 teaspoons beef bouillon granules
½ cup barley
½ cup orzo or tubitini

Put the beans into a stockpot, cover them with 2 to 3 inches of water, and cook over medium heat. Bring the liquid to a boil and simmer for 5 minutes, then remove from the heat, cover, and set aside for 2 hours. Drain and rinse. Set aside.

In a large stockpot or Dutch oven over medium heat, warm the oil, add the lamb shanks, and brown well on all sides. Add the carrots, celery, onion, garlic, green beans, soaked navy beans, salt and pepper, bouillon cubes, 10 cups of water, and barley to the stockpot. Bring to a boil, reduce the heat, and simmer for 1½ hours, stirring occasionally. Remove the shanks when they are tender, cut the meat into small pieces, and return the meat to the soup. Add the orzo and cook 10 minutes longer, or until tender. **Makes 6 to 8 servings.**

Dried Bean Conversions

- 1 cup dried beans = about 2½ cups soaked dried beans
- 1 pound dried beans = about 2 cups uncooked dried beans = 5 to 6 cups cooked
- 1 can (15 ounces) beans, drained = about 1½ cups cooked dried beans

Black Bean Soup With Grapefruit

If you do not have a grapefruit, substitute an orange, peeled and cut into small pieces, or a cup of seeded grapes.

1 pound dried black beans

1 cup finely chopped onion, for garnish

1 cup vegetable oil

1 cup red-wine vinegar

4 cups beef stock

½ pound cooked ham, cubed

1 grapefruit, peeled, seeded, and cut into small pieces

1 green bell pepper, finely chopped

1 clove garlic, minced

¼ cup dry sherry

1 teaspoon salt

3 cups cooked rice

Soak the beans in water overnight *(see tip, left)*. Put the chopped onion into a bowl. Combine the oil and vinegar, then pour over the onions and set aside to marinate. Drain and rinse the beans. Put them into a large stockpot, add the beef stock and 2 cups of water, and cook over medium-high heat to boiling. Reduce the heat and simmer until the beans are tender. Add the remaining ingredients except the rice and simmer for 30 minutes. Garnish each serving with marinated onions. Serve with the rice. **Makes 6 to 8 servings.**

Vermont Butternut Squash Soup
(recipe at right)

Vermont Butternut Squash Soup

Maple syrup brings out the butternut flavor.

3 tablespoons butter

2 tablespoons chopped onion

1 medium carrot, peeled and chopped

3 tablespoons all-purpose flour

4 cups warm chicken stock

2 pounds butternut squash, peeled,
    seeded, and cut into large cubes

1 clove garlic

1 tablespoon dried parsley

1½ cups milk

½ cup light cream

2 tablespoons maple syrup, or to taste

chopped fresh parsley, for garnish

freshly ground black pepper, for garnish

In a large stockpot, melt the butter over medium-low heat. Add the onion and carrot and cook for about 5 minutes, or until the onion is tender. Sprinkle the vegetables with the flour and, stirring constantly, continue cooking for 3 minutes. Remove the pot from the heat and add the chicken stock. Add the squash, garlic, and parsley, and simmer, covered, for 45 minutes. Set aside to cool for 10 minutes. In a blender or food processor, purée the mixture until smooth, in batches. Return the soup to the pot, add the milk, cream, and syrup, stir to incorporate, and heat through. Garnish with parsley and black pepper. **Makes 12 servings.**

MAKE AHEAD: *This soup can be prepared up to the purée stage, covered, and refrigerated for 4 days or frozen in an airtight container for 1 month. To use: For each serving, combine ½ cup of the thawed purée, 2 tablespoons of milk, 2 teaspoons of cream, and 1 teaspoon of maple syrup, then heat through.*

Save 'n' Store: Winter Squash

■ Here's one way to freeze winter squash: Wash the squash, peel it, slice it into sections, and remove the seeds. Cook the squash, mash it, let it cool, then place into freezer bags, leaving ½ inch of headspace. It will keep in the freezer for 8 to 12 months.

Chinese Cabbage Soup

A light meal that can be ready to eat in less than 30 minutes.

2 ounces shirataki or other translucent
    ("cellophane") noodles
6 cups chicken broth
1 egg
½ pound ground pork
1 teaspoon sherry
½ teaspoon freshly grated ginger
½ teaspoon salt
6 scallions, thinly sliced and separated
    into green and white parts
1 medium Chinese cabbage

Put the noodles into a large bowl. Pour boiling water over the noodles to cover and set aside for 10 minutes. Pour the broth into a large saucepan and bring to a boil. In a separate bowl, beat the egg. Add the ground pork, sherry, ginger, salt, and white parts of the scallions and stir to combine. Take up by teaspoonfuls and shape into meatballs. Carefully put the meatballs into the boiling broth. Reduce the heat so that the broth bubbles gently. Cook, uncovered, for 10 minutes, and as foam forms on the surface, remove it with a slotted spoon or skimmer. Slice across the cabbage, cutting it into inch-wide pieces. Add the pieces to the bubbling broth. Stir in the scallion greens and cook for 10 minutes, or until the cabbage is tender but still crisp. Drain the noodles and add them to the soup. Heat through. **Makes 6 servings.**

Peel-a-Pound Cabbage Soup

A perfect use for leftover turkey.

½ to 1 pound green cabbage, cut into
    bite-size pieces
1 green bell pepper, chopped
2 stalks celery, chopped
2 medium onions, chopped
8 tomatoes, peeled and chopped *(see tip, page 65)*, or
    1 can (16 ounces) whole tomatoes with liquid, chopped
3 cubes bouillon or 3 teaspoons bouillon granules
1 teaspoon celery seeds
1 teaspoon dried basil
2 teaspoons dried oregano
½ teaspoon garlic powder
salt and pepper, to taste
2 cups diced cooked turkey or beef

In a large saucepan or stockpot, combine all of the ingredients and add water to cover. Bring the liquid to a boil over medium heat, then reduce the heat and simmer for about 1 hour. Serve hot. **Makes 6 to 8 servings.**

In the Garden: Chervil

- Chervil is an annual or biennial herb that grows 12 to 24 inches tall. It does not like to be transplanted, so sow directly outdoors, ⅛-inch deep in moist soil in part shade. The flavor of the leaves resembles a milder form of parsley, with a dash of anise.

Cucumber Chervil Soup

¼ cup (½ stick) butter

2 scallions, chopped

3 large cucumbers, peeled, seeded, and sliced

salt and pepper, to taste

3 tablespoons all-purpose flour

3 cups chicken broth

½ cup fresh minced chervil

1 cup heavy cream

In a large saucepan, melt the butter over medium heat. Add the scallions and sauté until soft, but not brown. Add the cucumbers, salt and pepper, and 1 cup of water. Simmer for 15 minutes. In a small bowl, combine the flour and enough cold water to make a paste. Add the flour-water mixture and chicken broth to the saucepan. Stir constantly, until the liquid comes to a boil, then reduce the heat and simmer for 5 minutes. Set the soup aside for 10 minutes to cool. In a blender or food processor, purée the mixture, in batches. Return the soup to the saucepan, add the chervil and cream, and stir to blend. Serve hot or cold. **Makes 6 servings.**

Soup-Herb Advice

- Use dried herbs if your soup is going to cook for a long time. Fresh herbs are excellent for garnish.

Portuguese Bean Soup

Got cabbage, carrots, or watercress? Add them with the onion and parsley.

2 cups dried red beans, dried white beans,
    or dried lima beans

3 medium ham shanks

1 medium linguiça, cut into small slices

1 small soup bone

1 cup tomato sauce

¼ teaspoon cumin seeds

2 tablespoons oil

1 medium onion, sliced

3 tablespoons chopped fresh parsley

2 large potatoes, peeled and diced

salt, to taste

Soak the beans in water overnight *(see tip, page 44)*. Drain and rinse. In a stockpot, combine the ham shanks, linguiça, and soup bone with water to cover and boil over medium-high heat for 30 minutes. Add the beans and cook for 30 minutes, or until the beans are tender. Add the tomato sauce and cumin. In a skillet over medium heat, warm the oil. Add the onion and parsley and sauté until the onion is tender. Add the onion and parsley to the pot, with the potatoes, and cook for 30 minutes, or until tender. Season with salt. **Makes 12 to 14 servings.**

In the Kitchen: Broccoli and Cauliflower

■ Cabbageworms and other pests may hide in freshly picked broccoli or cauliflower. Before cooking, submerge the head in a pot or sink full of salted, cold water (1 teaspoon of salt per quart of water) for about 30 minutes. The pests will float to the surface. Skim off and discard them. Drain, then rinse the head in running cold water.

Broccoli Soup

1 large head fresh broccoli, chopped

3 cubes chicken bouillon or 3 teaspoons
    chicken bouillon granules

¼ cup minced onion

¼ cup (½ stick) butter

½ teaspoon salt

¾ cup minced peeled potatoes

½ teaspoon marjoram

½ cup heavy cream

2 strips bacon, cooked crisp and
    crumbled, for garnish

In a large stockpot, combine the broccoli, 3 cups of water, bouillon cubes, onion, butter, salt, potatoes, and marjoram and cook over medium heat, covered, for 15 to 20 minutes, or until the vegetables are tender. Remove the stockpot from the heat and set aside to cool for 10 minutes. In a blender or food processor, purée the mixture until smooth, in batches. Just before serving, add the cream, stirring to incorporate. Serve hot or cold. Garnish with bacon bits. **Makes 10 servings.**

MAKE AHEAD: *This soup can be prepared up to the purée stage, covered, and refrigerated for 4 days or frozen in an airtight container for 3 months.*

SOUPS

In the Kitchen: Fiddleheads

■ Raw fiddleheads contain a toxin and require special preparation before they can be eaten safely. For details on these edible ferns and how to prepare them, see page 121.

Cream of Fiddleheads Soup

1½ cups fiddleheads, finely chopped

2 tablespoons butter

2 cubes chicken bouillon or 2 teaspoons chicken bouillon granules

1 small onion, minced

1 clove garlic, minced

2 cups milk

2 cups heavy cream

salt and pepper, to taste

Steam the fiddleheads for 10 to 12 minutes, or until tender. Set aside. In a saucepan, melt the butter and bouillon cubes over medium heat. Add the fiddleheads, onion, and garlic and sauté for 10 minutes. Add the milk, stir frequently, and heat thoroughly. Add the cream, stir to incorporate, and season with salt and pepper. Serve steaming hot. **Makes 6 servings.**

Hearty Kale, Bean, and Zucchini Soup

Prepare this dish at the end of the summer, when kale and zucchini are both abundant. For the freshest flavor, add the kale, zucchini, and cilantro just before serving.

1 pound dried beans

2 onions, chopped

1 teaspoon minced garlic

8 cups chicken, beef, or vegetable stock

1 cup tomato sauce or stewed tomatoes

3 cups kale leaves, stemmed and sliced into ½-inch pieces

1 zucchini, quartered and sliced

3 tablespoons coarsely chopped cilantro

salt and pepper, to taste

Soak the beans in water overnight *(see tip, page 44)*. Drain and rinse. Place the beans in a stockpot and add the onions, garlic, and stock. Over medium-high heat, bring the liquid to a boil, reduce the heat, and simmer for 1½ hours, or until the beans are tender. Add the tomato sauce, kale, and zucchini. Bring the liquid to a boil again and cook, stirring constantly, for 2 to 3 minutes. Add the cilantro and season with salt and pepper. **Makes 8 to 10 servings.**

Classic Gazpacho

This quintessential summer soup has been a tradition in Spain for centuries. With all of the fresh flavor and nutrients of raw vegetables, it has aptly been called a liquid salad.

SOUPS

3 pounds tomatoes, diced

1 large onion, diced

1 large or 2 small green bell peppers, diced

1 large clove garlic, minced

½ cup olive oil

2 tablespoons sherry vinegar or other vinegar

1 slice white bread, crust cut off, saturated with cold water

¼ cup chopped fresh cilantro

¼ cup chopped fresh parsley

½ tablespoon hot-pepper sauce

2 teaspoons salt, or to taste

In a blender or food processor, purée the tomatoes, onion, and peppers (each separately) until smooth. In a large bowl, combine the processed vegetables, add the remaining ingredients, and stir to blend. Set the soup aside for 30 minutes to an hour to allow the flavors to marry. Serve cold. **Makes 6 servings.**

Pepper Heat

■ Hot peppers get their bite from a substance called capsaicin. In 1912, a test developed by Wilbur Scoville measured the amount of heat in one unit of pepper extract compared to the number of units of sugar solution needed to neutralize it—as judged by taste testers.

Today, we use a similar yet more sophisticated method that employs what are called Scoville heat units. Although a number of factors can cause the results to vary, here are a few common pepper types and their average ratings:

PEPPER TYPE	SCOVILLE UNITS
Sweet bell pepper	0
Ancho/Pasilla/Poblano	1,000–1,500
Jalapeño	2,500–5,000
Piquin/Cayenne/Tabasco	30,000–50,000
Habanero	150,000–300,000
Bhut Jolokia	1,001,304

Pure capsaicin is rated at between 15,000,000 and 16,000,000 Scoville units.

Classic Gazpacho
(recipe at left)

Lentil and Brown Rice Soup

¾ cup brown rice

1 cup dried lentils

1 onion, chopped

½ cup chopped celery

2 carrots, peeled and sliced

1 teaspoon dried basil

½ teaspoon dried oregano

½ teaspoon dried thyme

1 bay leaf

3 cups chicken broth

1 can (14 ounces) crushed tomatoes, with liquid

1 tablespoon cider vinegar

salt and pepper, to taste

In a large stockpot or Dutch oven, combine the rice, lentils, onion, celery, carrots, basil, oregano, thyme, bay leaf, chicken broth, and tomatoes. Bring to a boil and reduce the heat. Cover and simmer for 1 hour, or until the lentils and rice are tender. Remove and discard the bay leaf. Stir in the vinegar and season with salt and pepper. **Makes 6 servings.**

In the Kitchen: Lentils

■ Unlike many dried beans, most lentils commonly available in North America do not need to be presoaked. There are types, however, that do. Check package directions.

In the Garden: Celery

- Celery requires up to 140 days to mature, plenty of water, full sun, rich soil amended with compost, and cool temperatures. If your growing season is not that long, in early spring, sow the tiny seeds indoors in individual pots. Thin to one seedling per pot. Transplant outdoors after the last spring frost. Protect the plants as needed before the first fall frost.

Main Dish Minestrone

1 tablespoon olive oil

½ pound sweet or hot Italian sausage, crumbled

1 large onion, chopped

1 clove garlic, minced

½ cup chopped celery

½ cup chopped carrots

½ cup chopped green bell pepper

8 tomatoes, peeled (see tip, page 65), or 1 can (16 ounces) whole tomatoes, with liquid

4 cups chicken stock

2 cups shredded cabbage

2 tablespoons chopped fresh parsley

½ teaspoon dried basil

1 bay leaf

pinch of dried thyme

½ cup elbow macaroni

1 cup cooked kidney beans

freshly grated Parmesan cheese (optional)

In a large stockpot, warm the oil over medium heat. Add the sausage and cook until browned. Drain all but 1 tablespoon of the fat. Add the onion, garlic, celery, carrots, and green pepper and sauté for 5 minutes, or until the vegetables are soft. Add the tomatoes, chicken stock, cabbage, and herbs. Bring the liquid to a boil, cover, and simmer for 30 minutes. Add the macaroni and beans and cook for 30 minutes. Remove the bay leaf before serving. Sprinkle each serving with Parmesan cheese, if desired. **Makes 6 to 8 servings.**

Moussaka Soup

All the taste of the original Greek dish, without the calories.

½ **pound lean ground lamb**
3 cups beef broth
1 tablespoon minced onion
1 small eggplant, peeled and diced
2 stalks celery, cut into small pieces
7 plum tomatoes, peeled *(see tip,*
    page 65), **or 1 can (16 ounces) plum**
    tomatoes, with liquid
1 clove garlic, minced
1 teaspoon dried oregano
1 teaspoon dried basil
2 tablespoons chopped fresh parsley
6 slices (each 1-inch thick) French bread
2 tablespoons grated Gruyère cheese

Shape the lamb into teaspoon-size meatballs and place them on a cookie sheet. Preheat the broiler. Cook the meatballs, turning occasionally, until brown. Remove them from the sheet and drain off any fat. In a large stockpot over medium heat, bring the beef broth to a boil. Add the meatballs and the remaining ingredients, except the bread and cheese. Cover the stockpot and simmer for 30 minutes. Put one slice of French bread in the bottom of each soup bowl, sprinkle with cheese, and pour hot soup on top. **Makes 6 servings.**

Know Your Onions

- DRY, OR BULB, ONIONS include spring/summer sweet onions, such as Vidalia and Bermuda, and the stronger-flavor, fall/winter storage onions, such as Yellow Globe. They may be white, red, or yellow and are harvested after the tops have died down. Sweet onions have thin skins and a mild taste that makes them perfect for eating raw or using in briefly cooked dishes. Storage onions have thick layers of skin, are more pungent, and do well in dishes that cook for a while.

    Red onions are usually the mildest and often are eaten raw or grilled. White onions are a bit more pungent and often are sautéed and used in salsas or Mexican cuisine. Yellow onions have the strongest flavor; they are great for soups and other cooked dishes.

Cream of Onion Soup

The secret is the slowly cooked onion rings.

4 large sweet onions (Bermuda or Vidalia)

8 tablespoons (1 stick) butter, divided

3 cups milk

4 tablespoons all-purpose flour

2 cups chicken broth

⅛ teaspoon ground mace

1 cup heavy cream

½ teaspoon salt

white pepper or a pinch of cayenne pepper, to taste

snipped chives, for garnish

Thinly slice the onions, separating the slices into rings. In a wide saucepan, melt 4 tablespoons of the butter over medium-low heat. Add the onion rings and toss to coat. Reduce the heat to its lowest setting, cover the pan, and cook the onions until they take on a rich golden hue. Do not allow them to brown. Set aside. In another saucepan over medium heat, melt the remaining butter. Into a small third saucepan, pour the milk; heat it gently, but do not allow it to boil. Add the flour into the melted butter, whisking until the mixture foams. Remove the saucepan from the heat and immediately whisk in the warm milk. Return the saucepan to the heat and cook, stirring constantly, until the mixture thickens and boils. Remove from the heat and add the chicken broth, whisking constantly. Add the mace and whisk to blend. Transfer the onions to a blender or food processor. Add the white sauce base and purée until smooth, in batches. Pour the soup into a saucepan. Add the cream and stir to incorporate. Season with salt and pepper, and reheat briefly over medium heat. Serve garnished with snipped chives. **Makes 6 servings.**

■ True **GREEN ONIONS**, also called bunching onions, are bred specifically to have a small bulb and long stalks, both of which are edible. (Scallions fall into this category.) You can also use a dry onion as a green onion by harvesting the young green tops before the bulb has grown to full size.

■ **SHALLOTS** are milder than onions and often used in French cooking. The small bulbs grow in sections called cloves, similar to garlic. The skins can be reddish brown, yellow, or gray.

■ **PEARL ONIONS** are small (about 1 inch wide), mild onions with red, white, or yellow skins. Although commonly pickled and used in cocktails, they also can be cooked as a side dish or added whole to stews and casseroles.

Perfect Pumpkin Soup

Any pumpkin is edible, but two great choices for cooking are 'Sugar Treat' and 'Winter Luxury'.

5 cups chicken broth

2 pounds pumpkin, peeled and cut into 1-inch chunks

1 cup chopped onion

¼ teaspoon nutmeg

¼ teaspoon allspice

¼ teaspoon mace

½ teaspoon dried thyme

2 cups light cream or evaporated skim milk

⅛ cup dry sherry

croutons, for garnish

chopped fresh parsley, for garnish

In a large saucepan, warm the broth over medium heat. Add the pumpkin and onion and bring the liquid to a boil. Simmer for 20 minutes, or until the pumpkin is tender. Add the nutmeg, allspice, mace, and thyme in the last 5 minutes of cooking. Set aside for 10 minutes to cool. In a blender or food processor, purée the mixture until smooth, in batches. Return the soup to the pan and add the light cream and sherry, stirring to incorporate. Heat the soup thoroughly, stirring constantly so that it does not come to a full boil. Garnish with croutons and chopped parsley. **Makes 8 servings.**

Curried Pattypan Soup

2 tablespoons butter

¾ cup chopped onion

2 teaspoons curry powder

¼ teaspoon freshly ground black pepper

2 pounds pattypan squash, peeled and chopped

2 cups chicken broth

chopped chives, for garnish

In a large saucepan, melt the butter over medium heat. Add the onion and sauté until translucent. Add the curry powder and pepper and cook, stirring constantly, for 2 minutes more. Add the squash and broth and simmer, covered, until the squash is tender. Remove the pan from the heat and set aside for 10 minutes to cool. In a blender or food processor, purée the mixture, in batches. Serve hot or cold, garnished with chopped chives. **Makes 6 to 8 servings.**

> *What I say is that if a man really likes potatoes,*
> *he must be a pretty decent sort of fellow.*
>
> –A. A. Milne, English writer (1882–1956)

In the Garden: Potatoes

■ Potatoes like cool weather, so plant them in early spring. Depending upon the variety and weather conditions, potatoes planted in early April should be ready to harvest in late July.

Potato Chowder

This chowder's flavor improves with reheating, so make enough for another day.

CROUTONS:

¼ pound slab bacon (¼-inch thick), diced

4 slices pumpernickel bread, diced

CHOWDER:

2 quarts beef broth

1 pound (about 4 medium) potatoes, peeled and cut into ½-inch cubes

2 carrots, peeled and diced

3 tomatoes, diced

3 leeks, trimmed and thinly sliced

½ celery root (celeriac), diced (optional)

3 sprigs parsley, whole

1 small bay leaf

1 teaspoon dried thyme

salt and pepper, to taste

4 tablespoons sour cream or yogurt

For croutons: In a skillet over medium heat, fry the bacon until partially cooked. Add the pumpernickel cubes and fry, stirring occasionally, until the bacon is dark and the bread is crisp. Remove the bacon and bread from the pan and set them aside to drain.

For chowder: Put the beef broth into a large pot over medium heat and bring to a boil. Add the remaining ingredients except the sour cream and return to a boil, then reduce the heat, cover, and simmer for 30 minutes. When the vegetables are tender, remove the parsley and bay leaf. Add the sour cream and stir to incorporate. Adjust the seasonings to taste and simmer for 1 minute more. Serve garnished with bacon and croutons. **Makes 4 to 6 servings.**

In the Kitchen: Milk

■ To prevent formation of a "skin" when cooking milk or cream soups, cover the pan.

Autumn Garden Soup

(recipe at right)

Fun Food Fact: Rosemary

■ In the language of flowers, rosemary symbolizes remembrance.

Autumn Garden Soup

1 ham bone

¼ cup chopped salt pork

1 clove garlic

several sprigs parsley

2 onions, chopped

2 carrots, peeled and diced

3 stalks celery, chopped, or handful of celery leaves

1 cup fresh shell beans*

a few leaves each of mint, marjoram, basil, rosemary, and thyme

4 large tomatoes, peeled *(see tip, page 65)* and diced

½ pound fresh spinach or other greens, trimmed and chopped

1 cup puréed winter squash or pumpkin

salt and pepper, to taste

grated cheese, for garnish

Put the ham bone into a large stockpot, cover with water, and simmer over medium heat for 1 hour. In a frying pan, cook the salt pork until the fat is released. Add the garlic, parsley, onions, carrots, and celery and sauté lightly, without browning. Remove the ham bone from the pot and skim any fat from the stock. Cut off any bits of meat from the ham bone and return them to the soup. Add the onion and carrot mixture to the ham broth and simmer for 1 hour. Add the beans, herbs, tomatoes, spinach, and squash. Simmer for 30 minutes. Season with salt and pepper. Serve hot, with a sprinkling of grated cheese. **Makes 4 to 6 servings.**

You can substitute for fresh shell beans with ½ cup dried navy beans or soldier beans cooked in unsalted water, or fresh green or wax beans.

Root Soup

Inspired by a traditional Finnish recipe, this soup is delicious served with dark bread and sharp cheese.

2 tablespoons olive oil
1 medium onion, chopped
3 medium parsnips, peeled and sliced
4 to 5 medium carrots, peeled and sliced
1 sweet potato, peeled and sliced
1 ripe pear, peeled, cored, and chopped
3½ cups chicken or vegetable broth
½ cup white wine, apple cider, or
    apple juice
1 teaspoon freshly ground black pepper
¼ teaspoon ground cloves
¼ teaspoon nutmeg
¼ teaspoon ground ginger
¼ teaspoon ground cumin

In a large stockpot, warm the olive oil over medium-high heat. Add the onion, parsnips, carrots, sweet potato, and pear and sauté for 10 to 15 minutes. Add the broth, 2 cups of water, wine, and spices. Simmer for 20 minutes. Set aside to cool for 10 minutes, then purée in a blender or food processor until smooth, in batches. Return to the pot and reheat. **Makes 6 servings.**

What's the Difference?

■ A SWEET POTATO is not a potato but the elongated root of a vine in the morning glory family. Its smooth skin can be white, yellow, brown, red, or purple. White-flesh sweet potatoes aren't as sweet as the bright-orange types and have a drier texture. In North America, the orange types are often called yams—and therein lies the confusion.

■ A true YAM, sometimes called a tropical yam, is a tuber from one of several tropical vines. A yam can be similar in size to a sweet potato or grow more than 8 feet long in the wild. It has rough skin that can be cream, brown, or pinkish. The flesh is white, yellow, pink, or purple and is sweeter and moister than that of a sweet potato.

SOUPS

*I feel a recipe is only a theme,
which an intelligent cook can play
each time with variation.*

–Madame Benoit, Canadian writer (1904–87)

In the Garden: Spinach

■ For a late harvest of spinach, plant
broadleaf varieties such as 'Baker',
'St. Helens', 'Tyee', and 'Wolter' 6 to 8
weeks before the first fall frost.

Spinach, Basil, and Walnut Soup

*This soup derives its marvelous flavor and slightly thickened consistency from a walnut, garlic,
and basil paste—a version of the popular pesto sauce.*

¼ cup olive oil

¼ cup (½ stick) butter

1 clove garlic

¼ cup freshly grated Parmesan cheese

⅓ cup chopped walnuts

20 medium to large fresh basil leaves

6 cups chicken broth

1 pound spinach, trimmed and torn into
    bite-size pieces

salt and pepper, to taste

In a blender or food processor, combine the oil, butter, garlic, and Parmesan and blend until smooth. Add
the walnuts and basil and blend until the mixture is
vivid green, then transfer to a small bowl. Heat the
broth in a saucepan over medium heat. When the
broth bubbles gently, slowly add the basil paste, whisking constantly. Stir in the spinach and cook briefly over
medium heat, until the spinach is wilted. Season with
salt and pepper and serve immediately with additional
Parmesan. **Makes 6 servings.**

Spinach and Chicken Soup

For a heartier soup, add a cup of chopped cooked chicken.

2 quarts chicken stock

2 onions, chopped

1 cup diced tomatoes

4 cups finely chopped fresh spinach

salt and pepper, to taste

grated cheese, for garnish

In a large stockpot, combine the stock, onions, and tomatoes and simmer over medium heat for 15 minutes. Add the spinach and simmer for 5 minutes more, or until wilted. Season with salt and pepper. Serve with grated cheese sprinkled on top. **Makes 6 to 8 servings.**

Sorrel Soup With Rosemary

1 onion, chopped

¼ cup (½ stick) butter

3 cups chopped sorrel leaves

2 sprigs rosemary

1 quart chicken broth

3 potatoes, peeled, cooked, and
   mashed

1 cup cream

minced fresh parsley, for garnish

In a saucepan, sauté the onion in the butter until translucent. Add the sorrel leaves, rosemary, and broth and simmer for 15 minutes. Add the mashed potatoes and simmer for 15 minutes more. Add the cream, stir, and bring to a simmer. Garnish with minced parsley before serving. **Makes 6 servings.**

In the Kitchen: Sorrel

■ The sour, lemony leaves of sorrel are best used when young. Add the greens to salads but reduce any vinegar or lemon in the dressing, if it's homemade. Also use the leaves in soups, eggs, fish sauces, cream cheese, and poultry and pork dishes.

How to Peel and Seed a Tomato

- Bring a pot of water to a rolling boil. Stick a fork into the stem end of a tomato. Immerse the tomato fully in the water and hold it there for 5 seconds. Plunge the tomato immediately into ice-cold water for 3 to 5 seconds. With one hand, hold the fork with the tomato on it. With the other, slash the tomato skin with a sharp knife, pinch the skin between your thumb and the knife's blade, and peel the tomato.

- To seed the tomato, remove it from the fork, cut it in half crosswise (on its equator, not from the stem to the bottom), and scoop out the seeds with a small spoon.

Fresh Tomato Soup

¼ cup (½ stick) butter

½ cup coarsely diced celery

¼ cup minced onion

3 medium potatoes, peeled and chopped

3 medium carrots, peeled and chopped

4 large tomatoes, peeled, seeded (see tip, above), and coarsely cubed

6 cups chicken or vegetable stock

1 tablespoon brown sugar

1 bay leaf

½ teaspoon dried marjoram

½ teaspoon dried tarragon

salt and pepper, to taste

1 cup heavy cream

In a large stockpot, melt the butter over medium heat. Add the celery, onion, potatoes, and carrots and sauté, stirring frequently, for 5 minutes, or until lightly browned. Add the tomatoes, stock, brown sugar, and herbs and lower the heat to simmer, covered, for 1 hour. Remove the bay leaf. Set aside for 10 minutes to cool. Put the ingredients into a blender or food processor and purée until smooth. Season with salt and pepper. Just before serving, add the cream and stir to incorporate. Serve hot or cold. **Makes 16 servings.**

MAKE AHEAD: *This soup can be prepared up to the purée stage, covered, and refrigerated for 4 days or frozen in an airtight container for 3 months.*

Winter Vegetable Beef Stew

SOUPS

2 tablespoons vegetable oil, divided,
plus a bit more

1 clove garlic, minced

1 large onion, chopped

2 or 3 stalks celery with tops, cut into
1-inch pieces

2 carrots, peeled and cut into 1-inch
pieces

1 or 2 parsnips, peeled and cut into
1-inch pieces

1 large or 2 small turnips, peeled and
quartered

1 celery root (celeriac), peeled and diced

1 rutabaga, peeled and diced

1 small butternut squash, peeled and
diced

1 or 2 boiling potatoes, peeled and
quartered

2½ cups beef broth

dash Worcestershire sauce

1 cup red wine or water

3 to 4 pounds beef chuck, trimmed and
cut into 1-inch cubes

salt and pepper, to taste

1 tablespoon paprika

1 can (28 ounces) tomato purée

1 pound fresh mushrooms, wiped
clean and quartered

In a heavy stew pot, warm 1 tablespoon of the oil over medium heat. Add the garlic and onion and sauté for 5 minutes, or until soft. Add the celery, carrots, parsnips, turnips, celery root, rutabaga, squash, potatoes, beef broth, Worcestershire sauce, and wine, plus additional water to cover, if necessary. Raise the heat and bring to a boil. Reduce the heat to simmer, cover, and cook for 35 to 40 minutes, or until the vegetables are tender. Remove the pot from the heat and set aside for 10 minutes. Sprinkle the beef cubes with salt and pepper and paprika and set aside. With a slotted spoon, transfer the vegetables from the stew pot into a blender or food processor, in batches, and purée until smooth, adding a little liquid from the pot, if necessary. Return the puréed vegetables to the stew pot and add the tomato purée. Simmer. In a skillet or Dutch oven over medium heat, warm an additional 1 tablespoon of oil. Add the beef in three batches, raise the heat to high, and brown the meat. As the meat browns, add it to the stew pot. When all of the meat is cooked, put the mushrooms into the skillet and sauté until soft, adding more oil, if necessary. Add the mushrooms to the stew pot, cover, and simmer for 1 to 1½ hours, or until the meat is tender. **Makes 6 to 8 servings.**

How to Harvest: Carrots

■ Carrots can be picked when they reach a desired size, but they taste better after a frost—or two. Following the first hard frost, cover carrot rows with an 18-inch layer of shredded leaves to preserve them for harvesting later. For more about carrots, see page 99.

Turnips like a dry bed but a wet head.

–proverb

White Turnip Soup

3 tablespoons butter

4 medium white turnips, peeled, sliced, and coarsely chopped

1 large onion, coarsely chopped

salt and pepper, to taste

3 slices bread, dried in an oven on low heat and crumbled

2 egg yolks

½ cup heavy cream

finely minced fresh parsley, for garnish

In a large stockpot, melt the butter over medium heat. Add the turnips and onion and cook for 5 minutes. Put 6 cups of water into a saucepan and bring to a boil. Add the water to the vegetables, along with the salt, pepper, and bread. Simmer the soup for 30 minutes and set aside for 10 minutes to cool. Put the ingredients into a blender or food processor and purée until smooth, in batches. Return the soup to the stockpot and reheat on low. In a small bowl, beat the egg yolks with the cream. Add the egg mixture to the soup, stirring constantly to combine. Cook for 2 minutes. Serve at once, garnished with parsley. **Makes 6 servings.**

Vichyssoise (Potato Soup)

¼ cup (½ stick) butter

6 leeks (white part only), sliced into rings

1 large onion, finely chopped

3¾ cups chicken stock

4 to 5 potatoes, peeled and sliced

salt, to taste

1¼ cups milk

1¼ cups light cream

⅔ cup heavy cream

3 tablespoons chopped chives, for garnish

In a stockpot, melt the butter over medium heat. Add the leeks and onion, and sauté for 5 to 10 minutes, or until soft. Add the stock, potatoes, and salt, and cook gently for about 30 minutes, or until the potatoes are soft. Set aside for 10 minutes to cool. In a blender or food processor, purée the mixture in batches, return to the pot, add the milk and light cream, and bring slowly to a boil, stirring constantly. Remove the soup from the heat and set aside to cool. Refrigerate until chilled. Just before serving, add the heavy cream and stir to incorporate. Garnish each serving with chopped chives. **Makes 10 to 12 servings.**

Zucchini Potato Soup

A good reason never to say "No, thanks!" to zucchini.

5 cups chicken broth
1 pound zucchini, halved and thinly sliced
1 large potato, halved and thinly sliced
1 large onion, halved and thinly sliced
3 eggs
2 tablespoons fresh lemon juice
salt and pepper, to taste

In a large saucepan, bring the broth to a boil over medium-high heat. Add the zucchini, potato, and onion. Reduce the heat and simmer, covered, for 15 minutes. In a small bowl, beat the eggs. Add the lemon juice and ½ cup of the warm broth and whisk to combine. Add the eggs and lemon juice to the hot broth gradually and stir constantly, so that the mixture doesn't curdle. Increase the heat to medium and cook for 1 minute, stirring constantly, but do not boil. Season with salt and pepper and serve. **Makes 8 servings.**

How to Harvest: Summer Squashes and Zucchini

■ Summer squashes and zucchini are at their best when they're about 4 inches long. Pick them young, as more will follow. Cut the stem about 1 inch above the fruit.

Turkey and Potato Chowder

¼ pound bacon, diced
2 large onions, chopped
1 carrot, diced
4 stalks celery, chopped
¼ cup all-purpose flour
1 pound red-skin potatoes, diced
1 teaspoon dried thyme
½ teaspoon freshly ground black pepper
2 teaspoons salt
1 bay leaf
2 quarts turkey stock
1 cup white wine
2 cups diced cooked turkey
2 cups heavy cream
chopped fresh parsley, for garnish

In a large stockpot, cook the bacon over medium heat until it browns. Remove the bacon and set aside to drain, leaving the fat in the pan. Add the onions, carrot, and celery to the stockpot and sauté until soft. Sprinkle the flour on the vegetables, stir to combine, and cook for 2 minutes. Add the potatoes and cook for 2 minutes more. Remove the pot from the heat and add the thyme, pepper, salt, bay leaf, stock, and wine. Stir, then cook over low heat for 45 minutes. Add the turkey and cooked bacon and warm for 10 minutes, or until heated through. Add the cream, stir to incorporate, and cook for 5 minutes, but do not boil. Serve, garnished with parsley. **Makes 12 servings.**

CHAPTER 4

Salads

Shrimp, Arugula, and Chicory Salad. 70

Lobster Seaslaw Salad. 71

Carrot Salad. 72

Snow Pea and Carrot Salad. 73

Green Beans Piccata 73

Bean Salad With Summer Savory. 74

Sweet-and-Sour Bean Salad 74

Green Bean and Cauliflower Salad. 75

White Bean and Tuna Salad 77

Bean Salad With Lovage 78

Baby Beet Greens Salad 79

Apple and Beet Salad 79

Yellow Beans With Fresh Dill 80

Lima Bean Salad 80

Sorrel Salad 81

Beet, Egg, and Herring Salad. 82

Cucumbers With Feta Cheese Dressing 84

Orange and Onion Salad. 84

Crunchy Pear Salad 85

Strawberry Spinach Salad 86

Cantaloupe and Cucumber Salad 86

Tabbouli Salad 87

Root Vegetable Salad. 88

Marinated Vegetables 89

Confetti Salad With Calendula Petals. 91

Watermelon Salad. 92

Ruby Coleslaw With Caraway Dressing 92

Coleslaw With Salad Burnet 93

Slaw With Shrimp and Creamy Horseradish
    Dressing 94

New Potato Salad 94

Hot Potato Salad With Bourbon 95

Pizza Salad. 96

Green Goddess Dressing. 97

Mint Salad Dressing. 97

Shrimp, Arugula, and Chicory Salad

The dressing wilts the greens, so assemble the salad just before serving.

SALAD:
½ cup baby arugula leaves
1 bunch chicory, stemmed

DRESSING:
¼ cup olive oil
1 tablespoon minced garlic
1 onion, finely chopped
¼ cup chopped scallions
½ to ¾ pound shrimp, peeled, deveined,
  and cooked
3 tablespoons chopped fresh marjoram
  or parsley
1 tablespoon chopped fresh cilantro
  (optional)
3 tablespoons fresh lemon juice
2 tablespoons rice vinegar

For salad: Arrange the arugula and chicory on a serving platter.

For dressing: In a large skillet over medium heat, warm the olive oil and sauté the garlic, onion, and scallions for 3 minutes, stirring constantly. Add the shrimp and sauté for 2 minutes more, or until warmed through. Stir in the marjoram and cilantro, if using. Remove the skillet from the heat, add the lemon juice and vinegar, and stir to coat. Taste and adjust the seasonings, if necessary.

Pour the warm dressing over the salad and toss lightly. **Makes 2 to 4 servings.**

VARIATION: *Add ½ cup of diced ham along with the garlic. Or substitute ½ cup of diced chicken breast for the shrimp and cook for 3 minutes more, not 2.*

In the Garden: Chicory

- Chicory is a perennial herb closely related to radicchio and Belgian endive. It grows 3 to 5 feet tall, with ragged leaves and sky-blue flowers. In early spring, sow seeds in well-drained soil in full sun.

How to Harvest

- Chicory leaves are big enough to harvest in about 60 days. The roots can be boiled or slowly roasted. When ground after roasting, the root can be added to coffee for what is commonly considered a New Orleans-style brew.

Lobster Seaslaw Salad

SALAD:

3½ cups finely shredded cabbage

½ cup finely chopped green bell pepper

1 small Bermuda onion, quartered and
thinly sliced

¼ cup chopped fresh parsley

2 cups chopped, cooked lobster meat

12 cooked artichoke hearts, or 1 can
(14 ounces) artichoke hearts,
rinsed, drained, halved, and
thinly sliced

DRESSING:

3 tablespoons sherry

2 tablespoons fresh lemon juice

1 tablespoon red-wine vinegar

1 tablespoon olive oil

2 teaspoons honey

4 fresh basil leaves, coarsely chopped, or
¼ teaspoon dried basil

¼ teaspoon celery salt

pinch cayenne pepper

1 ripe honeydew melon, seeded, sliced,
and rind removed

18 extra-large shrimp, peeled, deveined,
and cooked

24 sprigs of watercress

For salad: In a large mixing bowl, combine the cabbage, green pepper, onion, parsley, lobster, and artichoke hearts.

For dressing: In a blender or jar with a lid, combine the sherry, lemon juice, vinegar, oil, honey, basil, celery salt, and cayenne pepper and process or shake to blend.

Pour the dressing over the salad ingredients and toss to coat. Cover and chill for 2 hours before serving. Toss several times while refrigerated.

Serve with the melon slices. Top with the shrimp and watercress sprigs. **Makes 6 servings.**

Save 'n' Store: Greens

■ It's best to use greens the same day that they are picked. If you need to store them briefly, refrigerate them, unwashed, until just before cooking. To prevent rotting, put a layer of newspaper and then a layer of paper towels under the greens in refrigerator bins to soak up any moisture.

Carrot Salad

Use slender and sweet carrots for best results.

SALAD:

1 pound carrots

DRESSING:

¼ teaspoon salt

¼ teaspoon paprika

1 small shallot, minced

2 tablespoons fresh lemon juice

6 tablespoons olive oil

**1 tablespoon chopped fresh chervil
   or parsley or 1 teaspoon dried
   chervil or parsley**

**1 teaspoon chopped fresh basil or
   ¼ teaspoon dried basil**

12 sprigs of watercress

For salad: With a soft-bristle brush, scrub the carrots under cold running water. Trim off the stem ends and leave the carrots whole. Put them into a saucepan and cover with cold water. Set the pan over high heat and bring the water to a gentle boil. Cook uncovered for 10 to 30 minutes, or until tender (the time will depend on the size of the carrots). Drain, then cover with cold water. When the carrots are cool, drain, then blot dry. Refrigerate for 1 hour.

For dressing: In a small bowl or jar with a lid, combine the salt, paprika, and shallot. Add the lemon juice and whisk with a fork or secure the lid and shake the jar to dissolve the salt and paprika. Gradually add the oil, whisking constantly, or add it all at once, cover the jar, and shake it vigorously. Add the chervil and basil and repeat the mixing process. Set the dressing aside at room temperature.

Arrange the sprigs of watercress on a plate. Before serving, whisk or shake the dressing to combine and pour over the chilled carrots. Spoon the carrots over the watercress. **Makes 4 servings.**

In the Garden: Carrots

■ **Mix radish seeds with carrot seeds before you sow. Radish sprouts will easily push through the soil, breaking it up for the later-sprouting carrots. As you harvest the radishes, space is made for the carrots to grow.**

SALADS

Snow Pea and Carrot Salad

SALAD:

2 cups fresh snow peas, cut diagonally

2 medium carrots, cut into matchsticks

DRESSING:

3 tablespoons sesame oil

1 tablespoon fresh lemon juice

1 teaspoon soy sauce

1 tablespoon sunflower seeds

½ teaspoon chopped fresh mint

For salad: Put the snow peas and carrots into a saucepan with a small amount of water. Simmer over medium heat for 3 to 5 minutes, or until barely soft. Drain, then rinse in cold water. Blot dry.

For dressing: In a small bowl or jar with a lid, combine the sesame oil, lemon juice, and soy sauce and whisk or shake to blend.

Preheat the oven to 300°F. Spread the sunflower seeds on a cookie sheet and toast in the oven for 5 minutes, or until golden brown.

Pour the dressing over the vegetables, sprinkle with the seeds and mint, and toss to coat. Serve warm or cold. **Makes 6 servings.**

Green Beans Piccata

This salad's dressing is refreshing and quite tart.

DRESSING:

2 cups dry white wine

½ cup olive oil

juice of 2 lemons

1 tablespoon cornstarch

3 cloves garlic, finely chopped

1 jar (3¼ ounces) capers, drained

salt and pepper, to taste

1 pound green beans, trimmed and
    cut into 1-inch pieces

For dressing: In a nonaluminum saucepan over medium heat, simmer the white wine until reduced by half. Pour the wine into a heatproof bowl and add the olive oil. Put the lemon juice into the saucepan and add the cornstarch. Return the saucepan to the heat and whisk the lemon and cornstarch mixture until it thickens. Add the wine and olive oil to the saucepan, whisking until the mixture boils and thickens to the consistency of cream soup. Remove the saucepan from the heat. Add the garlic and capers and season with salt and pepper. Set the dressing aside for about 2 hours.

Put the green beans into a saucepan and cover them with water. Over high heat, bring the water to a boil and cook, uncovered, for 5 to 8 minutes, or until tender. Drain, then put the beans into a bowl filled with ice water. When they are chilled, drain and blot dry. About 10 minutes before serving, toss the beans with the dressing. **Makes 4 servings.**

Bean Salad With Summer Savory

This "bean herb" makes for a peppery dish.

SALAD:

7 ounces dried white beans

1 carrot, sliced

1 stalk celery, sliced

1 Spanish onion, halved and divided

2 tablespoons chopped fresh summer savory

2 tablespoons chopped fresh parsley

DRESSING:

3 tablespoons olive oil

1 tablespoon white-wine vinegar

1 clove garlic, crushed

For salad: Put the beans into a large bowl and cover with cold water. Set aside to soak overnight or for at least 3 to 4 hours *(see tip, page 44)*. Drain and rinse the beans and then transfer them to a saucepan. Add water to cover and, over medium heat, bring the liquid to a boil. Add the carrot, celery, and half of the onion. Thinly slice the remaining half-onion. When the beans are soft, drain them and discard the vegetables. Transfer the beans to a bowl, add the sliced onion and the herbs, and stir.

For dressing: In a separate bowl, combine the oil, vinegar, and garlic and mix to blend. Add the dressing to the salad and toss to coat. Serve warm. **Makes 3 to 4 servings.**

Sweet-and-Sour Bean Salad

2 pounds wax beans, trimmed and cut into 1-inch pieces

½ cup white-wine vinegar

½ cup sugar

2 cloves

1 stick cinnamon

Put the beans into a saucepan, cover them with water, and cook over medium heat for 10 minutes, or until tender. Drain, rinse, and transfer to a bowl. In a saucepan over medium heat, combine 1 cup of water and the vinegar, sugar, cloves, and cinnamon. Bring the liquid to a boil and cook for 5 minutes. Pour over the drained beans. Chill for 2 hours or longer and serve. **Makes 8 servings.**

Cook's Glossary: Wax Beans

■ Wax beans are a type of snap bean with waxy pods that are yellow, light green, or purple. (Purple pods turn green when cooked.) Wax beans have a milder flavor than green beans.

Cook's Glossary: Green Beans

- Green beans are a type of snap bean (named for the sound made when they are broken into pieces). Green beans are also called string beans, for the stringy filaments found in the pods of some older varieties.

Green Bean and Cauliflower Salad

1½ pounds green beans, trimmed and cut into 1-inch pieces
1 head cauliflower, separated into small florets
1 teaspoon salt
2 teaspoons freshly ground black pepper
1 tablespoon chopped fresh mint
1 clove garlic, finely chopped
½ cup oil
2 tablespoons fresh lemon juice

Put the beans and cauliflower florets into separate pots of salted water over medium heat and boil for 5 minutes, or until the vegetables are tender but firm. Drain, rinse with cold water, and set them aside to cool separately. Sprinkle each vegetable with half of the salt, pepper, mint, and garlic. Arrange the beans and florets on a platter. In a small bowl or a jar with a lid, whisk or shake the oil and lemon juice to blend, then drizzle over the vegetables. Set aside to marinate for 30 minutes before serving. **Makes 4 servings.**

Cauliflower is nothing but cabbage with a college education.

– Pudd'nhead Wilson, *by Mark Twain,*
American writer (1835–1910)

White Bean and Tuna Salad
(recipe at right)

In the Garden: Lettuce

■ Lettuce requires frequent light watering. If the leaves wilt in hot weather, sprinkle them with water to cool.

White Bean and Tuna Salad

Serve this salad for lunch or as part of a soup-and-salad supper.

SALAD:

1 red bell pepper, cut into thin strips

2 cans (6½ ounces each) solid white tuna, drained

4 cups cooked cannellini beans

5 scallions, thinly sliced

2 tablespoons chopped fresh basil or parsley

1 teaspoon grated lemon zest

DRESSING:

½ teaspoon salt

1 clove garlic

2 tablespoons fresh lemon juice

6 tablespoons olive oil

freshly ground black pepper, to taste

Boston or romaine lettuce

1½ cups pitted black Greek or Italian olives, cut into quarters

For salad: Put the red pepper into a saucepan, add water to cover, and place over high heat. Bring to a boil and cook uncovered for 1 minute. Drain and set aside. Flake the tuna into a large bowl. Add the beans, scallions, red pepper, and basil. Stir to blend, then sprinkle with lemon zest.

For dressing: Using a pestle and small mortar, work the salt and garlic into a paste. Add the lemon juice and stir with the pestle until the salt is dissolved. Transfer the paste to a small bowl. Gradually add the oil, whisking constantly. Season with black pepper and whisk to blend.

Pour the dressing over the bean mixture and toss to coat. Serve on a bed of lettuce and top with black olives. **Makes 6 servings.**

Bean Salad With Lovage

Prepare this dish up to 4 hours ahead of serving time, tossing it occasionally during that time.

⅓ cup olive oil

2 tablespoons balsamic vinegar

1 teaspoon ground cumin

2 cups cooked black beans

2 cups cooked red kidney beans

2 cups cooked cannellini beans

½ cup chopped fresh lovage leaves and stems

1 red bell pepper, chopped

1 cup chopped red onion

⅓ cup chopped fresh cilantro

2 small jalapeños, seeded and chopped

salt and pepper, to taste

In a large bowl, combine the oil, vinegar, and cumin and whisk to combine. Add the beans, lovage, red pepper, onion, cilantro, and jalapeños and toss to coat. Season with salt and pepper. **Makes 6 servings.**

In the Kitchen: Lovage

■ Fresh lovage stems and leaves can be substituted for celery. Use smaller amounts, however, as lovage's taste, while similar, is more pronounced.

Baby Beet Greens Salad

If you grow your own beets, you'll have a good supply of these delicious and nutritious greens.

SALAD:

1 cup baby beet greens, stemmed

12 whole, cooked baby beets, peeled
    and sliced or diced *(see tip, page 82)*

1 cup sliced mushrooms (optional)

1 cup mixed salad greens

DRESSING:

3 tablespoons olive oil

2 tablespoons cider vinegar

1 tablespoon chopped fresh parsley or chervil or
    1 teaspoon dried parsley or chervil

For salad: Tear the beet greens, if they are too large. In a large bowl, toss together the beet greens, beets, mushrooms, and salad greens.

For dressing: In a small bowl or jar with a lid, combine the oil, vinegar, and parsley and whisk or shake to blend.

Pour the dressing over the salad and toss to coat. **Makes 2 to 4 servings.**

Apple and Beet Salad

SALAD:

1 head endive, trimmed and separated

1 small head Boston lettuce

2 to 3 tender, inner celery stalks, diced

2 medium cooked beets, peeled and
    diced *(see tip, page 82)*

1 large green apple, cored and diced

¾ cup walnut halves

2 scallions, thinly sliced

DRESSING:

¾ cup olive oil

¼ cup fresh lemon juice

1 teaspoon Dijon-style mustard

garlic cloves, to taste

fresh or dried basil, dill, rosemary,
    and/or tarragon, to taste

salt and pepper, to taste

For salad: Wash and drain the endive and lettuce, then tear the lettuce into bite-size pieces. Combine all of the ingredients in a salad bowl.

For dressing: In a bowl or jar with a lid, combine the olive oil, lemon juice, and mustard. Finely crush or chop the garlic cloves and add to the bowl or jar. Add as much of as many herbs as desired. (Some herbs are stronger than others and will dominate the flavor.) Season with salt and pepper. Whisk or shake to blend.

A few minutes before serving, pour the dressing over the salad and toss to coat. **Makes 6 to 8 servings.**

Yellow Beans With Fresh Dill

A dish as tasty as it is colorful!

SALADS

SALAD:

1 pound yellow beans, trimmed and
    cut into 1-inch pieces

¼ cup chopped red bell pepper

2 tablespoons chopped fresh dill

3 scallions, thinly sliced

DRESSING:

½ cup olive oil

3 tablespoons red-wine vinegar

¼ teaspoon freshly ground black
    pepper

½ teaspoon celery salt

For salad: In a saucepan over medium heat, steam the beans for 5 minutes, or until they are crisp-tender. Remove the pan from the heat, drain the beans, and rinse them under cold water. Pat them dry, then put them into a salad bowl with the red pepper, dill, and scallions.

For dressing: In a small bowl or jar with a lid, combine the olive oil, vinegar, black pepper, and salt and whisk or shake to blend.

Pour the dressing over the salad and toss to coat. Serve at room temperature or slightly chilled. **Makes 6 servings.**

In the Kitchen: Lima Beans

■ Raw lima beans contain linamarin, a toxic cyanide compound that is neutralized through cooking. Avoid eating them raw.

Lima Bean Salad

2 cups cooked lima beans, drained

½ cup minced ham or chopped bologna

½ cup chopped celery

1 tablespoon white-wine vinegar

oil and vinegar (or your favorite
    dressing), to taste

salt and pepper, to taste

2 hard-boiled eggs, chopped

lettuce leaves

In a medium bowl, combine the lima beans, ham, and celery. Drizzle with the white-wine vinegar, mix, and set aside to marinate for at least 1 hour. Just before serving, pour the oil-and-vinegar dressing over the marinated ingredients and toss to coat. Sprinkle with salt and pepper, add the eggs, and mix gently. Serve on a bed of lettuce. **Makes 2 to 4 servings.**

Fun Food Fact: Sorrel

■ In the language of flowers,
sorrel symbolizes affection.

Sorrel Salad

Simple and old-fashioned, with an unexpected flavor.

SALAD:

2 cups torn mild lettuce, such as Boston

4 cups torn sorrel

2 hard-boiled eggs, coarsely chopped

DRESSING:

1 small shallot, minced

salt and pepper, to taste

1 teaspoon or more Dijon-style mustard

½ cup olive oil

¼ cup white-wine vinegar

¼ cup heavy cream

For salad: Toss the lettuce and sorrel together. Toss the eggs with the greens.

For dressing: In a small bowl or a blender or food processor, combine the shallot, salt and pepper, and mustard. Add the olive oil and whisk or process to blend. Add the vinegar and cream, and whisk or process again. Adjust the seasonings to taste.

Pour the dressing over the salad and toss gently to coat. **Makes 4 servings.**

This rule in gardening never forget: to sow dry and to set wet.

Beet, Egg, and Herring Salad

A colorful salad—the perfect dish for a spring luncheon.

SALADS

2 medium potatoes, peeled, cooked, and diced

3 hard-boiled eggs, chopped

2 tart apples, cored, and diced

2 small carrots, peeled, cooked, and diced

1 small onion, minced

2 medium sour pickles, diced

¾ cup diced pickled herring

¼ teaspoon freshly ground black pepper

lettuce or baby spinach leaves

2 cups cooked beets, peeled and diced *(see tip, below)*

In a bowl, combine the potatoes, eggs, apples, carrots, onion, pickles, herring, and pepper. Refrigerate. Just before serving, line a bowl with lettuce. Add the beets to the chilled ingredients and toss. Spoon the mixture over the lettuce. **Makes 8 to 10 servings.**

How to Boil Beets

■ Select roots no larger than 2 inches in diameter and wash them thoroughly. Trim the leafy tops, leaving 1 to 2 inches of stem, but leave the root intact to reduce bleeding. Place the beets in a stain-resistant saucepan and add water to cover. Bring the water to a boil, reduce the heat, cover, and cook for 30 to 40 minutes, or until tender. Drain, then rinse in cold water. Slice off the stems and root end, then peel off the skin. Work on paper towels or similar material; beet juice may stain wood cutting boards, porous surfaces, fabrics, and skin.

Beet, Egg, and Herring Salad
(recipe at left)

Cucumbers With Feta Cheese Dressing

SALADS

SALAD:

1 head Bibb lettuce

2 large cucumbers, peeled and thinly
    sliced

2 medium Vidalia onions, thinly sliced

DRESSING:

¼ pound feta cheese

5 tablespoons olive oil, plus extra
    as needed

1 teaspoon minced fresh oregano

1 tablespoon fresh lemon juice

⅛ teaspoon freshly ground black pepper

For salad: Tear the lettuce into pieces and arrange them on a large salad plate. Place the sliced cucumbers and onions on the lettuce.

For dressing: In a blender or food processor, combine the feta cheese, olive oil, oregano, and lemon juice and blend until smooth. Add more olive oil as needed to reach desired consistency.

Just before serving, pour the dressing over the salad. Sprinkle with pepper. **Makes 6 to 8 servings.**

In the Garden: Cucumbers

- Spray cucumber vines with sugar water to attract bees and set more fruit.

Orange and Onion Salad

SALAD:

1 head Bibb lettuce

4 oranges, peeled, sliced in half rounds,
    and seeded

1 medium Bermuda onion, thinly sliced

20 pitted black olives, halved

DRESSING:

½ cup olive oil

¼ cup fresh lemon juice

½ teaspoon salt

1 teaspoon celery seed

⅛ teaspoon freshly ground black pepper

8 leaves fresh mint

1 tablespoon sugar

For salad: Tear the lettuce into bite-size pieces and place them in a salad bowl. Add the oranges, onion, and olives and toss. Chill the salad while preparing dressing.

For dressing: In a blender or food processor, combine all of the dressing ingredients and blend for 2 minutes.

Pour the dressing over the salad and serve. **Makes 8 servings.**

Crunchy Pear Salad

½ **cup chopped walnuts**

¾ **cup chopped celery**

¾ **cup golden raisins**

½ **cup mayonnaise**

1 **cup cottage cheese**

4 **ripe pears, halved and cored**

Bibb lettuce

In a small bowl, mix the walnuts, celery, raisins, mayonnaise, and cottage cheese to combine. Set aside in the refrigerator. Place the pear halves on a bed of lettuce and top each with a spoonful of the cottage cheese mixture. **Makes 4 servings.**

In the Kitchen: Onions

■ **To prevent shedding tears when peeling onions, cut them under running water. The water washes fumes and juice away before they reach your nose or eyes. Also, keep a few onions in the refrigerator. A well-chilled onion does not emit fumes into the air while it is being chopped.**

Strawberry Spinach Salad

Take this along to potluck suppers. Make it in smaller batches for a family dinner.

2½ pounds spinach, trimmed

8 cups strawberries, hulled and sliced

3 cucumbers, thinly sliced

1½ cups scallions, sliced

½ cup snipped fresh mint (optional)

1 bottle (16 ounces) ranch-style salad
    dressing

Tear the spinach into bite-size pieces. Put the spinach, strawberries, cucumbers, scallions, and mint into a large bowl and toss. Just before serving, drizzle the dressing over the spinach salad and toss to coat. **Makes 24 servings.**

Cantaloupe and Cucumber Salad

SALAD:

2 cantaloupes, peeled and seeded

2 cucumbers, peeled

DRESSING:

2 tablespoons fresh lime juice

6 tablespoons safflower oil

½ teaspoon salt

1 teaspoon finely chopped fresh mint

1 teaspoon finely chopped fresh chives

½ cup sour cream

crisp lettuce leaves

For salad: Cut the cantaloupes into bite-size pieces. Slice the cucumbers into thin rounds.

For dressing: In a small bowl, combine the lime juice, safflower oil, salt, mint, chives, and sour cream; mix well.

    Combine the cantaloupes and cucumbers and gently toss with the dressing. Serve on a bed of lettuce. **Makes 6 servings.**

A gift of wooden spoons brings good luck to the bride.

Tabbouli Salad

Popular in the Middle East, bulgur wheat is steamed and dried wheat that has been cracked into pieces, the smallest of which are best for tabbouli. You can usually find bulgur wheat in the rice or hot cereal section of a grocery or natural foods store.

2 cups boiling water

1 cup bulgur wheat

6 scallions, finely chopped

¾ cup finely chopped fresh parsley

4 tablespoons finely chopped fresh mint

3 medium tomatoes, finely diced

¼ cup olive oil

¼ cup fresh lemon juice

½ teaspoon salt

¼ teaspoon freshly ground black pepper

pitted black olives, for garnish

cucumber slices, for garnish

In a medium bowl, pour the boiling water over the bulgur and let it sit for 30 minutes. Drain the bulgur well through a fine strainer, pressing out the excess water. Transfer the bulgur to a mixing bowl and add the scallions, parsley, mint, tomatoes, oil, lemon juice, salt, and pepper. Mix the ingredients well to coat with the oil and lemon juice. Chill for 30 minutes before serving. (Do not chill salad for more than 1 hour because the wheat absorbs flavors and the salad will lose its taste.) Garnish with black olives and cucumber slices, if desired. **Makes 6 servings.**

Root Vegetable Salad

SALAD:

3 medium potatoes, peeled

2 medium carrots

2 medium beets, cooked, peeled, and diced *(see tip, page 82)*

3 small dill pickles, diced

½ cup chopped scallions, white part only

¼ cup finely chopped fresh dill

¼ teaspoon salt

⅛ teaspoon freshly ground black pepper

2 hard-boiled eggs, coarsely chopped

DRESSING:

½ cup plain yogurt

½ cup mayonnaise

3 tablespoons prepared horseradish

1 tablespoon fresh lemon juice

½ teaspoon sugar

freshly ground black pepper, to taste

For salad: In separate saucepans over medium heat, cook the potatoes and carrots in water until each is tender: about 20 minutes for potatoes and 10 minutes for carrots. Drain, then cut into a ½-inch dice. In a large bowl, combine the beets, potatoes, carrots, pickles, scallions, and dill. Toss gently, season with salt and pepper, and add the eggs. Cover and refrigerate.

For dressing: In a blender or food processor, combine the yogurt, mayonnaise, horseradish, lemon juice, and sugar and blend until smooth. Season with pepper.

Pour the dressing over the salad, toss to coat, and chill until served. **Makes 6 servings.**

In the Garden: Beets

■ To enable beet roots to develop quickly and uniformly, set the seeds into soil that is free of clumps and stones and has been worked well. For small beets, double the number of seeds in the row; crowding keeps the roots small.

Marinated Vegetables

SALAD:

½ head cauliflower, separated into small florets

2 cups bite-size broccoli florets and stems

2 carrots, sliced

2 stalks celery, sliced into ¼- to ½-inch pieces

1 small onion, sliced

1 green bell pepper, diced

¾ to 1 cup stuffed green olives or pitted black olives, drained

DRESSING:

¾ cup white or wine vinegar

½ cup olive oil

2 tablespoons sugar

1 teaspoon salt

½ teaspoon freshly ground black pepper

½ to 1 tablespoon chopped fresh oregano or ½ to 1 teaspoon dried oregano

For salad: In a large pot of boiling water, cook the cauliflower and broccoli for 1 minute. Drain, immediately plunge the vegetables into ice water to stop the cooking, then drain again. In a large bowl, combine the cauliflower, broccoli, carrots, celery, onion, green pepper, and olives.

For dressing: In a small bowl or jar with a lid, combine the vinegar, oil, sugar, salt, black pepper, oregano, and ¼ cup of water. Whisk or shake to blend.

Pour the dressing over the salad and toss to coat. Cover and refrigerate for at least 8 hours before serving. **Makes 8 to 12 servings.**

Fun Food Fact: Broccoflower

■ Broccoflower is a cross between cauliflower and broccoli. It is lime green and, when cooked, has a milder, slightly sweeter flavor than white cauliflower.

Confetti Salad With Calendula Petals

(recipe at right)

In the Garden: Calendula

- Calendula is an annual that resembles the marigold. Plant it in full sun and moderately fertile soil. This edible flower grows 1½ to 2 feet tall and produces lots of seeds, so it's easy to save some for next year. For more about calendula, see page 242.

Confetti Salad With Calendula Petals

This salad is almost too beautiful to eat.

SALAD:
8 cups torn mixed salad greens
⅓ cup shredded red cabbage
½ red bell pepper, thinly sliced
½ avocado, pitted, peeled, and sliced
¼ cup thinly sliced red onion
1 orange, peeled, sliced in half-rounds, and seeded
¼ cup sliced almonds, toasted
¼ cup fresh calendula petals

DRESSING:
2 tablespoons red-wine vinegar
6 tablespoons canola oil
salt and pepper, to taste

For salad: In a large bowl, mix the salad greens with the cabbage. Add the red pepper, avocado, onion, orange slices, almonds, and calendula petals.

For dressing: Put the vinegar, oil, and salt and pepper into a small bowl or jar with a lid and whisk or shake to combine.

Pour the dressing over the salad and toss to coat. **Makes 6 servings.**

–Diane Miller

Cook's Glossary: Mesclun

- Mesclun is a mix of young salad greens. The original combination came from Provence, France, and contained equal amounts of leaf lettuce, endive, arugula, and chervil. Today, a mesclun blend may also contain spinach, mustard, cilantro, and other greens. Before planting a mesclun mix, shake the seed packet to mix the seeds and ensure that your crops will be well distributed.

Watermelon Salad

Use a variety of red and green lettuces, and don't forget baby beet greens or spinach. The sweet-sour dressing perks up fruit or green salads.

SALAD:

6 cups torn mixed salad greens

3 cups cubed, seeded watermelon

½ cup sliced red onion

⅓ cup crumbled feta cheese

DRESSING:

2 tablespoons currant jelly

¼ cup puréed watermelon

2 tablespoons white-wine vinegar

¼ teaspoon garlic pepper

1 teaspoon vegetable oil

freshly ground black pepper, to taste

For salad: In a large bowl, combine the greens, watermelon, onion, and feta cheese.

For dressing: In a small saucepan over medium heat, melt the jelly. Set aside to cool. In a small bowl or jar with a lid, combine the jelly, puréed watermelon, vinegar, garlic pepper, and oil. Whisk or shake to blend, then refrigerate. Shake the dressing well before using.

Just before serving the salad, drizzle with the dressing, toss to coat, and season with black pepper. **Makes 6 servings.**

Ruby Coleslaw With Caraway Dressing

SALAD:

½ medium red cabbage, trimmed, cored, and grated

⅓ cup finely chopped Bermuda onion

5 radishes, grated

DRESSING:

½ cup mayonnaise

½ cup plain yogurt

2 teaspoons Dijon-style mustard

1 tablespoon sugar

2 teaspoons caraway seeds

½ teaspoon salt

⅛ teaspoon freshly ground black pepper

For salad: In a salad bowl, combine the cabbage, onion, and radishes.

For dressing: Put all of the ingredients into a small bowl and whisk to blend.

Pour the dressing over the salad and toss to coat. Chill before serving. **Makes 6 servings.**

Coleslaw With Salad Burnet

The flavor of salad burnet complements most salads, including this zesty coleslaw.

SALAD:

½ small head cabbage, cored and
   thinly sliced

½ medium onion, chopped

1 small carrot, chopped

¼ cup chopped fresh salad burnet
   leaves

DRESSING:

1 cup sour cream (or ½ cup plain
   yogurt and ½ cup sour cream)

1 teaspoon grated onion

1 teaspoon dill seed

½ tablespoon white-wine vinegar

¼ teaspoon sugar

½ teaspoon salt

freshly ground black pepper, to taste

For salad: In a medium bowl, combine the cabbage, onion, carrot, and salad burnet.

For dressing: Put all of the ingredients into a blender or food processor and blend until smooth.

Pour the dressing over the salad and toss to coat. Serve immediately. **Makes 4 servings.**

In the Kitchen: Salad Burnet

■ Salad burnet is a perennial herb with delicate, toothed leaves that taste like cucumber. Harvest fresh, young leaves before the plant starts to flower. They are a delicious addition to salads, cottage cheese, spreads and dips, herbal vinegars, and salad dressings. In olden days, a leafy sprig was added to wine, and it is still used to garnish beverages.

Slaw With Shrimp and Creamy Horseradish Dressing

SALAD:

1½ **pounds shrimp, peeled, deveined,
     cooked, and coarsely chopped**

1 **cup chopped red cabbage**

1 **cup chopped green cabbage**

½ **cup grated carrot**

2 **tablespoons chopped fresh parsley**

1 **tablespoon fresh lemon juice**

DRESSING:

½ **cup buttermilk**

½ **cup mayonnaise**

2 **tablespoons prepared horseradish**

1 **tablespoon minced fresh chives**

¼ **teaspoon salt**

⅛ **teaspoon freshly ground black pepper**

For salad: In a large bowl, combine the shrimp, cabbages, carrot, parsley, and lemon juice.

For dressing: In a small bowl, combine the buttermilk, mayonnaise, horseradish, chives, salt, and pepper and whisk to blend.

Pour the dressing over the salad and chill for 1 hour before serving. **Makes 6 servings.**

> ## Fun Food Fact: Horseradish
>
> ■ **The "horse" in horseradish may refer to the large size of the plant root or the strength of its flavor.**

New Potato Salad

The secret with this salad is to add the mayonnaise to the potatoes while they're still warm.

2 **pounds new potatoes**

½ **cup mayonnaise**

¼ **cup white wine**

1 **stalk celery, finely chopped**

1 **small onion, finely chopped**

1 **to 2 tart, firm apples, cored and
     coarsely chopped**

3 **sprigs fresh dill or** ½ **teaspoon dried dill**

3 **to 4 leaves fresh basil or** ½ **teaspoon
     dried basil**

salt and pepper, to taste

Boil the potatoes until just tender. Drain and set aside. In a small bowl, combine the mayonnaise and white wine, whisking to blend. In a large bowl, combine the celery, onion, apples, and herbs. Dice the still-warm potatoes and add to the celery mixture. Drizzle with the mayonnaise mixture and toss to coat. Season with salt and pepper. **Makes 6 to 8 servings.**

SALADS

Hot Potato Salad With Bourbon

6 small red-skin potatoes

2 slices bacon, each cut into 8 pieces

1 small onion, finely chopped

1 tablespoon all-purpose flour

½ cup hot water

2 tablespoons bourbon

1 teaspoon sugar

¼ teaspoon salt

freshly ground black pepper, to taste

¼ teaspoon dry mustard

Preheat the oven to 325°F (optional). Put the potatoes into a 6-quart pan and cover with cold water. Bring to a boil over medium heat. Cook uncovered until the potatoes are tender, then set them aside. In a skillet over medium heat, fry the bacon until it is browned. Remove from the skillet to drain. Reduce the heat to low and add the onion to the bacon drippings in the skillet. Cook until tender, stirring occasionally. Sprinkle the flour over the onions and increase the heat to medium-high. Stir continuously, and when the mixture foams, add the water and stir until smooth. Add the bourbon and cook, stirring, until thickened. Remove the skillet from the heat.

In a small bowl or mortar, blend the sugar, salt, pepper, and dry mustard. Add this mixture to the skillet and place over medium heat. Cook, stirring, until the sugar dissolves and the mustard is well incorporated. Remove the skillet from the heat and set aside.

Peel the warm potatoes, then slice into quarters. Place in a bowl and set aside to cool to room temperature, then cut each quarter into thin slices. Pour the bourbon-flavored sauce over the potatoes. Add the bacon and toss to coat. Serve at room temperature or heat for 15 to 20 minutes. **Makes 2 to 4 servings.**

In the Kitchen: Potatoes

- To seal in vitamin C, add a pinch of sugar—not salt—to potato-boiling water.

Pizza Salad

SALAD:

1½ cups cooked rice

1 cup shredded mozzarella cheese

¾ cup quartered pepperoni slices

1 large tomato, diced

¼ cup diced green bell pepper

¼ cup diced red bell pepper

3 scallions, thinly sliced

¼ cup thinly sliced mushrooms

¼ cup thinly sliced ripe black olives

DRESSING:

2 cloves garlic, minced

½ tablespoon chopped fresh oregano or ½ teaspoon dried oregano

½ tablespoon chopped fresh basil or ½ teaspoon dried basil

¼ teaspoon dried fennel

½ teaspoon salt

⅛ teaspoon freshly ground black pepper

⅔ cup olive oil

⅓ cup white-wine vinegar

1 tablespoon fresh lemon juice

For salad: In a large bowl, combine the rice, cheese, pepperoni, tomato, peppers, scallions, mushrooms, and olives.

For dressing: In a small bowl or with a mortar and pestle, grind the garlic with the herbs, salt, pepper, and enough oil to make a smooth paste. Add the remaining oil, vinegar, and lemon juice and stir to blend.

Pour ½ cup of dressing over the salad and toss to coat. Chill. Just before serving, add the remaining dressing and toss thoroughly. **Makes 6 servings.**

In the Kitchen: Garlic

■ A garlic bulb has 10 to 20 sections called cloves. Peel each clove before using: Press the flat part of a wide knife blade on a clove. Lift off the loosened skin with your fingers. Remove any green sprouts, as they are bitter and not easily digested.

Green Goddess Dressing

A classic salad or crudités dressing that tastes best when made with fresh herbs.

¼ teaspoon salt

⅛ teaspoon cayenne pepper

½ teaspoon sugar

¼ teaspoon dry mustard

1 clove garlic

2 anchovy fillets

2 tablespoons fresh lemon juice

6 tablespoons sour cream

½ tablespoon each chopped fresh chives, parsley, and tarragon
    or ½ teaspoon each dried chives, parsley, and tarragon

Blend the salt, cayenne, and sugar with the mustard *(see tip, below)*. Add the garlic and anchovy fillets and work into a paste. Add the lemon juice and blend until the salt, mustard, and sugar are dissolved. Transfer the mixture to a small bowl. Add the sour cream, whisking continuously to blend. Add the herbs and stir to incorporate. Cover and refrigerate for 1 hour. **Makes ½ cup.**

Mustard Mixing

■ **Dry mustard will dissolve more easily into a paste if you first disperse it into spices and other ingredients with a mortar and pestle.**

Mint Salad Dressing

Yogurt provides the creamy base for this dressing. Serve over chilled romaine lettuce or leaves of Belgian endive.

¼ teaspoon salt

½ teaspoon sugar

1 clove garlic

6 tablespoons plain yogurt, divided

1 tablespoon chopped fresh mint

freshly ground black pepper, to taste

In a small mortar and pestle, combine the salt and sugar. Add the garlic and work into a paste. Add 1 tablespoon of yogurt and blend. Transfer the mixture to a small bowl. Add the remaining yogurt, whisking continuously to blend. Add the mint and stir to incorporate. Season with pepper. Cover and refrigerate for 1 hour. **Makes about ½ cup.**

A BEGINNER'S
Vegetable Garden

*It is a pleasure to eat of the fruit of
one's toil, if it be nothing more than a
head of lettuce or an ear of corn.*

—*Charles Dudley Warner,
American editor (1829–1900)*

Follow these simple guidelines to become a successful gardener.

PLACEMENT. Avoid planting too near a tree, which will steal nutrients and shade the garden.

SUN. Vegetables require sunlight for at least 6 hours each day. Run the garden rows north and south, putting the tallest plants on the north end.

SOIL. Have well-drained soil that is rich in compost or aged organic matter.

WATER. Be ready: Vegetables need at least 1 inch of water per week.

CHECK FROST DATES.
Turn to page 305 for first and last frost dates in your area and be alert to your local conditions.

■ **Plant marigolds on the perimeter of the garden to discourage rabbits and other pests.**

- **When frost threatens, cover tender crops with old bedsheets to protect the plants and extend the growing season.**

The Seeds and Plants

Keep these ideas in mind and pay attention to the growing advice on your seed packets.

BUSH BEANS. For an early crop, start seeds in peat pots indoors and transplant outside when the soil is warm. Pinch bean pods off the plant when they reach a good length but do not yet show bulges where the seeds are developing.

BEETS. When seedlings are 3 inches tall, thin to 3 inches apart and use the thinnings in salads. Harvest leafy beet greens every week or two, but never take more than one-third. Dig the roots when they are 1½ to 3 inches in diameter.

- **Sprinkle wet cabbage with rye flour to discourage cabbageworms.**

CABBAGE. For large heads, space plants 20 inches apart. For small ones, plant 12 inches apart. Harvest when the head becomes firm. Cabbage plants can tolerate a frost; in fact, it improves their flavor.

CARROTS. Carrots like loose, sandy, well-turned soil. Thin seedlings by snipping them with scissors instead of pulling plants. Harvest when carrots reach a desired size.

LEAF LETTUCE. Lettuce thrives in cool weather and soil that has been fertilized. Thin seedlings to about 4 inches apart and use the thinnings in salads. Harvest outer leaves as needed, but don't wait too long: Lettuce may turn bitter in hot weather.

PEPPERS. Set plants in daylight when nights are above 55°F. Fertilize when the first blossoms open. For best flavor, pick peppers when they are fully developed.

RADISHES. Radishes like loose, well-drained soil and cool temperatures; they bolt (go to seed) in warm weather. Thin seedlings to 1 to 2 inches apart with scissors. Harvest 3 to 4 weeks after planting the seeds.

SUMMER SQUASHES. Plant seeds in warmed soil. Thin seedlings to the four strongest plants spaced evenly. Pick when young for tender squashes through the summer.

SWISS CHARD. Chard requires minimum care, if given a good start. To harvest, break off or peel outside leaves in a downward motion. Plants will produce all summer.

TOMATOES. Plant bushy, stocky, disease-resistant plants up to the first set of leaves when nights are above 55°F. In temperatures over 90°F, pick the fruit when they start to change color and let them finish ripening indoors. Use a knife, or gently twist the fruit off the stem.

Vegetable Dishes

Roasted Asparagus 102

Green Beans in Sour Cream 103

Green Beans With Mushrooms and

    Potatoes 103

Bombay Beans. 104

How to Grill Vegetables. 105

Lima Bean Timbales 106

Plymouth Succotash 106

Frijoles Rio Grande 107

Savory Baked Beans 108

Harvard Beets 109

Royal Broccoli Casserole. 109

Brussels Sprouts With Sun-Dried

    Tomatoes 110

Bubble and Squeak 112

Container Gardening. 113

Far East Celery. 114

Cheesy Corn Creole. 114

Farmer's Cabbage With White Sauce 115

Carrots Excelsior 116

Cauliflower Casserole 116

Apple Carrot Tzimmes. 118

Cinnamon Carrots 118

Curried Carrots 118

Carrots With Grapes 119

Cheddar Eggplant 120

Fennel and Parmesan Gratin. 120

Spring Fiddleheads 121

Easy Greens Pie 122

Kale With Feta and Olives. 123

Sautéed Chicory Greens 123

Spinach Pie. 124

Red Potatoes With Lemon Ginger

    Vinaigrette 125

Caraway and Tarragon Potatoes. 125

Use the Right Spud. 126

CHAPTER 5

Garlic Potato Soufflé 127

Buttermilk-Blue Potatoes

   Au Gratin 128

Bacon Cheddar Potato Kugelis 130

German Potato Casserole 131

Dill and Potato Cakes 131

Golden Onion Bake 132

Apple-Stuffed Acorn Squash 133

Rice-Stuffed Acorn Squash 133

Maple Squash Soufflé 134

Baked Summer Squash 134

Zucchini Casserole 135

Zucchini Provençal 136

Italian Zucchini Crescent Pie 136

Orange-Glazed Sweet Potatoes 137

Sweet Potato and Pineapple Casserole 139

Cheese Soufflé in a Tomato 140

How to Oven-Dry Tomatoes 141

Vegetable Cheese Bake 142

There's No Such Thing as Too Many

   Tomatoes 143

Italian Vegetable Popover Pizza 145

Ratatouille Pie 146

Spicy Stewed Okra 147

Vegetable Hash 148

Roasted Asparagus

1 pound asparagus, trimmed

2 tablespoons olive oil

salt and pepper, to taste

Preheat the oven to 400°F. Spread the asparagus in a single layer on a cookie sheet and drizzle with the oil. Season with salt and pepper, then toss to coat. Roast for 15 minutes, or until tender (time will depend on the thickness of the stalks). **Makes 4 servings.**

How to Harvest: Asparagus

■ Asparagus can be picked in the third year after planting. In the cool morning for 4 weeks, gather spears that are 6 to 9 inches long and at least ⅜-inch thick, and have tightly closed tips. Snap the stalks off at the base; don't use a knife, or you may injure the crown. Use immediately for best flavor. In ensuing years, extend the picking time to 6 to 8 weeks.

Save 'n' Store

■ To store for a week or two, wash asparagus spears in cold water and place a moist paper towel over their cut ends. Place the spears in a plastic bag and store in the vegetable crisper of the refrigerator.

To store for 2 to 3 days, trim the stems and stand the spears in 1 inch of water in a glass, cover with plastic, and refrigerate.

Green Beans in Sour Cream

1½ **pounds green beans, trimmed and cut into 1-inch pieces**

4 **slices bacon**

¼ **cup chopped onion**

2 **tablespoons chopped fresh parsley**

2 **tablespoons all-purpose flour**

1 **teaspoon salt**

1 **tablespoon cider or wine vinegar**

1 **cup sour cream**

In a saucepan over medium heat, steam or boil the beans until tender. In a large skillet over medium heat, cook the bacon, turning occasionally, until crisp. Remove the bacon and set aside to drain. Pour off all but 2 tablespoons of the bacon fat from the skillet. When the bacon is cool enough to handle, crumble it onto a small plate and set aside. In the same skillet over medium heat, warm the 2 tablespoons of bacon fat, add the onion and parsley, and sauté until tender. Add the flour and salt and cook, stirring constantly, for 1 to 2 minutes more. Remove the skillet from the heat. Put the cooked beans into a large bowl, drizzle with the vinegar, and toss to coat. Add the beans and sour cream to the onions in the skillet. Stir until blended. Heat thoroughly but do not boil. Before serving, sprinkle the crumbled bacon over the beans. **Makes 4 to 6 servings.**

Green Beans With Mushrooms and Potatoes

4 **tablespoons olive oil**

1 **teaspoon whole cumin seeds**

1 **medium onion, diced**

3 **medium potatoes, peeled and cut lengthwise into strips**

½ **pound mushrooms, sliced thickly**

1½ **pounds green beans, trimmed and cut into 1-inch pieces**

¼ **teaspoon ground turmeric**

½ **teaspoon cayenne pepper**

1 **tablespoon ground coriander seed**

1 **teaspoon salt**

In a stockpot over medium heat, warm the oil. Add the cumin seeds and cook for 1 minute, then add the onion and sauté until light brown. Add the potatoes, stir, and fry for 3 minutes. Add the mushrooms and cook for 1 minute more. Add the beans, spices, and salt and stir to blend. Add 1 cup of water and bring to a boil. Cover, reduce the heat, and simmer for 25 minutes, or until the vegetables are tender. Continue boiling to cook off nearly all of the liquid. **Makes 8 servings.**

In the Kitchen: Dried Beans

■ The flavor of dried beans melds well with cumin, garlic, rosemary, sage, savory, and thyme.

Bombay Beans

1 green chile (about 1¼ inches long),
   halved

1 pound green beans, trimmed

1 teaspoon salt

2 tablespoons butter or oil

4 slices sweet onion (each about ⅛-inch
   thick)

¼ cup grated fresh coconut or packaged
   unsweetened coconut

In a saucepan over medium heat, combine 1 cup of water with the chile, beans, and salt and cook until the beans are crisp tender. Discard the chile. Drain the beans and set aside. In a skillet over medium heat, melt the butter, then add the onion slices and gently sauté until soft. Add the coconut and cook, stirring, for 2 minutes. Add the beans and toss to coat. Reduce the heat to medium low, cover, and cook for 2 minutes more. **Makes 4 to 6 servings.**

In the Garden: Pole Beans

■ Pole beans grow 5 to 9 feet tall and need support to climb on, such as poles, strings, a trellis, or a tepee. Bush beans do not need support, as they grow only 1 to 2 feet tall.

How to Grill Vegetables

VEGETABLE	HOW TO PREPARE	GRILLING TIME
Artichokes	Cut in half lengthwise, apply pressure to spread the leaves open. Rub with olive oil and sprinkle with salt.	15 to 20 minutes per side, or until the base is tender. Remove the inedible choke before eating.
Asparagus	Roll spears in olive oil and sprinkle with salt and pepper.	5 to 10 minutes; turn every few minutes until tender.
Corn	Leave the stem and husk on. Pull back the husk, remove the silk, and soak for 15 minutes in cold water. Then carefully pull the husk back up, smoothing and twisting it if necessary so that it stays closed.	10 to 20 minutes; turn several times.
Eggplant	Cut in half lengthwise or into slices about ¼-inch thick. Brush with olive oil.	4 to 5 minutes per side.
Fennel	Remove the stalks and roots. Cut the bulb in half lengthwise. Brush with olive oil and sprinkle with salt. (Lightly steam large bulbs before grilling.)	5 to 6 minutes per side.
Leeks	Cut white portions in half lengthwise and wash well in warm water. Brush with olive oil. (Lightly steam large leeks before grilling.)	4 to 6 minutes per side.
Mushrooms	Use large caps, such as portobellos. Brush with olive oil and slice after grilling.	8 to 10 minutes per side.
Onions	Cut into ½-inch slices. Brush with olive oil and sprinkle with salt.	8 to 10 minutes per side.
Peppers	Cut bell peppers in half lengthwise, remove the seeds, and brush with olive oil.	6 to 10 minutes skin side down, then 3 to 4 minutes on the other side.
Summer Squashes/ Zucchini	Cut into thirds or halves lengthwise. Brush with olive oil and sprinkle with salt.	5 to 8 minutes per side.

Lima Bean Timbales

A timbale, French for "kettledrum," is a dish baked in a mold.

2 cups dried lima beans

1 cup bread crumbs

2 tablespoons butter, melted

2 tablespoons chopped pimiento

2 tablespoons minced onion

½ cup chopped unsalted peanuts

½ teaspoon salt

¼ teaspoon freshly ground black pepper

2 eggs, beaten

½ cup evaporated milk

Soak the beans in water overnight *(see tip, page 44)*. Drain, rinse, place in a stockpot, and add enough water so that the level reaches 1 inch above the beans. Bring the pot to a boil over medium-high heat and then reduce the heat to simmer. Cook for 45 minutes, or until tender. Preheat the oven to 350°F. Grease six timbale or ramekin dishes or a 1½-quart casserole. Drain the beans, then press them through a coarse sieve. In a large bowl, combine the beans, crumbs, butter, pimiento, onion, peanuts, salt, and pepper. Add the eggs and milk and stir to blend. Distribute the mixture equally among the prepared dishes (or put it all into a large one). Bake for 40 minutes. **Makes 6 servings.**

Plymouth Succotash

This is an old-time variation on the succotash theme.

8 cups dried navy beans

4 to 6 pounds corned beef

4 to 5 pounds chicken pieces

1 turnip, peeled and thinly sliced

6 potatoes, peeled and thinly sliced

16 cups hulled corn

salt, to taste

Soak the beans in water overnight *(see tip, page 44)*. Drain and rinse. Transfer the beans to a stockpot and add water to cover. Bring the liquid to a boil over medium-high heat, reduce the heat to a simmer, and cook for 1½ hours, or until soft enough to mash. In a large stockpot over medium-high heat, combine the beef and chicken. Cover with water and bring to a boil. When the meats are tender, remove them from the liquid. Add the turnip and potatoes to the beef-and-chicken stock and cook until tender. Remove the bones and skin from the chicken and cut both meats into 1½-inch cubes. Add the meat and beans to the vegetables and stock. Add the corn and enough water to cover amply. Simmer for 1 hour. Stir frequently to keep the ingredients from sticking, and add more water as necessary. Season with salt and serve. **Makes 16 to 20 servings.**

Cook's Glossary: Dried Beans

■ Dried beans are seeds of bean plants that have matured and dried in the pod. They include kidney beans, navy beans, and pinto beans.

Frijoles Rio Grande

2 cups dried navy beans

1½ cups dried split peas

½ pound ham hock or salt pork, chopped

2 cloves garlic, chopped

2 large onions, chopped and divided

1 teaspoon dried oregano

¼ teaspoon ground ginger

1 tablespoon salt

1 teaspoon freshly ground black pepper

4 stalks celery with tops, thinly sliced

4 medium carrots, thinly sliced

2 medium green peppers, sliced

2 fresh or dried chiles, seeded and chopped

1 teaspoon dried marjoram

2 cups red Burgundy wine

Soak the beans and split peas in water overnight *(see tip, page 44)*. Drain, rinse, place in a stockpot, and add enough water so that the level reaches 1 inch above the beans and peas. Bring the pot to a boil over medium-high heat and then reduce the heat to simmer. Cook for 30 minutes, or until tender. Add 6 cups of water and the meat, garlic, half of the chopped onion, oregano, ginger, salt, and black pepper, and simmer for 1½ hours. Add the remaining ingredients, except the wine, and cook for 25 minutes. Add the wine and cook for 5 minutes more. Serve hot. **Makes 10 to 12 servings.**

Save 'n' Store: Dried Beans

■ Cooked dried beans freeze well and will keep in an airtight container or freezer bag for up to 6 months.

How to Dry Beans

When the pods of dried bean varieties, such as kidney or navy beans, turn yellow or brown and start to shrivel, pull up the entire plant and hang it in a warm, dry place until the pods rattle (about a week). Or, leave the plant in the ground until the pods rattle. Pick and shell them singly by hand or do a bunch at a time: Put fistfuls of pods into an old pillowcase and walk on it until the pods are crushed. Separate the debris from the beans by pouring them back and forth between two bowls in front of a fan.

Then, spread the beans on a cookie sheet and place in a 150°F oven for 30 minutes. To test readiness, bite down on a cooled bean. If your teeth barely make a dent, remove the sheet and set the beans aside to cool. Bag and freeze the beans for at least 2 days to kill any insects. Store them in a sealed container in a cool, dry area.

Savory Baked Beans

2 pounds dried soldier, Great Northern,
 or navy beans
½ pound salt pork
2 onions, chopped
¼ cup fresh parsley, chopped
½ tablespoon fresh thyme or
 ½ teaspoon dried thyme
2 teaspoons dry mustard
1 scant teaspoon ground ginger
1 teaspoon salt
¼ cup molasses
¼ cup packed brown sugar
freshly ground black pepper, to taste
boiling water

Soak the beans in water overnight (see tip, page 44). Drain, rinse, place in a stockpot, and add enough water so that the level reaches 1 inch above the beans. Bring the pot to a boil over medium-high heat and then reduce the heat to simmer. Cook for 1 to 2 hours, or until tender. Drain, reserving the liquid. Preheat the oven to 275°F. Cut the salt pork in half and score both halves with cuts ½-inch deep. Place one piece on the bottom of a beanpot. Cover the pork with a layer of prepared beans. In a small bowl, combine the onions, parsley, and thyme. Spoon some of the onion mixture over the beans. Add another layer of beans. Repeat the alternate layers until both are used up, ending with beans on top. Place the remaining salt pork on top of the beans. Put a pot or kettle of water on to boil. In a medium bowl, combine the reserved bean liquid, mustard, ginger, salt, molasses, brown sugar, and pepper and whisk to blend. Pour the mixture over the beans. Add boiling water to cover the beans. Cover the beanpot and bake for 6 to 8 hours. Uncover for the last hour of baking. **Makes 12 to 14 servings.**

Harvard Beets

12 medium beets
3 tablespoons butter
1 tablespoon cornstarch
½ cup brown sugar
¼ cup white-wine vinegar
salt, cloves, and nutmeg, to taste

In a stockpot, combine the beets with enough water to cover. Bring to a boil, then reduce the heat to simmer. Cook for 30 to 45 minutes, or until tender. Remove the beets to cool, reserving 1½ cups of the cooking liquid. When the beets are cool to the touch, peel and dice them. In a saucepan over low heat, melt the butter. Add the cornstarch and the cooking liquid and whisk to blend. Cook, stirring constantly, until smooth and thick. Add the sugar and vinegar, and then the salt, cloves, and nutmeg. Stir to blend. Add the beets, mix to coat, and serve. **Makes 6 servings.**

Cook's Glossary: Harvard Beets

■ This is a sweet/sour dish of beets cooked with sugar, vinegar, cornstarch, and other flavorings. The dish may have been created by a Harvard University student, or the name might just reflect the school's colors. Another theory says that a Russian immigrant opened a restaurant in Boston and served a beet dish famous at an English pub named Harwood's, which was misinterpreted as "Harvard."

Royal Broccoli Casserole

2 cups cooked, chopped broccoli
2 tablespoons butter
1 large onion, chopped
1 teaspoon salt
¾ teaspoon chopped fresh tarragon or
   marjoram, or ¼ teaspoon dried
   tarragon or marjoram
⅛ teaspoon freshly ground black
   pepper
1 pint sour cream

Preheat the oven to 325°F. Grease a 1-quart casserole. Place the broccoli in the casserole. In a skillet over medium heat, melt the butter. Add the onion and sauté until soft. Transfer the onions to the casserole. Add the remaining ingredients and stir to blend. Smooth the top. Cover and bake for 25 minutes. **Makes 4 servings.**

Brussels Sprouts With Sun-Dried Tomatoes

1½ **pounds brussels sprouts**

¼ **cup oil-packed, sun-dried tomatoes**

¼ **cup rice wine vinegar**

¼ **cup olive oil**

1 **clove garlic, minced**

½ **tablespoon sugar**

dash of hot-pepper sauce

salt and pepper, to taste

2 **scallions, thinly sliced**

¼ **cup chopped fresh parsley**

Trim off the stem ends of the brussels sprouts and remove any wilted outer leaves. Cook the sprouts in 6 cups of boiling, salted water just until crisp-tender. Drain, then submerge the sprouts in ice water to cool. Drain, then transfer to a large bowl. Cut the tomatoes into thin strips and add them to the brussels sprouts. Toss and set aside. In a glass bowl, whisk together the vinegar, oil, garlic, sugar, hot-pepper sauce, and salt and pepper. Pour this sauce over the sprouts and tomatoes. Add the scallions and parsley. Stir, cover, and refrigerate for at least 2 hours. **Makes 10 servings.**

NOTE: *To boil brussels sprouts, use 1 cup of water for every cup of sprouts.*

How to Harvest: Brussels Sprouts

■ Pick brussels sprouts when they are about an inch in diameter and firm. Harvest at the base of the stem first and work upward. Twist off the sprouts by hand or cut them off with a sharp knife.

Brussels Sprouts With Sun-Dried Tomatoes

(recipe at left)

Bubble and Squeak

Some say that this British classic gets its name from the way it looks and sounds as it cooks.

4 or 5 medium potatoes
½ pound bacon cut into 1-inch pieces
1 head cabbage, cut into ¼-inch slices
salt, to taste

Put the potatoes into a deep saucepan, cover with water, and bring to a boil over medium-high heat. Cook until just tender, remove from the heat, and set aside. Put the bacon into a large, cast-iron skillet over medium heat and sauté until lightly brown. Remove the bacon and set aside to drain, reserve 2 to 3 tablespoons of grease, and pour off the remainder. Return the reserved grease to the skillet, then add the cabbage and ½ cup of water. Cover and cook over low heat for 20 minutes. Peel and dice the potatoes. Add the potatoes and cooked bacon to the cabbage. Season with salt and stir to combine. Cook for 10 minutes more, adding more water if needed during the cooking; during the last few minutes, let the mixture brown. **Makes 4 to 6 servings.**

In the Kitchen: Cabbage

■ While cooking, cabbage releases hydrogen sulfide, which has an odor that some people find unpleasant. (Cooking in an aluminum pan may increase the odor.) To minimize the smell, use the freshest cabbage available; cut it into small pieces so that it will cook faster; and boil it, uncovered, until just tender.

Container Gardening

Growing herbs, fruits, and vegetables in containers is an easy way to garden, especially when you lack yard space. Here are some pointers:

- Choose plants that can be easily transplanted. Purchase transplants from local nurseries or start seeds at home.

- Select smaller varieties. For example, try 'Patio' tomatoes, 'Spacemaster' cucumbers, and 'Topcrop' bush beans. Dwarf fruit trees and smaller berry plants, including strawberries and dwarf blueberries, work well in containers.

- Consider the size of each plant at maturity when choosing a container. Tomatoes and cucumbers will require larger pots than radishes and lettuce. Avoid small containers, as they often can't store enough water to get through hot days.

- Clay pots are usually more attractive than plastic ones, but plastic pots retain moisture better. To get the best of both, slip a plastic pot into a slightly larger clay pot. Make sure that there are drainage holes in the pots.

- Add about 1 inch of coarse gravel to the bottom of the container to improve drainage.

- Use a good soil mix that is recommended for pots and the type of plant you are growing. Consult your garden nursery for advice.

- Place containers where they will receive maximum sunlight (at least 6 hours) and good ventilation.

- Feed container plants at least twice a month with liquid fertilizer, following the instructions on the label. An occasional application of fish emulsion or compost will add trace elements.

- Keep the plants watered. Some containers or devices found in garden supply centers help to maintain even moisture.

- Watch for and control insect pests.

Far East Celery

Try this side dish with steak or chicken.

4 cups celery, cut into 1-inch pieces
salt, to taste
1 can (5 ounces) water chestnuts,
    drained and sliced
1 can (10¾ ounces) cream of chicken
    soup
1 small jar (4¼ ounces) pimientos,
    drained and chopped
2 tablespoons butter
½ cup slivered almonds
½ cup bread crumbs

Preheat the oven to 350°F. Grease a 1-quart casserole. In a saucepan over medium heat, combine the celery with water to cover, salted to taste. Bring to a boil and cook for 8 minutes. Drain. In the casserole, combine the celery, water chestnuts, soup, and pimientos and mix to coat. In a skillet over medium-low heat, melt the butter. Add the almonds and toast, lightly. Add the bread crumbs, mix to combine, then sprinkle the mixture over the vegetables. Bake for 35 minutes. **Makes 6 servings.**

Cheesy Corn Creole

2 tablespoons vegetable oil
½ cup chopped green bell pepper
1 large onion, chopped
2 cups peeled tomatoes *(see tip, page 65)*
    or 2 cups canned tomatoes, drained
1 teaspoon sugar
½ teaspoon salt
⅛ teaspoon freshly ground black pepper
⅛ teaspoon cayenne pepper
2 cups corn
1½ cups shredded cheddar cheese
2 slices bacon, cooked crisp and
    crumbled

In a skillet over medium heat, warm the oil. Add the pepper and onion and sauté for 5 minutes, or until soft. Add the tomatoes and sugar and cook for 10 minutes, stirring occasionally. Add the salt, black and cayenne peppers, and corn and cook until tender, about 5 minutes. Remove the pan from the heat, sprinkle with the cheese and bacon. Cover only long enough to melt the cheese. **Makes 8 servings.**

In the Garden: Corn

■ **The deeper corn seeds are planted, the harder it is for crows to find them. Plant at least 2 inches deep, especially for late plantings in warm or dry weather, when it is important to keep the seeds moist. In wet weather, plant corn only an inch deep, so that the seeds won't rot.**

Cook's Call: Steaming vs. Boiling Vegetables

- Steamed vegetables, such as greens, tend to retain their color, texture, flavor, and certain nutrients. Cooking time is usually shorter, and it's less likely that the vegetables will be overdone.

- Boiled vegetables run the risk of turning into mush if cooked too long. This method usually takes more time than steaming and can discolor foods. Also, water-soluble nutrients can leach out of fresh vegetables and into the water. However, boiling is handy for durable fare such as corn and potatoes, which can hold up to the vigorous motion of the bubbling water. Some studies show that certain nutrients, such as carotenoids *(see page 308)* in carrots, hold up better to boiling than to steaming.

Farmer's Cabbage With White Sauce

CABBAGE:
1 head cabbage
salt and pepper, to taste

WHITE SAUCE:
3 tablespoons butter
3 tablespoons all-purpose flour
⅜ teaspoon salt
freshly ground black pepper, to taste
1½ cups milk

1½ tablespoons butter
¾ cup bread crumbs

For cabbage: Preheat the oven to 400°F. Shred the cabbage and put it into a greased baking dish. Season with salt and pepper.

For sauce: In a skillet over medium heat, melt the butter. In a cup or small bowl, combine the flour and seasonings, then add to the butter. Stir or whisk until blended. Add the milk gradually, stirring constantly. Bring the mixture to a boil and cook for 2 minutes. Remove from the heat.

In a skillet over medium heat, melt the 1½ tablespoons of butter. Add the bread crumbs and stir for 1 to 2 minutes. Remove the skillet from the heat and set aside. Add the white sauce to the cabbage and mix well. Cover with bread crumbs. Bake until brown, about 20 minutes. **Makes 6 servings.**

—Linda Wilcoxen

Carrots Excelsior

2½ cups diced carrots

salt and pepper, to taste

2 eggs, separated

1 cup bread crumbs

1 tablespoon finely chopped onion

1½ cups milk

In a saucepan over medium heat, steam or boil the carrots until tender. Drain, then mash the carrots and season with salt and pepper. Preheat the oven to 350°F. Grease a 1½-quart casserole. In a small bowl, beat the egg yolks. In another bowl, combine the carrots, egg yolks, bread crumbs, onion, and milk. In a large, chilled bowl, beat the egg whites until stiff. Gently fold the whipped whites into the carrot mixture. Turn into the prepared casserole. Bake for 45 to 60 minutes, or until a toothpick comes out clean. Serve hot. **Makes 6 to 8 servings.**

Cauliflower Casserole

1 head cauliflower, separated into florets

1 cup tomato sauce

2 tablespoons chopped fresh parsley

3 tablespoons chopped ripe olives

3 tablespoons grated Parmesan cheese

¼ cup bread crumbs

1 tablespoon melted butter

Preheat the oven to 400°F. Lightly grease a 2½-quart casserole. In a saucepan over medium heat, steam the cauliflower for 8 minutes, or until crisp tender. In the casserole, combine the tomato sauce, parsley, and olives. Add the cauliflower and sprinkle with the cheese, bread crumbs, and butter. Bake for 10 minutes, or until browned. **Makes 4 servings.**

Carrots Excelsior
(recipe at left)

Apple Carrot Tzimmes

Tzimmes is a sweet stew of Jewish origin. It can be any combination of fruit, vegetables, and (sometimes) meat.

1 apple, peeled, cored, and grated

4 cups grated carrots

1 tablespoon pearl barley

½ cup (1 stick) butter, melted

2 teaspoons sugar

1 teaspoon fresh lemon juice

¼ teaspoon nutmeg

½ teaspoon salt

In a heavy saucepan over medium heat, combine all of the ingredients plus ½ cup of water. Bring to a boil, reduce the heat to low, cover, and simmer for 2 hours, or until the barley is soft, adding more water if necessary. **Makes 6 servings.**

Cinnamon Carrots

This carrot dish is tasty and incredibly easy to make.

1 to 1½ pounds carrots, sliced

⅓ cup butter, at room temperature

½ cup sugar

1 teaspoon salt

¼ to ½ teaspoon cinnamon

⅓ cup boiling water

Preheat the oven to 350°F. Place the carrots in a 1½-quart casserole or baking dish. Cream together the butter, sugar, salt, and cinnamon. Add the boiling water and stir to blend. Pour the mixture over the carrots. Bake for 1 hour, or cover and cook on high in a microwave for 10 minutes. **Makes 6 servings.**

Curried Carrots

A simple yet exotic dish.

1 pound carrots, sliced 1-inch thick

2 tablespoons butter

2 to 3 teaspoons curry powder

¼ teaspoon freshly ground black pepper

1 tablespoon fresh lemon juice

1 tablespoon honey

⅓ cup chopped pecans or walnuts

In a saucepan over medium heat, combine the carrots with water to cover, bring to a boil, and simmer for 15 to 20 minutes, or until tender. Drain and return the carrots to the pan. Add the remaining ingredients, stir to blend, and cook over low heat until warmed through. Serve immediately. **Makes 4 to 6 servings.**

Carrots With Grapes

Serve as a side dish with chicken or turkey.

2 pounds carrots, cut into julienne strips

2 tablespoons chopped fresh basil or
    2 teaspoons dried basil

1 clove garlic

½ cup (1 stick) butter

1 tablespoon chopped fresh chervil or
    1 teaspoon dried chervil

¼ teaspoon celery salt

2 cups seedless white grapes, halved

2 tablespoons fresh lemon juice

In a saucepan over medium heat, combine the carrots, basil, and garlic. Add water to cover and cook for 20 minutes, or until tender. In a separate saucepan, melt the butter and add the chervil and celery salt. When the carrots are cooked, drain, then discard the garlic. Add the carrots, grapes, and lemon juice to the butter mixture, toss to coat, and heat until the grapes are warm. **Makes 12 servings.**

Save 'n' Store: Carrots

■ **To store freshly harvested carrots, twist or cut off the tops. Scrub the carrots clean, using a vegetable brush, if necessary, in a pot of cold water. Rinse and drain in a large colander. Place the carrots in a perforated plastic bag and refrigerate for up to 4 weeks.**

Cheddar Eggplant

A soufflé-like way to serve this vegetable.

2 small eggplants, peeled and cut into
  ¼-inch-thick slices
2 tablespoons vegetable oil, divided
salt and pepper, to taste
2 tablespoons butter
8 slices firm white toast, crusts
  removed
2 cups grated cheddar cheese, divided
1 egg
1 cup milk
¾ teaspoon chopped fresh marjoram
  or ¼ teaspoon dried marjoram

Preheat the broiler. Spread the eggplant slices on a cookie sheet, brush with oil, and season with salt and pepper. Broil for 4 minutes, or until lightly browned. Turn the eggplant over, brush with oil, season, and broil for 3 minutes, or until lightly browned. Preheat the oven to 375°F. Grease a 2½-quart casserole. Butter the toast and cut each slice into eighths. In the casserole, layer half of the toast. Cover it with half of the eggplant. Spread half of the cheese on the eggplant. Repeat the layers. In a small bowl, beat the egg until light. Add the milk and marjoram and whisk to blend. Pour the egg mixture over the cheese, eggplant, and toast layers. Bake for 30 minutes. **Makes 6 servings.**

Fennel and Parmesan Gratin

2 pounds fennel bulbs, trimmed
½ cup grated Parmesan cheese
3 tablespoons butter
salt and pepper, to taste

Preheat the oven to 400°F. Cut each fennel bulb in half lengthwise. Bring a stockpot of water to a boil. Add the fennel and cook for 10 minutes. Drain. When cool enough to handle, cut the bulbs in half crosswise and arrange, cut side up, in a shallow baking dish. Sprinkle to cover with the Parmesan cheese, dot with the butter, and season. Bake for 20 minutes, or until the cheese is browned. **Makes 4 servings.**

In the Garden: Fennel

■ Common fennel looks like a giant dill plant, as it has feathery leaves and grows 3 to 5 feet tall. In spring, select a site in full sun and sow seeds ¼-inch deep in light, well-worked soil of average fertility.

The garden and late crops will require attention, else the weeds will take possession.

–The Old Farmer's Almanac, *1898*

How to Prepare Fiddleheads

■ Fiddleheads are the shoots of edible ferns. Ostrich ferns are the safest to eat; not all ferns are edible. When the fern emerges from the ground, the shoots are coiled in a shape similar to the scrolled top of a violin. Harvest them at this stage.

Raw fiddleheads contain a toxin that can cause digestive distress and require special preparation before they can be eaten safely. Use your fingers to remove as much of the brown papery husk, or chaff, as possible. Trim off the browned ends and wash the fiddleheads in several changes of cold water. Boil fiddleheads for at least 15 minutes or steam them for 10 to 12 minutes, or until tender. Discard the boiled water. Do not cook fiddleheads in the microwave, as this method may not remove all toxins.

Spring Fiddleheads

2 pounds fiddlehead ferns, cleaned
    (see tip, above) and picked over
½ cup (1 stick) butter
4 cloves garlic, minced
2 tablespoons minced shallots
2 tablespoons fresh lemon juice
salt and pepper, to taste

Prepare the fiddleheads for cooking as directed above. In a stockpot of lightly salted water over medium heat, boil the fiddleheads for at least 15 minutes. Drain and rinse under cold water. In a skillet over medium heat, melt the butter, add the garlic and shallots, and sauté until aromatic but not browned. Add the fiddleheads and sauté for 1 to 2 minutes more. Season with lemon juice and salt and pepper. **Makes 6 servings.**

Easy Greens Pie

Use escarole, spinach, Swiss chard, broccoli rabe, or any other greens you like.

3 tablespoons olive oil, divided
1 large onion, minced
½ to 1 cup chopped, blanched, and squeezed greens
4 eggs
2 cups cottage cheese, drained,* or 2 cups low-fat Ricotta cheese
¼ cup freshly grated Parmesan cheese
salt and pepper, to taste

*For best results, drain the cottage cheese in a coffee filter over a small bowl for 30 minutes. The cooking time will vary depending on the moisture in the cottage cheese.

Preheat the oven to 350°F. Grease an 8-inch square baking dish. In a large skillet over medium heat, warm 2½ tablespoons of oil. Add the onion and sauté for 4 minutes, or until soft but not browned. Add the greens and continue cooking until warmed through. Remove the pan from the heat and set it aside to cool slightly. In a large mixing bowl, beat the eggs. Add the cottage cheese, Parmesan cheese, and salt and pepper and stir to combine. Add the cooked greens and stir to coat. Pour the mixture into the prepared dish. Drizzle with the remaining ½ tablespoon of olive oil. Bake for 35 to 40 minutes, or until firm. **Makes 6 to 8 servings.**

VARIATION: *Substitute ⅔ cup of cooked, chopped asparagus for the greens and add 1 teaspoon of chopped fresh tarragon with the Parmesan cheese.*

How to Blanch Greens

■ Place the greens in boiling water for 2 minutes, then remove, place in a colander, and plunge immediately under cold running water or into a pot of iced water for 2 minutes. Drain. This process sets the color and flavor, especially before freezing.

VEGETABLE DISHES

Kale With Feta and Olives

Kale doesn't mind the cold, providing nutritious greens throughout the winter season.

2 pounds kale, stemmed and torn into pieces
3 tablespoons olive oil, divided
1 large onion, thinly sliced
2 cloves garlic, minced
salt and pepper, to taste
2 teaspoons fresh lemon juice
1 to 1½ tablespoons balsamic vinegar
1 cup crumbled feta cheese, for garnish
10 kalamata olives, pitted and halved, for garnish

Put the kale into a stockpot, add ¼ cup of water, cover, and cook over medium heat for 12 minutes, or until tender. Drain in a colander and set aside to cool. In a large, nonreactive skillet over medium heat, warm 1½ tablespoons of oil. Add the onion and sauté for 8 to 9 minutes, or until translucent. Add the garlic, stir, and sauté for 30 seconds. Add the kale and the remaining oil and toss to coat. Season with salt and pepper. Reduce the heat to low, cover, and cook for 2 to 3 minutes. Meanwhile, in a small bowl, whisk together the lemon juice and vinegar. Uncover the skillet, sprinkle the kale with the lemon-vinegar mixture, and remove from the heat. Transfer the kale to a serving dish and garnish with the feta cheese and olives. **Makes 4 to 6 servings.**

Sautéed Chicory Greens

Not enough chicory greens? Substitute dandelion greens.

2 pounds fresh green tops of chicory
¼ cup olive oil
2 large cloves garlic, minced
½ teaspoon hot red-pepper flakes
½ teaspoon salt

Strip the leaves from the chicory and cut them crosswise into 4-inch pieces. In a stockpot of boiling, salted water, cook the greens for 4 to 5 minutes, or until they are tender at the leaf ribs. Drain, then rinse the greens with cold water. Drain again, pressing out any excess water. In a heavy skillet over medium heat, warm the oil until it is hot but not smoking. Add the garlic and cook, stirring, until golden. Increase the heat slightly and add the greens, red-pepper flakes, and salt. Sauté, stirring, for 4 minutes, or until all of the liquid evaporates. **Makes 4 servings.**

NOTE: *If substituting dandelion greens, remove the tough stems first. In the boiling, salted water, cook for 5 minutes, or until tender.*

Spinach Pie

¾ cup melted butter, divided

2 medium onions, finely chopped

1 bunch scallions, thinly sliced

1 pound spinach, chopped

⅓ cup finely chopped fresh parsley

1 tablespoon chopped fresh basil or
    1 teaspoon dried basil

½ tablespoon chopped fresh oregano
    or ½ teaspoon dried oregano

1 teaspoon cumin

¾ teaspoon salt

¼ teaspoon freshly ground black pepper

¼ teaspoon nutmeg

1 pound feta cheese, crumbled

4 eggs, beaten

1 package frozen phyllo dough, thawed

Preheat the oven to 350°F. Grease a 16x10-inch baking dish. In a large skillet over medium heat, add 1 tablespoon of the melted butter. Add the onions and sauté for 2 minutes. Add the scallions and cook for 3 minutes more. Add the spinach and herbs and spices, stirring to coat. Simmer for 5 minutes. In a large bowl, combine the feta cheese, spinach mixture, and eggs. Stir to blend and set aside. Spread a sheet of the phyllo dough in the prepared dish. Brush well with the melted butter. Repeat for 10 layers. Spread the spinach filling over the phyllo layers and fold any edges over the filling. Add the remaining sheets of phyllo dough (do at least eight), buttering between the layers and on top of the final sheet. Bake for 30 minutes, or until golden brown. **Makes 8 servings.**

Lighter Phyllo

■ For a lighter, healthier pie, spray a light coating of olive oil on each phyllo sheet, instead of using butter.

Red Potatoes With Lemon Ginger Vinaigrette

3 pounds small red-skin potatoes

¼ cup white-wine vinegar

zest and juice of 2 lemons

2 teaspoons peeled, grated fresh ginger

2 teaspoons chopped fresh dill

¼ cup canola oil

½ cup olive oil

salt and pepper, to taste

¼ cup chopped red onion

2 tablespoons chopped fresh chives

fresh parsley sprigs, for garnish

In a stockpot of boiling, salted water, cook the potatoes for 15 minutes, or until just tender. Drain well, cool slightly, and cut the potatoes in half. Return the potatoes to the pot and keep warm. In a large bowl, combine the vinegar, lemon zest and juice, ginger, and dill. Slowly add the canola and olive oils, whisking constantly until well blended. Season with salt and pepper. Transfer the warm potatoes to the bowl, add the red onion and chives, and toss gently to coat. Garnish with the parsley sprigs and serve warm or at room temperature. **Makes 8 servings.**

Caraway and Tarragon Potatoes

¼ cup (½ stick) butter

2 tablespoons white wine

zest of one lemon

½ teaspoon lemon pepper

1 teaspoon caraway seeds

2 tablespoons fresh tarragon, minced,
or 2 teaspoons dried tarragon

4 large potatoes, cut into strips

1 bunch scallions, thinly sliced

¼ cup grated Parmesan cheese

In a large skillet over medium heat, combine the butter, wine, lemon zest, lemon pepper, caraway seeds, and tarragon and cook until the butter melts. Add the potatoes and scallions and mix well. Cover and cook for 15 to 20 minutes, or until the potatoes are tender and slightly browned. Sprinkle with the cheese. Cover and cook for 1 minute longer, or until the cheese softens. **Makes 6 to 8 servings.**

Use the Right Spud

Potatoes come in several different colors, sizes, shapes, and textures, and with different cooking qualities. Potatoes high in starch do well when mashed or baked but do not keep their shape when boiled. Types low in starch are best for boiling.

POTATO	DESCRIPTION	KITCHEN NOTES
Russet	Medium to large, oblong potato with thick, rough, netted, brown skin and dry, white flesh. High in starch.	Does not hold shape as well as other types when cooked, but comes out light and fluffy when baked or mashed.
Round white or long white	Thin, white to tan skins and white, creamy flesh. Low to medium starch content.	Hold their shape well when cooked. All-purpose.
Yellow, including 'Yukon Gold'	Thin gold skin and yellow, creamy, buttery-tasting, waxy flesh. Low to medium starch content.	All-purpose.
Blue or purple	Blue or purple inside and out. Flesh has slightly nutty flavor. Low to medium starch content.	Color holds up best when cooked in the microwave.
Fingerling	Slender; about 2 to 4 inches long. Thin skin; can be gold, red, yellow, and purple. Flesh is yellow, waxy, firm, flavorful. Usually low in starch.	Holds up well when cooked.
Red	Small to medium. Thin, red skin and firm, smooth, moist, waxy, white flesh. Low in starch.	Holds shape well when cooked. Excellent as new potatoes.
New	Any potato that is harvested before maturity. Has thin skin and waxy, moist, creamy flesh.	Best cooked whole; holds shape well.

Some potatoes are more suitable for certain cooking techniques than others. Here are a few suggestions.

PURPOSE	TYPE
Baking	Blue/purple, fingerling, russet, yellow
Boiling	Fingerling, red, white
French fries	Russet, white, yellow
Mashing	Russet, white, yellow
Pancakes	Yellow, 'Yukon Gold'
Panfrying	Red
Purées	Fingerling
Roasting	Red, russet, white, yellow
Salads, scalloped dishes, gratins	Blue/purple, red, white
Soups, chowders	Red, white
Steaming	Blue/purple, fingerling, white, yellow

Garlic Potato Soufflé

3 eggs, separated

3 cups hot mashed potatoes

¼ cup melted butter

¼ teaspoon salt

1 cup hot milk

2 cloves garlic, minced, or ¼ teaspoon garlic powder

¼ teaspoon nutmeg

paprika

Preheat the oven to 350°F. Grease an 8-inch square baking dish. In a large mixing bowl, beat the egg yolks until light yellow. Add the mashed potatoes, butter, salt, milk, garlic, and nutmeg and beat to blend. In a separate large bowl, beat the egg whites until stiff. Gently fold them into the potato mixture. Pour the mixture into the prepared baking dish, sprinkle with paprika, and bake for 25 minutes, or until the top is golden brown. **Makes 6 servings.**

Buttermilk-Blue Potatoes Au Gratin

7 medium russet potatoes, parboiled, peeled, and thinly sliced

2½ tablespoons butter

1 clove garlic, crushed

2 shallots, minced

2 tablespoons all-purpose flour

1½ cups milk, at room temperature

1 teaspoon white pepper

¼ cup mayonnaise

1 teaspoon Dijon-style mustard

½ teaspoon Worcestershire sauce

¼ cup chopped fresh parsley

2 ounces blue cheese, crumbled, divided

1 cup buttermilk, at room temperature

3 cups sliced mushrooms

1 cup grated Monterey Jack cheese

1½ cups coarsely crushed potato chips

2 cups chopped broccoli

1 tablespoon diced pimiento, for garnish

Preheat the oven to 350°F. Grease a shallow 2½-quart casserole. Arrange half of the potato slices in the bottom of the prepared dish and set aside. In a medium saucepan over low heat, melt the butter. Add the garlic and shallots and sauté for 1 minute. Add the flour, stir or whisk to blend, and cook for 3 minutes more. Add the milk. Cook, stirring constantly, until the sauce thickens and bubbles. Remove the saucepan from the heat. Add the pepper, mayonnaise, mustard, Worcestershire sauce, parsley, and half of the blue cheese and stir to incorporate. Add the buttermilk and stir. Layer the mushrooms over the potatoes in the casserole. Spread half of the sauce on top, then sprinkle with the Monterey Jack cheese. Layer the remaining potatoes over the cheese and cover with the remaining sauce. Sprinkle with the remaining blue cheese. Bake for 45 minutes. Distribute the potato chips on top and bake for 10 minutes more. In a saucepan over medium heat, steam or boil the broccoli until crisp-tender. Arrange the broccoli around the outer edge of the casserole and garnish with pimiento. Bake for 5 minutes more. **Makes 6 servings.**

Show me your garden and I will tell you what you are.

–Alfred Austin, English poet (1835–1913)

Buttermilk-Blue Potatoes Au Gratin
(recipe at left)

The Potato-in-Water Test

■ To determine what kind of potatoes you have, drop one in a pot containing 11 parts water to one part salt. Waxy potatoes, best for salads, will float. Mealy potatoes, best for baking or mashing, will sink.

Bacon Cheddar Potato Kugelis

Kugelis is a baked potato pudding of Lithuanian origin.

2 slices bacon, diced

1 cup finely chopped onion

2 eggs

1 teaspoon salt

¼ teaspoon white pepper

1 tablespoon all-purpose flour

¼ cup half-and-half

4 large russet potatoes, peeled and cubed

1 cup shredded sharp cheddar cheese

Preheat the oven to 425°F. Grease a 9-inch square baking pan. In a skillet over medium heat, combine the bacon and onion and cook until the bacon is crisp and the onion is soft and golden. Set the pan and ingredients aside to cool. In a large bowl, combine the eggs, salt, pepper, flour, and half-and-half and whisk until smooth. Put the potatoes into a food processor and pulse until coarsely ground. Add the potatoes to the egg mixture and stir until well combined. Add the bacon and onions, along with any pan drippings, and stir to blend. Pour the mixture into the prepared pan. Bake for 30 minutes. Reduce the oven temperature to 375°F and bake for 13 to 15 minutes more, or until firm and golden. Sprinkle with the cheese and bake for 5 minutes more. Cut into squares and serve warm. **Makes 8 servings.**

Water Reuse

■ Remember to save cooled cooking water for the garden or houseplants.

German Potato Casserole

This casserole is a perfect accompaniment to roast pork or lamb.

5 medium potatoes, peeled and diced

2 small rutabagas, peeled and diced

2 tablespoons butter

2 tablespoons all-purpose flour

1½ cups milk, warmed

⅛ teaspoon white pepper

¼ teaspoon salt

⅛ teaspoon nutmeg

6 slices bacon, cooked crisp and crumbled

Preheat the oven to 350°F. Grease a 2-quart casserole. In a stockpot of boiling, salted water, cook the potatoes and rutabagas until tender, but not mushy (they should hold their shape). Drain well and set the vegetables aside in the pot to keep warm. In a saucepan over medium heat, melt the butter. Add the flour and stir or whisk constantly until bubbly and well blended. Add the warm milk slowly and continue stirring until the sauce comes to a boil. Add the pepper, salt, and nutmeg and stir to blend. Remove the pan from the heat and pour the sauce over the potatoes and rutabagas. Transfer the mixture into the prepared casserole. Sprinkle the crumbled bacon on top and cover. Bake for 15 minutes. Remove the cover and bake for 15 minutes more, or until golden. **Makes 8 servings.**

Dill and Potato Cakes

A great way to use leftover mashed potatoes.

2 tablespoons butter, softened

pinch of salt

1 tablespoon finely chopped dill

1 cup self-rising flour*

2 cups mashed potatoes

⅛ to ¼ cup milk, as required

*If you do not have self-rising flour, you can substitute 1 cup of all-purpose flour plus 1¼ teaspoons baking powder plus ¼ teaspoon salt.

Preheat the oven to 400°F. Grease a cookie sheet. In a bowl, combine the butter, salt, and dill. Sift the flour on top. Add the mashed potatoes and ⅛ cup of milk. Mix to incorporate the ingredients and turn them into a soft dough, adding more milk, 1 teaspoon at a time, if necessary. Use your hands to form round cakes (or patties) about 3 inches in diameter and ½-inch thick. Place the cakes onto the prepared sheet. Bake for 15 to 20 minutes, without turning, until golden. Serve warm. **Makes 10 to 12 cakes.**

To remove onion odors from your hands, rub dry mustard onto them and then rinse it off.

Golden Onion Bake

Vidalia onions work best in this dish.

8 sweet onions, quartered
2 tablespoons butter
1 teaspoon salt
½ teaspoon paprika
¼ cup tomato juice
3 tablespoons honey
2 tablespoons herbed bread crumbs

Preheat the oven to 300°F. Grease a shallow baking pan. Place the onions in the pan. In a small saucepan over medium heat, melt the butter. Add the salt, paprika, tomato juice, and honey. Stir to combine, and cook for 2 minutes. Drizzle the mixture over the onions. Sprinkle with the bread crumbs. Cover and bake for 1 hour. **Makes 6 servings.**

In the Garden: Onions

- Onions look perfectly healthy even when they're bone-dry; don't let fat green stalks fool you. Give onions plenty of water for best flavor. Drought stress makes onions more pungent.

In the Kitchen

- Scallions and other green onions have a small white bulb at the base and a white stalk that turns into green leaves at the top. All parts are edible. The white parts are often used in cooking, while the green parts are usually eaten raw but can be cooked.

Apple-Stuffed Acorn Squash

3 medium acorn squashes
2 tablespoons butter
3 cups peeled, cored, and chopped tart apples
1 cup chopped onion
½ cup golden raisins
2 tablespoons light-brown sugar
1 teaspoon cinnamon
1½ cups grated cheddar cheese

Preheat the oven to 350°F. Cut the squashes in half lengthwise and scoop out the seeds and strings. Place in a baking dish and bake, cut side down, in ½ inch of water for 40 minutes, or until tender. In a skillet over medium heat, melt the butter. Add the apples and onion and sauté for 10 minutes, or until both are tender. In a large bowl, combine the apples and onion with the raisins, brown sugar, cinnamon, and cheese. Stir to blend. Place the cooked squashes on a lightly greased cookie sheet and spoon the apple stuffing into the cavities in equal portions. Bake for 20 minutes, or until the apples are soft and the cheese has melted. **Makes 6 servings.**

In the Garden: Winter Squashes

▪ **Winter squashes—such as acorn, butternut, delicata, hubbard, and turban—generally take longer to ripen than summer types, since they are harvested when the seeds are mature and the skin has toughened.**

Rice-Stuffed Acorn Squash

2 medium acorn squashes
1 tablespoon butter, melted
¼ teaspoon salt
¼ teaspoon cinnamon
⅛ teaspoon nutmeg
2 cups cooked rice
1 cup applesauce
½ cup finely chopped celery
½ cup chopped, toasted pecans
¼ cup packed brown sugar
¼ teaspoon ground ginger

Preheat the oven to 350°F. Lightly grease a cookie sheet. Prepare the squash as for the Apple-Stuffed version above. Brush the inside of each cooked squash with butter and sprinkle with the salt, cinnamon, and nutmeg. In a bowl, combine the rice, applesauce, celery, pecans, brown sugar, and ginger. Stir to blend. Spoon the rice stuffing into the cavities in equal portions. Place the squash on the prepared sheet. Bake for 25 to 30 minutes. **Makes 4 servings.**

Maple Squash Soufflé

3 cups cooked winter squash
¼ cup milk
3 tablespoons all-purpose flour
3 eggs, beaten
½ teaspoon salt
¼ teaspoon nutmeg
freshly ground black pepper, to taste
3 tablespoons maple syrup

Preheat the oven to 350°F. Grease a 1-quart casserole. In a large bowl, combine all of the ingredients and beat to blend. Spoon the mixture into the prepared casserole. Bake for about 35 minutes, or until the top is golden. **Makes 6 to 8 servings.**

Baked Summer Squash

This can be prepared a day ahead and stored in the refrigerator until you're ready to bake it.

3 pounds yellow squash or zucchini, sliced
½ cup chopped onion
2 eggs, lightly beaten
1 tablespoon sugar
1 teaspoon salt
½ teaspoon freshly ground black pepper
½ cup (1 stick) butter, melted and divided
1 cup bread crumbs

Preheat the oven to 375°F. In a saucepan over medium-high heat, boil or steam the squash for 3 to 5 minutes, or until tender. Drain, then return the squash to the pan and mash it. Add the onion, eggs, sugar, salt, pepper, and half of the melted butter to the squash. Stir to incorporate. Spoon the mixture into a 2-quart casserole. In a small bowl, drizzle the remaining butter on the bread crumbs and toss to coat. Sprinkle the bread crumb mixture over the squash. Bake for 45 minutes. **Makes 6 servings.**

In the Garden: Squashes

■ Squash plants thrive in compost and will produce better if fertilized. When the first blooms appear, apply a small amount of fertilizer as a side dressing and water thoroughly. After harvest begins, fertilize occasionally for vigorous growth and an abundant yield.

Zucchini Casserole

**1½ pounds zucchini or yellow squash,
cut into bite-size pieces**

**¼ cup chopped fresh dill or 1 tablespoon
dried dill**

¾ teaspoon garlic powder

salt and pepper, to taste

6 tablespoons (¾ stick) butter, divided

2 tablespoons all-purpose flour

⅔ cup milk

1 cup herb stuffing mix

Preheat the oven to 350°F. Grease a shallow, 1½-quart casserole. Put the zucchini into a saucepan and cover with water. Add the dill and garlic and simmer over medium heat for 3 minutes. Cover, reduce the heat, and cook for 5 minutes, or until the zucchini is tender. Drain and reserve the cooking water. Pat the zucchini dry, season with salt and pepper, and put into the prepared casserole. In a saucepan over low heat, melt 3 tablespoons of butter. Add the flour and cook for 2 minutes, stirring or whisking constantly. Add the milk, stir or whisk, and cook for 5 minutes, or until the sauce thickens. Pour it over the zucchini and toss lightly to cover. Prepare the stuffing mix according to package directions, using the remaining 3 tablespoons of butter and the zucchini cooking water. Spread the stuffing over the zucchini. Bake for 30 minutes. **Makes 4 servings.**

MAKE AHEAD: *The zucchini and cream sauce can be made early in the day, covered, and refrigerated. It can also be frozen, defrosted, and baked. For best results, prepare and spread the stuffing just before baking.*

In the Kitchen: Zucchini

■ When zucchini are plentiful, grate 1- or 2-cup portions and freeze to use in soups, stews, and nut breads throughout the winter.

Zucchini Provençal

VEGETABLE DISHES

3 tablespoons olive oil

⅔ cup chopped onion

4 ounces mushrooms, sliced

2½ pounds zucchini, cut into ¼-inch-thick slices

⅔ cup grated Parmesan cheese, divided

2 cans (6 ounces each) tomato paste

1 clove garlic, minced

1 teaspoon salt

⅛ teaspoon freshly ground black pepper

Preheat the oven to 350°F. In a large saucepan over medium heat, warm the oil. Add the onion and mushrooms and sauté for 3 minutes, or until the onion is soft. Add the zucchini and cook for 4 minutes, or until just tender. Remove the saucepan from the heat and add half of the cheese. Stir to incorporate. Add the tomato paste, garlic, salt, and pepper and mix well. Turn the mixture into a 2-quart casserole and sprinkle the remaining cheese on top. Bake for 20 minutes, or until heated through. **Makes 6 to 8 servings.**

Italian Zucchini Crescent Pie

The easiest-ever "pizza"!

3 tablespoons butter

4 cups thinly sliced zucchini

1 cup chopped onion

½ cup chopped fresh parsley or 2 tablespoons dried parsley

½ teaspoon salt

½ teaspoon freshly ground black pepper

¼ teaspoon garlic powder

¾ teaspoon chopped fresh basil or ¼ teaspoon dried basil

¾ teaspoon chopped fresh oregano or ¼ teaspoon dried oregano

2 eggs, beaten

2 cups shredded mozzarella cheese

1 can (8 ounces) crescent dinner rolls

2 teaspoons prepared mustard

Preheat the oven to 375°F. In a large skillet over medium heat, melt the butter. Add the zucchini and onion and sauté for 10 minutes, or until the onion is golden. Remove the pan from the heat. Add the parsley, salt, pepper, garlic powder, basil, and oregano and stir to blend. In a bowl, combine the eggs and mozzarella and stir, then add to the zucchini mixture. Place the crescent roll dough in an ungreased 10-inch pie plate. Press the dough over the bottom and up the sides to form a crust. Spread the mustard on the dough. Spread the vegetable mixture on top. Bake for 18 to 20 minutes, or until the center is set. If the edges begin to brown before the center is set, cover with aluminum foil. Let stand for 10 minutes before serving. **Makes 6 to 8 servings.**

Orange-Glazed Sweet Potatoes

6 sweet potatoes

3 tablespoons butter

1 tablespoon cornstarch

1 cup fresh orange juice

⅓ cup sugar

⅓ cup light-brown sugar

pinch of salt

Cook the sweet potatoes in boiling, salted water for 30 minutes, or roast in the oven at 450°F for 30 minutes. When cool enough to handle, peel, slice in half lengthwise, and place in a 2-quart casserole. Set aside.

Set the oven at 350°F. In a small saucepan over medium heat, melt the butter. Add the cornstarch and stir or whisk until it is dissolved and the consistency is smooth. Add the orange juice, then the sugars and salt, and cook until the sauce thickens, stirring or whisking constantly. Pour the sauce over the sweet potatoes. Bake for 30 minutes. **Makes 6 servings.**

MAKE AHEAD: *The sauce can be made a few days ahead. Refrigerate it until you're ready to use it.*

In the Garden: Sweet Potatoes

■ **A 50-foot row of sweet potatoes yields about 60 pounds.**

Sweet Potato and Pineapple Casserole
(recipe at right)

Sweet Potato and Pineapple Casserole

For the sweet potato aficionado or "sweet tooth."

4 to 6 small sweet potatoes

⅛ teaspoon allspice

⅛ teaspoon ground cloves

⅛ teaspoon nutmeg

½ teaspoon salt

1 can (8 ounces) crushed pineapple, with liquid

½ cup miniature marshmallows

½ cup honey

Grease a 1-quart casserole. Cook the sweet potatoes in boiling, salted water for 30 minutes, or roast in the oven at 450°F for 30 minutes. When cool enough to handle, peel and cut into ½-inch slices. Set the oven at 350°F. In a small bowl, combine the spices and salt. Layer the sweet potatoes in the prepared casserole. Sprinkle the spice mixture over the sweet potatoes. Layer the pineapple over the spice mixture. Top with the marshmallows and pour the honey over it all. Bake for 10 minutes. **Makes 4 servings.**

In the Kitchen: Sweet Potatoes

■ A medium sweet potato cooked in a microwave on high will be done in 5 to 7 minutes. If it still feels firm, let it stand for 5 minutes to soften.

In the Garden: Tomatoes

■ Except for dwarf types, tomato plants need support as they grow. Not only does this save space, but also it lessens the chance of fruit rot and makes it easier to control pests. Stakes and cages work well for all nondwarf tomatoes, including determinate types, which fruit at the tips of the plant and then stop growing. Indeterminate tomatoes, which grow continuously, also thrive on trellises. Support tomatoes when the plants reach 1 foot tall.

Cheese Soufflé in a Tomato

¼ cup (½ stick) butter
⅓ cup all-purpose flour
¾ cup milk
2 eggs, separated
¾ cup grated Swiss or cheddar cheese
½ teaspoon salt
¼ teaspoon freshly ground black pepper
6 firm medium tomatoes
chopped fresh chives, for garnish

Preheat the oven to 350°F. In a saucepan over medium heat, melt the butter. Add the flour and stir or whisk to blend. Add the milk gradually, stirring or whisking constantly until the sauce thickens. Remove the pan from the heat, add the egg yolks, and beat to blend. Add the cheese and mix until combined. Add the salt and pepper and mix, then set aside. Slice the tops off of the tomatoes and scoop out the pulp, leaving a ½-inch-thick shell wall. Invert the tomato shells onto paper towels and set aside to drain. In a large, chilled bowl, beat the egg whites until stiff but not dry. Gently fold the whites into the cheese mixture. Set the tomato shells into six small soufflé dishes or custard cups or side-by-side in a 9x9-inch (or similar) baking dish. Spoon the cheese soufflé mixture into the tomatoes. Bake for 35 to 40 minutes, or until puffed and light brown. Garnish with chopped chives. **Makes 6 servings.**

How to Oven-Dry Tomatoes

■ Dried tomatoes add color and flavor to salads, pizza, soups, stir-fries, pesto, and sauces. Paste types work best, as they have less water.

Preheat the oven to 150°F. Wash about 5 pounds of tomatoes. Peel the skins, if desired *(see tip, page 65)*. Remove the stems and blemishes. Cut the tomatoes in half, take out the seeds, and then cut the halves into ½- to ¾-inch slices.

Place the tomato slices on cookie sheets so that they do not touch each other. Sprinkle with seasonings or salt, as desired. Place in the oven and bake for 6 to 24 hours, depending on the variety, size, and moisture content of the tomatoes. Use an oven thermometer to monitor the temperature periodically and make sure that it is correct; adjust as needed. Check the tomatoes every so often and switch sheets from top to bottom racks and back to front. Turn the tomatoes over occasionally.

The tomatoes are done when they turn dark red and are leathery and dry; they should be flexible and not hard or brittle. If they are tacky or moist, keep baking. When ready, remove the sheets from the oven and cool the tomatoes to room temperature. Place in plastic bags, squeeze out the air, and store in the refrigerator for 2 to 4 weeks or in the freezer for 8 to 12 months.

For more on how to dry tomatoes, see page 143.

VEGETABLE DISHES

In the Garden: Tomatoes

■ Years ago, farmers planted tomatoes on the south side of stonewalls edging their fields because stones heat up during the day and release their warmth at night, keeping the plants comfortable. Try adding rocks to your garden. Place them close to, but not touching, tomato stems.

VEGETABLE DISHES

Vegetable Cheese Bake

2 tablespoons vegetable oil
1 large onion, chopped
1 large green bell pepper, cubed
1 medium eggplant, cubed
8 ounces fresh mushrooms, sliced
1 large tomato, chopped
1 teaspoon salt
1 tablespoon chopped fresh thyme or
**   ¾ teaspoon dried thyme**
⅛ teaspoon freshly ground black
**   pepper**
1 cup herb stuffing mix
12 ounces Swiss cheese, shredded and
**   divided**

Preheat the oven to 350°F. Grease a 2-quart casserole. In a skillet over medium heat, warm the oil. Add the onion and green pepper and sauté for 3 minutes. Add the eggplant and mushrooms, toss lightly to mix, and sauté for 3 minutes more. Add the tomato and seasonings, stir, and cook for 1 minute. Spread the stuffing mix in the bottom of the casserole. Spread half of the vegetable mixture over the stuffing. Sprinkle with 1 cup of the shredded cheese. Top with the remaining vegetables. Bake, uncovered, for 30 minutes. Sprinkle with the remaining cheese and bake for 10 minutes more, or until the cheese is melted. **Makes 6 to 8 servings.**

In the Garden: Peppers

■ Before the first frost, bring pepper plants indoors. Keep them in a bright, sunny location and you may enjoy fresh peppers until mid-December.

There's No Such Thing as Too Many Tomatoes

Enjoy the fresh taste of summer year-round by preserving tomatoes using these methods:

DRYING

■ Perhaps the easiest way to dry tomatoes is with an electric food dehydrator. If you don't have one, you can use a conventional oven (*see tip, page 141*).

■ Sun drying is not recommended for tomatoes, unless you live in an area with less than 60 percent humidity and daily temperatures that reach at least 90°F. Below this temperature, the tomatoes may dry too slowly, encouraging the growth of mold or bacteria.

■ A solar dehydrator takes less time than sun drying, so it is safer. However, all foods dried outdoors should then be frozen in sealed bags in the freezer for at least 2 days or baked on a cookie sheet in the oven at 160°F for 30 minutes, to destroy any insects or their eggs.

FREEZING

To preserve your harvest quickly, freeze the tomatoes whole. Separate the tomatoes on a cookie sheet and put them into the freezer. Once frozen, place the tomatoes in plastic freezer bags, then seal, label, and return to the freezer.

Season tomatoes after they are thawed rather than before freezing. Freezing may strengthen or weaken the flavor of herbs, garlic, or onions, changing the flavor of the dish.

When defrosted, the tomatoes will be mushy and best suited for cooked foods such as stews, sauces, and casseroles.

AS SAUCE

Wash and quarter the tomatoes, then simmer them in a stockpot with the lid on for about 40 minutes. Let cool. The pulp will settle to the bottom. As the liquid rises to the top, ladle off the clear juice. Repeat several times. Or, simmer the tomatoes slowly, uncovered, until the sauce is thickened. Strain the pulp; toss out the skins and seeds. To preserve, pour into sterilized jars and process them in a boiling-water bath.*

See proper canning procedures on page 150.

VEGETABLE DISHES

**Italian Vegetable
Popover Pizza**

(recipe at right)

Italian Vegetable Popover Pizza

The "crust" is on top.

3 tablespoons vegetable oil, divided

2 cups sliced zucchini

⅓ cup chopped green bell pepper

1 cup sliced carrots

1 pound mushrooms, sliced

⅓ cup diagonally sliced celery

½ cup chopped broccoli

2 cups homemade tomato sauce or
   2 cans (8 ounces each) tomato sauce

2 tablespoons tomato paste

½ cup red wine

1 tablespoon chopped fresh oregano or
   1 teaspoon dried oregano

1 tablespoon chopped fresh basil or
   1 teaspoon dried basil

¾ teaspoon chopped fresh marjoram or
   ¼ teaspoon dried marjoram

1 clove garlic, chopped

¾ teaspoon salt, divided

12 ounces mozzarella cheese, shredded

2 large eggs

1 cup milk

1 cup all-purpose flour

½ cup grated Parmesan cheese

Preheat the oven to 400°F. Grease a 13x9-inch baking pan. In a large frying pan over medium heat, warm 2 tablespoons of the oil. Add the zucchini, green pepper, carrots, mushrooms, celery, and broccoli and cook for 5 to 7 minutes, or until soft; strain, if needed. Add the tomato sauce, tomato paste, wine, oregano, basil, marjoram, garlic, and ¼ teaspoon of the salt and stir well. Reduce the heat and simmer for 20 minutes. Spoon the mixture into the prepared baking pan. Sprinkle with the mozzarella. Set the pan in the oven to keep warm. In a large bowl, combine the eggs, milk, and remaining tablespoon of oil and beat to blend. Add the flour and remaining ½ teaspoon of salt and beat until smooth. Remove the vegetable mixture from the oven and pour the egg mixture over it, covering the ingredients completely. Sprinkle with the Parmesan cheese. Bake for 30 minutes, or until puffed and golden brown. **Makes 9 servings.**

How to Roast Peppers

■ Preheat the broiler. Cut the peppers in half and remove the core and seeds. Lay the peppers on a broiler rack or cookie sheet, cut side down, and place under the heat until the skin is blackened. Transfer the hot peppers to a brown paper bag, close the top tightly, and let the peppers steam for 10 minutes. Remove from the bag and peel off the charred skin. Use or store in the refrigerator.

Ratatouille Pie

This recipe can be frozen unbaked.

¾ cup olive oil

1 large onion, chopped

1 clove garlic, minced

1 large eggplant, peeled and cubed

2 cups cubed zucchini

1 red bell pepper, cubed

2 cups peeled, seeded, and cubed
   tomatoes *(see tip, page 65)*

1 tablespoon chopped fresh basil

salt and pepper, to taste

1 teaspoon red-wine vinegar

1 unbaked 9-inch double piecrust *(see
   recipe, page 272)*

Preheat the oven to 500°F. In a heavy frying pan over medium heat, warm the olive oil. Add the onion and garlic, lower the heat, and cook for 10 minutes, or until the onion begins to wilt. Add the eggplant, stir, and cook for 5 minutes. Add the zucchini, bell pepper, and tomatoes, toss lightly, and cook for 5 minutes. Add the basil, salt and pepper, and vinegar and stir to blend. Cover, raise the heat to medium, and cook for 30 minutes, or until the mixture cooks down a bit. If there is too much liquid, remove the cover and cook until the juice has been reduced. Pour the mixture into the piecrust and finish with a lattice top *(see tip, page 272).* Bake for 10 minutes, then reduce the heat to 350°F and cook for 15 minutes, or until golden. **Makes 4 to 6 servings.**

Spicy Stewed Okra

1 tablespoon vegetable oil

¾ cup chopped onion

3 cups seeded, chopped tomatoes

1 jalapeño, seeded and diced

1 cup corn

2 tablespoons lemon juice, divided

⅛ teaspoon ground cloves

1 pound fresh young okra pods, washed
 and trimmed *(see tip, below)*

¾ cup vegetable or chicken broth

½ teaspoon salt

¼ teaspoon freshly ground black
 pepper

rice (optional)

In a stockpot or large saucepan over medium heat, warm the oil. Add the onion and sauté for 5 minutes, or until translucent. Raise the heat to medium-high, add the tomatoes and jalapeño, and cook for 5 minutes. Add the corn, 1 tablespoon of lemon juice, and the ground cloves and simmer for 5 minutes, or until heated through. Cut the okra into slices and add to the tomato mixture. Add the remaining lemon juice and the broth. Cook, stirring gently, for 10 minutes, or until the okra is tender. Stir in the salt and pepper and remove the pot from the heat. Serve over rice, if desired. **Makes 6 to 8 servings.**

In the Kitchen: Okra

■ Okra can get slimy when exposed to moisture, which is helpful in gumbo and sauces but not as pleasant in other dishes. To lessen the effect: Choose small pods and wash and dry them thoroughly before trimming with a dry knife. Soak the pods in vinegar or lemon juice; drain and dry them completely before adding to recipes. Stir-fry whole or sliced okra quickly, uncovered, or roast or grill the pods. Do not add salt until the end of cooking.

Vegetable Hash

This can easily be multiplied to feed a crowd. The flavor will vary depending on the vegetables and proportions used.

1 tablespoon vegetable oil

6 cups coarsely shredded raw winter
vegetables (squashes, carrots,
rutabaga, turnips, parsnips, sweet
potatoes, etc.)

5 tablespoons cream, half-and-half,
or reduced-fat sour cream

¼ teaspoon nutmeg, or to taste

salt, to taste

In a large, heavy skillet over medium heat, warm the oil. Add the shredded vegetables and sauté, turning often to prevent burning, for 15 minutes, or until the vegetables are lightly browned and soft. Add a few drops of water as needed to prevent sticking. Add the cream, nutmeg, and salt and stir to coat. Heat through and serve warm. **Makes 4 to 6 servings.**

VEGETABLE DISHES

Canning & Preserving

When Putting Things By 150

Sweet Refrigerator Pickles 154

Sweet-and-Sour Wax Beans 155

Dilly Beans 155

String Bean Pickles 156

Garden Relish 156

Corn Relish 157

Apple Pepper Relish 157

End-of-the-Garden Relish 158

Peach Preserves With Fennel 159

Nasturtium Capers 159

Curried Apricot-and-Peppercorn Chutney 161

Watermelon Marmalade 161

Zesty Apple Chutney 162

Cherry Almond Chutney 163

Spiced Green-Pear Chutney 164

Cherry-Raspberry Conserve 164

Watermelon Apple Chutney 165

Blueberry Butter 166

Pear Butter 166

Spiced Grape Butter 166

Blueberry Conserve 167

Pumpkin Conserve 167

Cantaloupe and Peach Conserve 168

Apricot Jam 168

Mixed Fruit Jam 169

Crab Apple Jelly 170

Apple Mint Jelly 170

Grape Jelly 171

Sweet Green-Pepper Jelly 172

Harvest Jelly 172

NOTE: *Recipe yields in this chapter are approximate and will depend on the size and ripeness of the fruit and vegetables used.*

When Putting Things By . . .

. . . the containers are as important as the contents.

■ Use only jars that are specifically designed for home canning, such as mason or Ball jars. Most canning jars are sold with two-piece lids—a round metal screw band and a removable flat metal lid that has a rubber-type sealing compound around the outer edge. The screw band can be reused if it is cleaned well and does not rust. To ensure a tight seal, do not reuse the flat metal lids.

■ Before every use, thoroughly wash empty jars and lids in hot water and detergent and rinse well.

To sterilize empty jars just before filling, put them right side up in a stockpot. Fill the pot and jars with water to 1 inch above the tops of the jars. Boil for 10 minutes. Turn off the heat and keep the jars in the hot water until ready to use, taking them out one at a time as needed.

To sterilize screw bands, place them in a small saucepan. Add enough water to cover and bring to a simmer (do not boil) over medium heat. Keep the bands hot until ready to use. Keep any flat metal lids at room temperature.

■ For a strong seal, fill each jar to the proper level, leaving the right amount of air space, called headspace, between the top of the food or liquid and the inside of the jar lid. In general, allow:

¼ inch of headspace for jams, jellies, juices, pickles, and relishes

½ inch of headspace for acid foods such as tomatoes and fruits

1 inch of headspace for low-acid foods such as meats and most vegetables (if tomatoes are mixed with meats or other vegetables, consider the mixture low-acid)

■ After the food has been placed in a jar, remove all air bubbles by sliding a nonmetallic spatula in an up-and-down motion around the inside of the jar a few times.

■ When the jars are filled, wipe them clean and seal. Process, if required *(see next page)*. Label and date the jars and store them in a clean, cool, dark, dry place. Do not store near heat or direct sunlight or in extreme cold. Under these conditions, food will lose quality and may spoil. Dampness may corrode metal lids and break seals.

Canning Processing Methods

THE BOILING-WATER BATH

■ In this procedure, jars of food are completely covered with boiling water and heated for a specific amount of time. (Follow the directions provided by your canning jars' manufacturer.) Use this method to safely can tomatoes, fruit, jams, jellies, and pickles with high acidic content. Acidic foods are usually safe for about 18 months.

THE PRESSURE CANNER

■ In this procedure, jars of food are set in 2 to 3 inches of water in a pressure canner and cooked at a high temperature for a specific amount of time. (Follow the directions provided by the manufacturer of your pressure canner.) Use this method to safely can many foods with a low acidic content and a pH of 4.6 and higher, including meat, seafood, poultry, dairy products, and vegetables.

WHAT'S THE DIFFERENCE?

■ In the boiling-water bath process, food is heated to 212°F, which kills many harmful microorganisms. The spores of *Clostridium botulinum* survive, however, enabling the bacteria to grow again in low-acid foods.

■ During the pressure-canning method, the temperature of the food reaches 240°F, completely destroying the spores.

What You'll Need

Knives (for cutting and preparing fruits and vegetables)

Cutting board

Jars, screw bands, and flat lids

Jar funnel (for pouring and packing liquid and small food items into canning jars)

Jar lifter (for removing hot jars from the canning bath)

Tongs (for removing sterilized bands from hot water)

Clean cloths (for wiping jar rims and spills)

Timer or clock (for monitoring food-processing time)

Hot pads or mitts (for handling hot jars)

Large pot, boiling-water canner, or pressure canner

How to Can Like a Blue-Ribbon Winner

Ever wonder why some home-canned goods are uncannily delicious? Here are some clues:

■ The best fruit and vegetables are fresh, firm, and free of spoilage. Avoid any fruit or vegetables that have been waxed. Measure or weigh amounts carefully; the proportion of fresh food to other ingredients will affect the flavor.

■ Use canning or pickling salt. Using plain table salt may cause the pickles to turn too dark or a white sediment to form in the jar.

■ White distilled and cider vinegars of 5 percent acidity are recommended. Use white vinegar when a light color is desirable, as with fruit and cauliflower.

■ White granulated and brown sugars are used most often. Sugar serves as a preserving agent, contributes flavor, and aids in gelling. Corn syrup and honey can be used to replace part of the sugar, but too much will mask the fruit flavor and alter the gel structure. Do not try to reduce the amount of sugar in traditional recipes. Too little sugar prevents gelling and may allow yeasts and molds to grow.

How Much Is Enough?

FRUIT	POUNDS PER QUART CANNED	VEGETABLE	POUNDS PER QUART CANNED
Apples	2½ to 3	Asparagus	2½ to 4½
Blackberries	1½ to 3½	Beans	1
Blueberries	1½ to 3	Beets	2 to 3½
Cherries	2 to 2½	Cauliflower	3
Grapes	3	Corn	3 to 6
Peaches	2 to 3	Cucumbers	1½
Pears	2 to 3	Peas	3 to 6
Raspberries	1½ to 3	Peppers	3
Strawberries	1½ to 3	Spinach	2 to 3
		Tomatoes	2½ to 3½

In a Pickle?

IF THE PROBLEM IS . . .	THE POSSIBLE CAUSE IS . . .
Soft and slippery pickles	Pickles were stored in a warm spot. The brine was too weak. The jars didn't seal properly. The cucumbers were not covered with brine.
Dark pickles	Table salt was used. Ground spices or too many spices were used. The canning lids were corroded.
Shriveled pickles	The brine was too salty. The cucumbers were not fresh. The pickles were overprocessed.
White sediment in the jar	Table salt was used. The temperature during fermentation was not constant.

Pickling Proportions

■ When pickling, measure or weigh carefully. The proportion of fresh produce to other ingredients will affect flavor and your health. (An imbalance of acidic ingredients could result in botulism.) Here are some useful measures:

1 pound pickling salt = 1⅓ cups

1 pound granulated sugar = 2 cups

1 pound brown sugar = 2¼ to 2¾ cups, firmly packed

1 pound honey = 1½ cups

1 tablespoon fresh herbs = 1 teaspoon crushed dried herbs

In the Kitchen: Cucumbers

■ Cucumber blossoms may contain an enzyme that causes excessive softening of pickles. When pickling fresh cucumbers, remove and discard a $\frac{1}{16}$-inch slice from the blossom end to lessen the risk of a bad batch.

Sweet Refrigerator Pickles

These can be eaten right away, but the flavor is better after about a week.

8 cups sliced cucumbers (6 to 8 medium cucumbers)

2 large onions, sliced

2 large red bell peppers, sliced

3 hot peppers, sliced

1 tablespoon pickling salt

2 cups cider vinegar

2 cups sugar

2 teaspoons celery seed

2 teaspoons mustard seed

In a large bowl, combine the cucumber slices, onions, and peppers. Sprinkle with the salt and set the bowl aside for 1 hour. Drain and discard the liquid. In a bowl or jar with a lid, combine the vinegar, sugar, and seeds and whisk or shake until the sugar is dissolved. Pour the liquid over the cucumbers. Transfer the cucumbers to a glass or plastic covered container for storage and refrigerate. These will keep for up to 3 months. **Makes about 4 quarts.**

Sweet-and-Sour Wax Beans

**2 pounds wax beans, cut diagonally
  into 1-inch pieces**

salt, to taste

1 cup white vinegar

½ cup sugar

1 teaspoon celery seed

pinch of ground ginger

**1 tablespoon chopped fresh summer
  savory or 1 teaspoon dried
  summer savory**

4 small bay leaves

Put the beans into a saucepan and add water to cover. Season with salt and cook over medium heat until just barely tender. Drain the beans, reserving the liquid. Set the beans aside. Return the liquid to the pan and add the vinegar, sugar, celery seed, ginger, and savory. Add more water, if needed, to have enough liquid to fill the packed jars. Bring the liquid to a boil, add the beans, return to boiling, and remove from the heat. Pack into sterilized jars. Add a small bay leaf to each jar. Seal and process. **Makes 4 pints.**

Cook's Glossary:
Butter Beans

■ **Yellow wax beans are sometimes
  called butter beans. Don't confuse
  them with lima beans, which are also
  known by this alternate name.**

Dilly Beans

2 pounds whole green beans, trimmed

1 teaspoon cayenne pepper

4 cloves garlic

4 heads dill

2½ cups white vinegar

¼ cup pickling salt

Pack the beans lengthwise into sterilized 1-pint jars. Slice off the tops of the beans by running a sharp knife along the top of the jar. To each jar, add ¼ teaspoon of cayenne pepper, 1 garlic clove, and 1 head of dill. Combine 2½ cups of water with the vinegar and salt, heat to boiling, and immediately pour over the beans. Seal and process. **Makes 4 pints.**

String Bean Pickles

8 pounds green or wax beans,
    trimmed
6 cups sugar
1½ cups all-purpose flour
½ cup dry mustard
1 tablespoon turmeric
1 tablespoon celery seed
2 quarts cider vinegar

In a large stockpot of boiling, salted water, cook the beans slowly, until just tender. Do not overcook; the hot pickling sauce added later will cook them more. Drain the beans thoroughly. Divide and place in sterilized quart jars. In a large saucepan, combine the sugar, flour, spices, and vinegar and cook over low heat until thick. Stir almost constantly to prevent sticking. Pour the sauce over the cooked beans, seal, and process. **Makes about 8 quarts.**

Garden Relish

4 cups coarsely chopped onion
4 cups coarsely chopped cabbage
5 cups coarsely chopped green bell
    pepper
3 cups coarsely chopped red bell
    pepper
½ cup pickling salt
6 cups sugar
1 tablespoon celery seed
2 tablespoons mustard seed
1½ teaspoons turmeric
4 cups apple cider vinegar

Combine the coarsely chopped vegetables in a large bowl, sprinkle with the salt, and set aside overnight. Rinse and drain the vegetables, discarding the liquid. Put the vegetables into a large stockpot. In a large bowl, combine the remaining ingredients with 2 cups of water, whisk to blend, and then pour over the vegetables. Heat to boiling and simmer for 3 minutes. Remove from the heat. Pack into sterilized jars, seal, and process. **Makes about 5 quarts.**

Corn Relish

12 ears sweet corn

2 onions, chopped

2 green bell peppers, chopped

1 red bell pepper, chopped

1 cup chopped cabbage

2 tablespoons pickling salt

¼ teaspoon freshly ground black
  pepper

1½ tablespoons dry mustard

1 cup sugar

2 cups cider vinegar

Cut the corn kernels from the cobs but do not scrape the ears. In a large stockpot, combine the corn kernels, onions, peppers, and cabbage and toss to mix. Add the remaining ingredients and cook the mixture over medium-low heat for 1 hour, stirring occasionally. Pour the relish into sterilized jars, seal, and process. **Makes about 5 half-pint jars.**

In the Garden: Corn

■ **Plant corn seeds where beans and peas were planted last season. Corn loves the nitrogen-rich soil that these legumes leave behind.**

How to Harvest

■ **Corn is ready to pick when a pierced kernel squirts white milk.**

Apple Pepper Relish

4 red bell peppers, cut into chunks

5 large sweet onions, cut into quarters

6 apples, peeled, cored, and sliced

2 tablespoons lemon zest

⅔ cup fresh lemon juice

2 cups sugar

2 teaspoons salt

In a food processor, coarsely grind the peppers, onions, and apples. Transfer the mixture to a large stockpot, add the lemon zest and juice, and stir. Over medium heat, bring the ingredients to a boil. Add the sugar and salt and boil for 40 minutes, stirring occasionally, until thick. Remove from the heat. Pack into sterilized jars, seal, and process. **Makes about 2 pints.**

End-of-the-Garden Relish

2 cups chopped green or yellow beans

2 large carrots

1 cup celery

4 white onions

**1 each small red, green, and yellow bell
    peppers**

1 small head cabbage

1 head cauliflower

4 green tomatoes

2 cups lima beans

2 cups corn (optional)

6 cups cider vinegar

4 cups sugar (part brown, part white)

⅓ cup salt

2 tablespoons mustard seed

2 tablespoons celery seed

Finely chop all of the vegetables, except for the lima beans and corn, then combine all in a large stockpot and cook until just tender. Drain, then put the mixture back into the pot. Pour the vinegar, sugar, salt, and spices over the vegetables. Over medium-high heat, bring the mixture to a boil. Remove from the heat. Pack into sterilized jars, seal, and process. **Makes 6 quarts.**

Peach Preserves With Fennel

½ cup anisette liqueur

2 cups sugar

3 pounds fresh peaches, peeled, halved, and pitted

4 sprigs (6 inches each) fresh green or bronze fennel

In a large saucepan over medium-high heat, combine 2½ cups of water with the anisette and sugar and cook, stirring frequently, until the mixture boils and the sugar is dissolved. Add the peach halves and simmer for 3 minutes. Fill sterilized jars with the fruit and fennel sprigs, leaving ½ inch of headspace. Pour the remaining hot liquid over the fruit until just covered. Seal and process. **Makes 2 quarts.**

How to Harvest: Fennel

■ Before fennel blooms, snip stems and leaves as needed for recipes. Harvest seeds when they start to turn brown by cutting off the whole seed head and placing it in a paper bag. Set the bag aside, away from heat, and let the seeds dry. Shake the bag to release the seeds from the head. Store the seeds in an airtight container.

Nasturtium Capers

You can use these in place of real capers.

1 tablespoon pickling salt

6 peppercorns

2 cups wine vinegar

1 clove garlic

3½ to 4 green nasturtium seedpods

In a sterilized quart jar, combine the salt, peppercorns, vinegar, and garlic. Fill the jar with green nasturtium seedpods, seal, and store a month before using. After opening, store in the refrigerator. **Makes 1 quart.**

For more ideas on how to use edible flowers in recipes, see pages 242–243.

Curried Apricot-and-Peppercorn Chutney
(recipe at right)

Curried Apricot-and-Peppercorn Chutney

¾ cup dried apricot halves

1 small red bell pepper, finely chopped

1 small mild or medium-hot red pepper,
   finely chopped

2 large yellow onions, thinly sliced

½ orange, thinly sliced

½ lemon, thinly sliced

1 clove garlic, crushed

1½ teaspoons curry powder

½ cup golden raisins

½ tablespoon black peppercorns or
   1 teaspoon black onion seed

1 teaspoon kosher salt

1 teaspoon prepared mustard

2¼ cups white vinegar

2 cups sugar

Put the dried apricots into a small bowl, add water to cover, and let them soak overnight. Drain and quarter. In a large nonreactive stockpot, combine all of the ingredients. Cook the chutney over medium heat, uncovered, stirring occasionally, until the mixture boils. Reduce the heat to low and cook for 1 hour more, or until the ingredients collapse, darken, and thicken. Stir every 15 to 20 minutes: Sugar and fruit scorch easily. The chutney will be done when the onions are soft and nearly invisible. Ladle immediately into sterilized jars, seal, and process. **Makes about 3 pints.**

Watermelon Marmalade

4 cups chopped watermelon rind (no
   red flesh)

4 apples, peeled, cored, and chopped

2 oranges, chopped with peels on, and
   seeded

juice of 3 lemons

4 cups sugar

In a large stockpot, combine all of the ingredients with 2½ cups of water, mix thoroughly, and boil for 2½ hours, or until thick, stirring occasionally to prevent sticking. Remove the pot from the heat, pour the marmalade into sterilized jars, seal, and process. **Makes six 6-ounce jars.**

Zesty Apple Chutney

12 tart apples, cored, peeled, and
  chopped
3 cups chopped green tomatoes
1 red bell pepper, chopped
1 lemon, chopped
2 cloves garlic, chopped
1 quart cider vinegar
1 tablespoon salt
1 pound dark-brown sugar
2 sweet onions, chopped
1 pound raisins
¼ cup freshly grated ginger or 3 ounces
  crystallized ginger
½ teaspoon cayenne pepper

In a large stockpot over medium heat, combine all of the ingredients and simmer for at least 1 hour, or until the sauce thickens. Put the hot chutney into sterilized jars, seal, and process. **Makes 4 pints.**

How to Harvest: Apples

■ An apple is ripe when it is in full color, firm, crisp, and juicy. To pick, lift the apple and gently twist the stem; it should release effortlessly. Handle with care: Apples bruise easily.

Cherry Almond Chutney

SPICED VINEGAR:

12 whole cloves

1 cinnamon stick

12 allspice berries

1¾ cups white or cider vinegar

CHUTNEY:

1 cup dried apricot halves

1 apple, peeled, cored, and chopped

1 ripe pear, peeled, cored, and chopped

1 small onion, diced fine

¾ cup dried sweet cherries

½ cup sliced or slivered almonds

½ cup currants

½ cup apple cider

½ lemon, quartered, and finely chopped

½ teaspoon ground ginger

½ teaspoon almond extract

3 drops Angostura bitters

¼ cup honey

1¼ cups sugar

1 teaspoon whole coriander seeds (optional)

For spiced vinegar: Combine all of the ingredients in a glass jar. Let stand for 6 to 12 hours. Strain out the spices before using.

For chutney: Put the dried apricots in a small bowl, add water to cover, and let them soak overnight. Drain, quarter, and set aside. In a large nonreactive stockpot, combine the spiced vinegar with the chutney ingredients. Cook the chutney over medium heat, uncovered, stirring occasionally, until the mixture boils. Reduce the heat to low and cook for 1 hour more, or until the ingredients collapse, darken, and thicken. Stir every 15 to 20 minutes: Sugar and fruit scorch easily. Ladle immediately into sterilized jars, seal, and process. **Makes about 3 pints.**

Save 'n' Store: Sweet Cherries

- Fresh sweet cherries are best eaten immediately. If you need to store them temporarily, place them unwashed, with their stems, in a plastic bag in the refrigerator. They will keep for up to 4 days.

Spiced Green-Pear Chutney

2 pounds (about 4 large) hard green
    pears, peeled, cored, and thinly
    sliced
1 ripe mango, peeled and sliced off the
    pit (about 1¼ cups fruit or pulp)
1 cup raisins
zest and juice of 1 large lemon
1 onion, thinly sliced
¼ cup ginger preserves, or ¼ cup
    marmalade and 1 teaspoon
    ground ginger
2⅓ cups cider vinegar
2⅓ cups brown or white sugar
1 rounded teaspoon kosher salt
½ teaspoon cinnamon
¼ teaspoon ground cloves
⅛ teaspoon nutmeg
⅛ teaspoon cayenne pepper

In a large nonreactive stockpot, combine the ingredients. Cook the chutney over medium heat, uncovered, stirring occasionally, until the mixture boils. Reduce the heat to low and cook for about 1 hour more, or until the ingredients collapse, darken, and thicken. Stir every 15 to 20 minutes: Sugar and fruit scorch easily. The chutney will be done when the onions are soft and nearly invisible and the mango pieces are translucent. Ladle immediately into sterilized jars, seal, and process. **Makes about 3 pints.**

Cherry-Raspberry Conserve

3 cups tart red cherries, pitted
3 cups raspberries
4½ cups sugar
½ cup chopped blanched almonds
    (or other nuts)

In a large stockpot over medium heat, combine the cherries and ⅓ cup of water, then cook until tender. Add the raspberries and sugar, stir, and cook until the mixture is thick. Add the nuts, stir, and cook for 5 minutes more. Transfer the conserve to sterilized jars, seal, and process. **Makes about 5 pints.**

Watermelon Apple Chutney

Let the flavors marry for a day before serving.

2 cups finely chopped watermelon rind
(no red flesh)

2 cups chopped tart apples

1 cup chopped red bell pepper

1 cup brown sugar

½ cup raisins

2 tablespoons chopped onion

1 clove garlic, minced

¾ cup cider vinegar

½ cup apple juice

1¼ teaspoons ground ginger

⅛ teaspoon cayenne pepper

In a large nonreactive stockpot over medium heat, combine all of the ingredients and mix well. Bring the ingredients to a boil, reduce the heat, and simmer for 35 to 40 minutes, stirring occasionally, or until the watermelon rind is tender and the liquid is partially reduced. Cool and store, covered, in the refrigerator. **Makes 4 pints.**

In the Garden: Watermelons

- Amaze your friends by growing a SQUARE watermelon. In rich, well-drained soil, sow seeds for small (5- to 15-pound) watermelons. When a fruit is pea-size, place a rectangular cinder block nearby and hang the little melon over one of the holes in the block. Fertilize and water the plant regularly. When the watermelon is ripe and snugly fills the block hole, break the block with a sledgehammer and harvest the watermelon.

Blueberry Butter

8 cups blueberries

8 large green cooking apples, peeled, cored, and chopped

8 cups sugar

1 teaspoon allspice

1 teaspoon mace

1 teaspoon nutmeg

In a large stockpot over medium-high heat, combine all of the ingredients. Bring the mixture to a boil, lower the heat, and simmer for 1 hour, or until the mixture is thick, stirring occasionally. Spoon the butter into sterilized jars, seal, and process. **Makes 8 pints.**

Pear Butter

4 cups apple cider

6 cups pears, peeled, cored, and sliced

honey, to taste

cinnamon, ground cloves, and allspice, to taste (optional)

In a large stockpot over medium-high heat, combine the cider and 2 cups of water and bring to a boil. Add the pears carefully. Return the liquid to a boil, then reduce the heat to medium and simmer until the mixture is a thick, deep-dark-brown mass. Stir frequently to prevent sticking. When the mixture is very thick, the slices will fall apart as you stir. Taste, and if it needs sweetening, add honey and stir. Add cinnamon, ground cloves, and/or allspice, if desired. Return the mixture to a boil, then remove the pot from the heat. Spoon the butter into sterilized jars, seal, and process. **Makes 6 pints.**

Spiced Grape Butter

1½ pounds Concord grapes

1 tablespoon orange zest

2¼ cups sugar

½ teaspoon cinnamon

¼ teaspoon ground cloves

Remove and reserve the grape skins. In a large saucepan over medium heat, cook the grape pulp for 20 minutes, or until it softens. Press the pulp through a sieve to remove the seeds. Return the pulp to the saucepan, add the orange zest and 1 cup of water, and cook for 10 minutes. Add the grape skins, stir, and heat to boiling. Add the sugar and spices and cook until thick, stirring occasionally. Remove the saucepan from the heat, pour the butter into sterilized jars, seal, and process. **Makes six 6-ounce jars.**

Blueberry Conserve

2 oranges, peeled (reserve rinds)
juice of 1 lemon
1 quart blueberries
⅔ cup sugar for each cup cooked fruit

Cut the orange rinds into thin strips. Remove the pith, then cut the oranges into thin slices. In a saucepan over medium heat, combine the orange and rind, lemon juice, blueberries, and ½ cup of water. Bring the mixture to a boil. In a heatproof measuring cup, measure the cooked ingredients. Return the ingredients to the saucepan, add the sugar, and stir. Simmer until the mixture is thick. Transfer the conserve to sterilized jars, seal, and process. **Makes about 3 pints.**

Pumpkin Conserve

This is delicious with roast beef.

3 pounds pumpkin, peeled, seeded,
**   and chopped**
6 cups sugar
½ cup cider vinegar
rind of 1 orange, chopped
pulp of 2 oranges, chopped
1 cup raisins, chopped
juice of 2 lemons
½ cup chopped walnuts

In a large stockpot over medium heat, combine the pumpkin with the sugar and vinegar. Bring to a boil and maintain the boil for 30 minutes, stirring occasionally. Add the chopped orange rind, pulp, and raisins to the pumpkin mixture and cook for 30 minutes more. Add the lemon juice and walnuts and stir. Pour into sterilized jars, seal, and process. **Makes about 4 pints.**

Cantaloupe and Peach Conserve

1 large cantaloupe, peeled and diced

3 cups diced peaches

juice of 2 lemons

juice of 1 orange

4½ cups sugar

1 cup walnuts, chopped (optional)

In a large stockpot over medium heat, combine the cantaloupe, peaches, juices, and sugar, then cook until thick and clear. Add the nuts and stir. Transfer the ingredients into sterilized jars, seal, and process. **Makes about 4 pints.**

Apricot Jam

8 cups diced apricots

6 cups sugar

¼ cup fresh lemon juice (optional)

In a large stockpot over medium-high heat, cook the apricots, sugar, and lemon juice. Stir to dissolve the sugar, bring the mixture to a boil, stirring frequently, and boil for 20 to 40 minutes, or until the syrup is at a desirable consistency. Remove the pan from the heat. Stir once, skim, then pour the jam into sterilized jars, seal, and process. **Makes about 4 pints.**

In the Garden: Apricots

■ Apricot trees bloom in early spring, making the flowers vulnerable to late frosts. In cold regions, choose late-blooming varieties—in fact, choose two: Most apricots are self-fertile, but fruit set is better with a different variety nearby.

Fruit Jams and Jellies

Preparing your own jams and jellies is easy once you get the knack of it.

- Some fruit, such as apples, gooseberries, and certain plums, naturally contain enough pectin to form a gel. Strawberries, cherries, blueberries, and other fruit must be combined with fruit high in pectin or with commercial pectin products for gel to form.

- Fully ripened fruit has less pectin; one-fourth of the fruit used for jellies without added pectin should be underripe.

- Fruit that is low in acid needs lemon juice or another acid added in order for gel to form.

- To make an attractive gift, cover the top of the jar with a round piece of fabric whose diameter is 2 inches larger than that of the jar. Secure it with several turns of cord or ribbon.

Mixed Fruit Jam

3 cups fresh pineapple, shredded
4 cups strawberries, hulled
2 cups rhubarb, cut up
dash of salt
4½ cups sugar

In a large stockpot over medium heat, cook the pineapple for 10 minutes, stirring occasionally so that it doesn't stick to the pan or burn. Add the strawberries, rhubarb, and salt and cook for 20 minutes, stirring occasionally. Add the sugar and bring the mixture to a boil, stirring to dissolve the sugar and prevent scorching. Allow the mixture to boil rapidly for 25 to 30 minutes, or until the jam thickens, stirring frequently. Remove the pan from the heat. Skim, pour into sterilized jars, seal, and process. **Makes about 5 pints.**

If a crab apple tree hangs over the well and blooms out of season,
there will be marriage and fertility.

Crab Apple Jelly

3 pounds crab apples, halved
1 cup sugar for each cup strained juice

In a large nonreactive stockpot over medium-high heat, combine the crab apples with enough cold water to almost cover (about an inch of the apples should be uncovered). Bring to a boil, reduce the heat to medium, and cook until the apples are soft. Mash the fruit slightly. Wet a jelly bag or cheesecloth and strain the apples through it. (For clear jelly, do not squeeze.) Measure the juice, then simmer for 5 minutes. Skim any foam that appears, then add sugar. Simmer for about 10 minutes, until the jelly thickens. Remove from the heat. Skim, pour into sterilized jars, seal, and process. **Makes 2 pints.**

Apple Mint Jelly

8 tart apples, cored and quartered
(reserve cores)
½ cup sugar for each cup strained juice
½ cup fresh mint leaves, tied at stem
ends and bruised

Place the apples and cores in a saucepan and almost cover with cold water (about an inch of the apples should be uncovered). Cook over low heat, uncovered, until the apples are very soft. Pour the apples into a jelly bag (or a colander lined with wet cheesecloth) over a large bowl and allow the juice to drip into the bowl. (Don't try to hurry the process by squeezing the bag.) Measure the juice, then transfer to a saucepan and regulate the heat to simmer. Spoon off and discard any foam that rises to the top. Add the sugar. Simmer (do not boil), until the juice thickens and falls in sheets from a spoon. Remove the pan from the heat. Hold the mint leaves by the stems and swish them through the jelly until the jelly attains the desired flavor. Discard the mint. Pour the jelly into sterilized jars, seal, and process. **Makes about 2 pints.**

In the Garden: Apples

- Apple trees like well-drained soil—especially sandy loam. Plant trees in early spring in full sun and water well.

In the Garden: Grapes

■ Grapes provide many more benefits than just the sweet fruit: Grapevines offer shade and privacy when grown on an arbor or fence. Later, pieces of vine can be woven into wreaths and baskets. Plus, the mild-tasting younger leaves can be picked and stuffed with rice or lamb and spices—that is, if the plant has not been treated with pesticides.

Grape Jelly

Wild grapes or underripe Concord grapes make the best jelly.

3 pounds grapes
¾ cup sugar for each cup strained juice

Put the grapes into a large stockpot, mash roughly, and cook over medium heat for 10 minutes, or until the juice flows freely. Add a tablespoon of water at a time, if necessary to prevent scorching or sticking. Pour the grapes into a jelly bag (or a colander lined with wet cheesecloth) over a large bowl and allow the juice to drip into the bowl overnight in the refrigerator. Pour off the juice carefully and discard any sediment. Measure the juice, then simmer for 5 minutes. Skim any foam that appears, then add sugar. Simmer for about 10 minutes, until the jelly thickens. Remove from the heat. Skim, pour into sterilized jars, seal, and process. **Makes about 4 pints.**

Sweet Green-Pepper Jelly

To best retain juice when chopping peppers, use a blender at "chop" speed or chop finely in a bowl.

¾ cup chopped green bell pepper
¼ cup chopped red bell pepper
6 cups sugar
1½ cups cider vinegar
1 bottle (6 ounces) liquid pectin
½ to 1 teaspoon green food coloring

In a large saucepan, combine the peppers, sugar, and vinegar and bring to a boil. Continue a full, rolling boil for 10 minutes. Add the pectin and return to boiling for 2 minutes. Remove the saucepan from the heat, skim, and cool. When the jelly is tepid, add the coloring and stir. Pour the jelly into sterilized jars, seal, and process. **Makes 2 pints.**

Harvest Jelly

2 pounds underripe Concord grapes
6 ripe tomatoes, sliced
6 medium cooking apples, sliced
1 cup sugar for each cup strained juice

Mash the grapes. In a large stockpot over medium heat, combine the tomatoes, fruit, and ½ cup of water and cook for 15 minutes. Pour the mixture into a jelly bag (or a colander lined with wet cheesecloth) over a large bowl to strain the liquid. Measure the liquid, return it to the pot, and add the sugar. Raise the heat and boil the mixture rapidly until syrup coats the spoon. Pour the jelly into sterilized jars, seal, and process. **Makes about 3 pints.**

*Go out on a limb—
that's where the fruit is.*

–attributed to Mark Twain,
American writer (1835–1910)

CHAPTER 7

Poultry

Chicken With Avocado and Almonds 174

Roasted Lemon-Balm Chicken 175

Chicken Chasseur. 175

Rosemary Chicken With Spinach 176

Chicken With Rice 178

Poached Chicken With Niçoise Sauce 179

Braised Chicken Breasts With Raspberry

    Sauce 179

Brunswick Chicken Pie 180

Skillet Chicken With Fresh Tomatoes 181

Chicken-Stuffed Tomatoes 181

Cock-a-leekie Pie. 182

Chicken Salad With Cashews 183

Marinated Chicken Salad 183

Chicken Noodle Salad 184

Turkey and Grape Salad 184

Turkey Cacciatore 185

Turkey With Cheese Sauce 185

Turkey-Stuffed Eggplant 187

Turkey-Stuffed Cucumbers 187

Duck With Turnips 188

Celery Stuffing 189

Eggplant Stuffing 189

Apple Stuffing 190

Sauerkraut Stuffing 190

Potato Walnut Stuffing 190

How to Poach a Chicken

■ Put a 3-pound chicken into a soup pot, add enough cold water to cover, and bring to a boil. Skim the foam from the top, reduce the heat, and add ½ of a fresh lemon, 1 bay leaf, 1 clove, and a stalk of celery. Stir and simmer for 30 minutes. Remove the chicken from the pot and set aside until it is cool to the touch. Discard the skin and bones and cut the meat into bite-size pieces. Discard the lemon, bay leaf, clove, and celery. Reserve the stock.

Chicken With Avocado and Almonds

A dish combining the best of a fricassee and chow mein. The avocados add striking color and flavor.

4 cups chicken broth

4 chicken bouillon cubes or 4 teaspoons
    chicken bouillon granules

½ cup slivered almonds

3 to 4 cups chopped cooked chicken
    (see tip, above)

3 cups diced zucchini

1 can (8 ounces) water chestnuts,
    drained and coarsely chopped

½ cup (1 stick) butter

½ cup all-purpose flour

½ cup grated Monterey Jack cheese

2 medium avocados, pitted, peeled, and
    thinly sliced

Preheat the oven to 350°F. Grease a large casserole. In a medium saucepan over medium heat, warm the broth, add the bouillon cubes, and stir to dissolve. Spread the almonds in a single layer on a cookie sheet. Bake until lightly browned, about 5 minutes, then set aside to cool. Put the chicken, zucchini, and chestnuts into the casserole and set aside. In a separate, large saucepan over low heat, melt the butter, add the flour, whisk to combine, and cook for 1 minute, stirring constantly. Slowly add the chicken broth, stirring constantly, and cook until the sauce is smooth and thickened, about 5 minutes. Pour the liquid over the ingredients in the casserole. Bake covered for 30 minutes. Sprinkle the grated cheese on top and return to the oven uncovered to bake for 15 minutes, or until the cheese melts. Arrange the avocado slices on top of the casserole. Sprinkle with almonds. **Makes 6 to 8 servings.**

Roasted Lemon-Balm Chicken

With a fresh and surprising taste and aroma, this is no ordinary roasted chicken.

2 tablespoons olive oil

15 to 20 lemon balm leaves on sprigs

¼ cup (½ stick) butter, softened

salt and pepper, to taste

1 large roasting chicken

1 teaspoon paprika

Preheat the oven to 400°F. Grease a large roasting pan with the olive oil. Trim the lemon balm leaves from the sprigs. Set the sprigs aside. Chop two-thirds of the leaves and combine them with the butter, salt, and pepper. Rinse the chicken and pat it dry. Loosen the chicken's skin in several places and insert lemon balm butter underneath. Rub the chicken with salt, pepper, and paprika. Insert the lemon balm sprigs into the chicken cavity. Place the chicken breast side down in the prepared pan. Bake for 30 minutes, then turn the chicken over. Bake for 20 minutes longer. Strew the remaining lemon balm leaves on the chicken before serving. **Makes 4 to 6 servings.**

POULTRY

In the Kitchen: Lemon Balm

■ **For best aroma and taste, use fresh lemon balm leaves. The herb is used whole, crushed, or chopped in beverages, fruit cups, teas, jams, salads and dressings, sauces, and soups. Add chopped fresh leaves to fish, chicken, or mushroom dishes or mix into soft cheese, as well as vinegars, wines, and liqueurs.**

Chicken Chasseur

salt, to taste

3 pounds chicken pieces

2 tablespoons butter

1 cup chicken stock

3 shallots, minced

1 tablespoon chopped fresh chervil

½ teaspoon chopped fresh thyme

1 tablespoon all-purpose flour

1½ cups sliced mushrooms

¼ cup dry white wine

Sprinkle salt on the chicken. In a Dutch oven over low heat, melt the butter. Add the chicken, cooking slowly to brown on all sides. Add the stock and simmer for 10 minutes. Add the shallots, chervil, and thyme and simmer for 5 minutes. Add the flour and whisk until smooth. Add the mushrooms and wine, cover, and simmer for 15 minutes, or until the chicken is tender. **Makes 4 servings.**

Rosemary Chicken With Spinach

4 chicken breast halves, with skin

salt and pepper, to taste

2 cloves garlic, 1 finely chopped, 1 thinly
   sliced

1 tablespoon chopped fresh rosemary or
   1 teaspoon dried rosemary

3 tablespoons olive oil, divided

3 tablespoons red-wine vinegar, divided

1 pound spinach, stemmed

½ teaspoon sugar

Place the chicken breasts on a plate. Season them with salt and pepper. Sprinkle them with the chopped garlic and rosemary, turning once or twice to coat evenly. In a small bowl, whisk together 2 tablespoons of the oil and 1 tablespoon of the vinegar. Pour this over the chicken and set aside to marinate for 20 to 30 minutes. In a large, heavy skillet over medium-high heat, place the chicken breasts, skin side down. Reduce the heat to medium and cook for 8 minutes, or until browned. Turn the chicken over, cover the pan, and cook for 5 minutes. Remove the cover and continue cooking for 3 minutes, or until the chicken is cooked through.

Meanwhile, steam the spinach until barely wilted. Place 1 tablespoon of olive oil and the sliced garlic in a medium skillet and heat just until the garlic sizzles. Remove from the heat. Add the spinach and toss to coat.

Remove the chicken from the large skillet when cooked. Add the sugar and remaining 2 tablespoons of vinegar to the large skillet and boil, stirring until blended and reduced by half, about 1 minute. Drizzle a little of this glaze over each chicken breast. Serve on a bed of the cooked spinach. **Makes 4 servings.**

Herbs in a Window Box

■ These herbs do well in a
   window box placed under a
   sunny south- or west-facing
   window:

UPRIGHT HERBS
'Opal' and bush basil, chives,
lavender, rosemary, sage

TRAILING HERBS
marjoram, nasturtium,
prostrate rosemary, thyme

Rosemary Chicken With Spinach
(recipe at left)

The Easiest Garden Ever: Herbs in a Bag

■ Turn an ordinary bag of potting soil into a "grow bag."

1. Lay the bag of soil flat on the ground.
2. Poke a few drainage holes in the top surface.
3. Roll the bag over, then cut a few holes in the new top surface.
4. Insert herb seedlings into the holes and firm the soil around the roots.
5. Water and fertilize as you would a regular garden bed.
6. Set the bag into a wheelbarrow or child's wagon and move it into and out of the sunlight as needed.

BEST HERBS FOR A BAG:
basil, chives, marjoram, oregano, parsley, sage, thyme

Chicken With Rice

A fine dish for lunch or dinner. Accompany with broccoli, peas, or another green vegetable.

5 to 6 pounds chicken pieces
1 bay leaf
2 carrots, peeled and sliced
2 cloves garlic, sliced
2 onions, sliced
6 peppercorns
3 tablespoons butter
1 cup sliced mushrooms
1 green bell pepper, diced
2 tablespoons all-purpose flour
1 tablespoon chopped fresh tarragon
    or 1 teaspoon dried tarragon
½ cup heavy cream
salt and pepper, to taste
⅔ cup grated cheddar cheese
4 cups cooked rice

Put the chicken into a stockpot and add cold water to cover. Add the bay leaf, carrots, garlic, onions, and peppercorns. Cover the pot, raise the heat to medium high, and bring it to a boil. Reduce the heat and simmer for 30 minutes, or until the chicken is tender. Remove the chicken, separate the meat from the skin and bones, and chop it. Discard the skin and bones. Strain the stock and reserve.

Preheat the oven to 425°F. Grease a 2-quart casserole. In a large saucepan over medium heat, melt the butter. Add the mushrooms and green pepper and sauté until the vegetables are soft. Sprinkle with the flour and tarragon and stir to blend. Add 2 cups of the reserved stock and stir until smooth. Slowly add the cream and stir until blended. Season with salt and pepper. Add the cheese and stir until it melts. Spread the chopped chicken in the bottom of the casserole. Top with a layer of rice and then a layer of sauce. Repeat, ending with the sauce. Bake for 30 minutes, or until bubbling. **Makes 6 to 8 servings.**

Poached Chicken With Niçoise Sauce

1 cup diced roasted red bell pepper

1 cup diced tomato

8 Kalamata olives, pitted and chopped

1 tablespoon capers, rinsed and drained

1 tablespoon olive oil

2 teaspoons red-wine vinegar

1 clove garlic, minced

¼ teaspoon crushed fennel seeds

salt and pepper, to taste

4 boneless, skinless chicken breast halves, poached and thinly sliced *(see tip, page 174)*

In a medium bowl, combine the red pepper, tomato, olives, and capers. In a small bowl, combine the olive oil, vinegar, garlic, and fennel seeds. Whisk to blend, then season with salt and pepper. Pour the sauce over the vegetables and mix to coat. Arrange the chicken slices on serving plates and top each with a spoonful of the vegetables. Serve the remaining vegetables on the side. **Makes 4 servings.**

Braised Chicken Breasts With Raspberry Sauce

CHICKEN:

6 boneless, skinless chicken breast
    halves

¼ teaspoon salt

⅛ teaspoon freshly ground black pepper

½ teaspoon chopped fresh marjoram or
    ¼ teaspoon dried marjoram

⅛ teaspoon freshly grated nutmeg

2 tablespoons vegetable oil

SAUCE:

½ cup (1 stick) butter

1 cup sugar

2 tablespoons all-purpose flour

½ cup cider vinegar

½ cup raspberry vinegar

1½ cups raspberries

2 ounces Chambord liqueur

For chicken: Season both sides of the chicken with salt, pepper, marjoram, and nutmeg. In a large skillet over medium heat, warm the oil, then add the chicken breasts. Sauté the chicken for 8 to 10 minutes, or until it is golden brown on both sides. Remove from the pan and set aside.

For sauce: In a saucepan over medium heat, melt the butter. Add the sugar and stir to blend. Reduce the heat to low and cook until the sauce begins to darken slightly, stirring constantly. Add the flour, whisk to blend, and continue stirring until well mixed. Add the vinegars and stir until the sugar dissolves. Bring the liquid to a slow boil and cook until it is reduced by half, about 15 minutes, and thickens. Remove the pan from heat and stir in the raspberries and Chambord.

Preheat the oven to 350°F. Lightly grease a large baking dish. Using tongs, dip the browned chicken pieces in the sauce and arrange them in the baking dish. Bake uncovered for 20 minutes, or until the chicken is tender. Reheat the remaining sauce on low heat and serve with the chicken. **Makes 6 servings.**

Brunswick Chicken Pie

A wonderful, hearty, winter meal from the bounty of summer's harvest.

4 to 5 pounds chicken pieces

**½ tablespoon chopped fresh thyme
    or ½ teaspoon dried thyme**

¼ teaspoon plus 2 tablespoons butter

salt and pepper, to taste

1 cup corn

1 large onion, diced

**1½ cups peeled, seeded, and cubed
    tomatoes *(see tip, page 65)***

1 cup lima beans

1 cup diced okra

¼ pound slab bacon, diced

3 tablespoons all-purpose flour

**1 unbaked 9-inch double piecrust
    *(see recipe, page 272)***

Into a heavy saucepan over medium heat, put the chicken, thyme, ¼ teaspoon of butter, salt, and pepper. Add cold water to cover, bring the liquid to a boil, reduce the heat, cover, and simmer for 1 hour, or until the chicken is done. Remove the chicken from the broth to cool. Strain and reserve the broth. When the chicken can be handled, separate the meat from the skin and bones and discard them. Cut the chicken into pieces and set aside.

Preheat the oven to 500°F. Put the corn, onion, tomatoes, lima beans, okra, bacon, and reserved broth into a large, heavy stockpot over medium heat. Add water, if necessary, to cover. Bring the liquid to a boil, lower the heat, and simmer gently until the vegetables are just barely cooked. Remove the pot from the heat, strain, and reserve the broth. In a small saucepan over low heat, melt the remaining 2 tablespoons of butter. Add the flour and whisk to blend. Add 2 cups of the broth and whisk until well blended and the liquid thickens. In a large bowl, mix the chicken, vegetables, and sauce together. Pour the ingredients into the piecrust, then add the piecrust top. Pierce the top crust with a fork several times. Bake for 15 minutes, then lower the heat to 375°F and bake for 20 minutes, or until golden. **Makes 4 to 6 servings.**

In the Garden: Thyme

- Plant thyme near cabbage to deter cabbageworms.

POULTRY

Skillet Chicken With Fresh Tomatoes

Serve this dish over pasta or rice.

1 tablespoon cooking oil

1 pound boneless, skinless chicken
     breasts, cut into ½-inch pieces

1 teaspoon minced garlic

1 pound tomatoes, cored and coarsely
     chopped

¼ cup fresh chopped basil

½ teaspoon salt

½ teaspoon crushed fennel seed

1 teaspoon lemon zest

⅛ teaspoon freshly ground black pepper

¼ cup chopped scallions

In a large skillet over medium heat, warm the oil. Add the chicken pieces and garlic and cook for 5 to 8 minutes, or until the chicken is no longer pink. Remove the chicken and set aside. Add the remaining ingredients to the skillet. Cook for 5 to 8 minutes, or until the tomatoes are soft. Add the chicken and stir, until the chicken is warm. **Makes 4 servings.**

Chicken-Stuffed Tomatoes

4 large, firm tomatoes

1½ cups diced cooked chicken

1 cup diced celery

1 tablespoon chopped fresh chervil or
     1 teaspoon dried chervil

1 tablespoon chopped fresh basil or
     1 teaspoon dried basil

½ tablespoon chopped fresh thyme or
     ½ teaspoon dried thyme

3 tablespoons heavy cream

salt and pepper, to taste

butter, to taste

parsley, for garnish

Preheat the oven to 350°F. Grease a large baking dish. Core the tomatoes and scoop out the seeds, leaving the tomato wall at least ¼-inch thick. Place the tomatoes in the baking dish. In a medium bowl, combine the chicken, celery, chervil, basil, and thyme, and mix well. Add the cream and toss until everything is coated. Season with salt and pepper. Spoon the chicken mixture into the tomato shells. Dot the top of each tomato with butter and bake for 20 minutes. Garnish with parsley. **Makes 4 servings.**

Save 'n' Store: Leeks

- To freeze leeks, remove the tough green leaves and the root end. Slice length- or crosswise, and wash with cold water to remove any grit. Pat dry. Put the pieces into freezer bags, squeeze out any air, seal, label and date, and place in the freezer. Use within 3 months.

Cock-a-leekie Pie

This recipe is based on an old favorite from the British Isles.

1 chicken (4 to 5 pounds), cut up
1 medium onion, diced
1 carrot, sliced
2 stalks celery, sliced
2 tablespoons minced fresh parsley
1 bay leaf
1 pound cooked ham, diced
¼ cup (½ stick) butter
6 leeks, trimmed and chopped
¼ pound fresh mushrooms, chopped
3 tablespoons all-purpose flour
2 tablespoons sherry
1 unbaked 9-inch double piecrust
   (see recipe, page 272)

Place the chicken, onion, carrot, celery, parsley, and bay leaf in a large stockpot. Cover with water, bring to a boil over high heat, reduce the heat to low, and simmer gently, covered, for about 1 hour, or until the chicken is tender. Remove the pot from the heat and the chicken from the pot. Strain the broth into a large saucepan and reserve. Discard the vegetables and herbs. Preheat the oven to 500°F. When the chicken is cool, separate the large pieces of the meat from the skin and bones. Discard the skin and bones and dice the meat. Place the diced chicken and ham in a medium bowl and set aside. In a large skillet, melt the butter over medium heat. Add the leeks and mushrooms and sauté until tender. Add the flour and stir until well blended. Add the sherry and 2½ cups of the reserved chicken broth. Whisk gently until a light cream sauce forms. Add the chicken and ham, stir to coat, and pour the ingredients into the bottom piecrust. Add the piecrust top, then pierce with a fork several times. Bake for 15 minutes, then lower the heat to 375°F and bake for 20 minutes, or until golden. **Makes 4 to 6 servings.**

Chicken Salad With Cashews

Chicken, fruit, and nuts give varied texture and taste to this salad.

1 tablespoon fresh lemon juice

1 cup peeled, cored, and chopped apple

1 chicken (3 pounds), poached *(see tip, page 174)*, **skinned, boned, and cut into bite-size pieces**

¾ cup chopped celery

½ cup cashews

½ cup mayonnaise

¼ teaspoon curry powder

salt and pepper, to taste

lettuce leaves

sliced cherry tomatoes, for garnish

sliced hard-boiled eggs, for garnish

In a small bowl, whisk to combine 1 tablespoon of water and the lemon juice. Add the apple and toss to coat. In a large bowl, mix the apple, chicken, celery, and cashews together. In a separate bowl, combine the mayonnaise with the curry. Add the mayonnaise mixture to the large bowl and mix the ingredients to coat. Season with salt and pepper. Put the salad in a ring mold and chill until ready to serve on a bed of lettuce. Garnish with the cherry tomatoes and hard-boiled eggs. **Makes 8 servings.**

Marinated Chicken Salad

Serve on beds of lettuce, garnished with clusters of grapes.

4 cups diced cooked chicken

1 green bell pepper, chopped

1 cucumber, peeled and chopped

1 stalk celery, chopped

1 carrot, peeled and chopped

2 cups dry white wine

1 cup mayonnaise

In a large bowl, combine the chicken, pepper, cucumber, celery, and carrot. Add the wine, toss to coat, and refrigerate for 3 to 4 hours. Drain the salad, reserving the liquid. Add the mayonnaise to the chicken mixture and stir to coat. Thin, if desired, with reserved liquid. **Makes 4 to 6 servings.**

Chicken Noodle Salad

This salad's flavor improves as the pasta absorbs the oil and vinegar, so prepare it the night before serving, if possible.

linguine
4 tablespoons olive oil
3 tablespoons sesame oil
⅛ teaspoon chili powder
3 tablespoons red-wine vinegar
1 cup diced cooked chicken
½ cup chopped fresh parsley
½ cup chopped fresh chives
¼ teaspoon salt

Cook the linguine according to the package directions for 6 servings, drain, then put into a large bowl. Add the olive oil and sesame oil and toss to coat. Add the chili powder, vinegar, chicken, parsley, chives, and salt. Mix well and refrigerate for at least 10 hours. **Makes 6 servings.**

Turkey and Grape Salad

Arrange on a bed of lettuce and garnish with tomato wedges.

2 cups diced cooked turkey
1 cup halved and seeded grapes
¼ cup chopped pecans
¼ cup diced celery
¼ cup mayonnaise
¼ cup sour cream
1 tablespoon milk (optional)
¼ teaspoon dry mustard
salt and pepper, to taste

In a medium bowl, combine the turkey, grapes, pecans, and celery. Toss until blended. In a separate bowl, mix together the mayonnaise and sour cream. Thin, if desired, with milk. Stir the mayonnaise mixture into the turkey mixture. Season with the mustard and salt and pepper and chill for several hours. **Makes 4 servings.**

Turkey Cacciatore

Use chicken if turkey is not available.

spaghetti or rice

2 tablespoons butter

½ cup sliced mushrooms

2 cloves garlic, minced

1 onion, chopped

1 green bell pepper, chopped

½ tablespoon chopped fresh oregano
   or ½ teaspoon dried oregano

10 tomatoes, peeled and chopped *(see tip, page 65)*, or 1
   can (20 ounces) peeled tomatoes, chopped, with juice

1 can (6 ounces) tomato paste

1 cup chicken stock

½ teaspoon salt

2 cups diced cooked turkey

Prepare the spaghetti according to the package directions for 4 to 6 servings and set aside. Melt the butter in a Dutch oven over medium heat. Add the mushrooms, garlic, onion, and pepper and sauté until soft. Add the oregano, tomatoes, tomato paste, stock, and salt. Cook for 15 minutes. Add the turkey, cover, and simmer for 15 minutes. Serve over the spaghetti. **Makes 4 to 6 servings.**

POULTRY

Turkey With Cheese Sauce

TURKEY:

2 tablespoons butter

1 cup sliced mushrooms

2 cups diced cooked turkey

1 cup diced cooked potatoes

SAUCE:

3 tablespoons butter

3 tablespoons all-purpose flour

2 cups milk

1 teaspoon prepared mustard

2½ cups grated cheese, divided

salt and pepper, to taste

For turkey: Preheat the oven to 400°F. Grease an 8-inch square baking dish. In a skillet over medium heat, melt the butter. Add the mushrooms and sauté until soft. Add the turkey and potatoes. Remove from the heat.

For sauce: Melt the butter in a saucepan. Add the flour and stir with a whisk until blended. Add the milk, stirring constantly until smooth. Add the mustard and 2 cups of the cheese and simmer until the cheese melts and the sauce is thick. Season with salt and pepper.

Measure 2 cups of the sauce and mix into the turkey. Pour the mixture into the prepared baking dish, sprinkle with the remaining ½ cup of cheese, and bake for 15 minutes. **Makes 4 to 6 servings.**

Turkey-Stuffed Eggplant

(recipe at right)

How to Harvest: Eggplants

- Eggplants are ready to pick when they are not quite full-size but still glossy and firm. Wear gloves, as some varieties have prickles. Use a knife or pruning shears to cut the stem just above the eggplant's leafy top, called the calyx.

Turkey-Stuffed Eggplant

Use this stuffing to fill tomato or pepper shells as well.

2 medium eggplants
6 tablespoons (¾ stick) butter
1 pound mushrooms, diced
2 onions, diced
2 cups diced cooked turkey
¼ cup dry white wine
salt and pepper, to taste
¼ cup grated cheese
chopped fresh oregano,
    for garnish

Preheat the oven to 400°F. Grease a cookie sheet. Cut the eggplants in half lengthwise and carefully scoop out the pulp. Dice the pulp and set aside. In a skillet over medium heat, melt the butter. Add the diced eggplant pulp, mushrooms, and onions and sauté for 15 minutes, or until the vegetables are soft. Add the turkey and stir to blend. Add the wine and season with salt and pepper. Spoon the mixture into the eggplant shells, mounding it above the shell rims, if necessary. Place the shells on the cookie sheet. Sprinkle the shells with cheese and bake for 15 minutes. Garnish with oregano. **Makes 4 servings.**

Turkey-Stuffed Cucumbers

1 to 2 tablespoons butter
1 cup dry bread crumbs
4 medium cucumbers
salt, to taste
2 tomatoes, peeled and chopped
    (see tip, page 65)
1 onion, minced
2 cups minced cooked turkey
1 tablespoon tomato sauce
1 cup heavy cream
freshly ground black pepper, to taste

Preheat the oven to 350°F. Grease a cookie sheet. In a small pan over low heat, melt the butter. Add the bread crumbs, stir to blend, and set aside. Cut the cucumbers in half lengthwise. Scoop out the pulp and reserve in a bowl. Sprinkle the cucumber shells with salt and place them on the cookie sheet. In a medium bowl, combine the cucumber pulp, tomatoes, onion, turkey, tomato sauce, and cream and stir to mix. Season with salt and pepper. Fill the cucumber shells with the vegetable mixture, sprinkle each shell with crumbs, and bake for 25 to 30 minutes. **Makes 8 servings.**

Duck With Turnips

Versions of this recipe appear in many cookbooks dating from the turn of the 20th century.

1 duck (4 pounds)

salt

3 tablespoons oil

2 cups chicken stock

1 bay leaf

2 stalks celery with leaves, chopped

2 onions, sliced

1 carrot, peeled and sliced

3 tablespoons butter

4 medium turnips, peeled and diced

lemon wedges, for garnish

parsley, for garnish

Preheat the oven to 325°F. Rub the duck with the salt, prick its skin with a fork, and truss. In a heavy skillet over medium heat, warm the oil. Put the duck into the skillet and brown it slowly on all sides. Place the duck on a rack in a small roasting pan. Add the stock, bay leaf, celery, onions, and carrot. Cover the pan and roast for 1 hour. In the skillet over low heat, melt the butter. Add the turnips and sauté until just lightly browned. Set the turnips aside. Remove the duck from the pan and strain the juices into a bowl. Let the juices sit for several minutes, then remove as much fat as possible. Discard the roasted vegetables. Return the duck to the pan. Arrange the turnips around the duck, then add the pan juices to cover the turnips. (Add more stock, if necessary.) Cover and bake for 15 minutes, or until the turnips are tender. Place the duck on a platter and surround with the turnips. Garnish with lemon wedges and parsley. **Makes 4 servings.**

Truss-worthy

■ Trussing is a way of tying poultry to keep the bird's wings and legs from cooking unevenly and/or prevent them from becoming too dry. A trussed bird browns evenly and is also easier to handle.

Celery Stuffing

6 cups stale bread crumbs

2 cups corn bread crumbs

2 small onions, chopped fine

2½ cups chopped celery

½ cup chopped fresh parsley

¼ teaspoon freshly ground black pepper

2½ teaspoons salt

½ tablespoon chopped fresh thyme or
   ½ teaspoon dried thyme

½ tablespoon chopped fresh sage or
   ½ teaspoon dried sage

1½ cups chicken stock, divided

½ cup (1 stick) butter, melted

1 apple, peeled, cored, and finely chopped

3 eggs, beaten

Preheat the oven to 200°F. Spread the bread crumbs on a cookie sheet and bake to dry, but do not brown. Set the crumbs aside to cool. In a large bowl, combine the bread crumbs, onions, celery, parsley, and seasonings. Add ½ cup of stock and mix to moisten. Add the melted butter and mix well. Add the apple and the eggs and stir to moisten. Add more stock, in small portions, using just enough to bind the stuffing. (The stuffing should not be wet or pasty.) Mix to combine. **Makes 12 cups.**

Eggplant Stuffing

1 large eggplant, peeled and diced

3 onions, chopped

1 sweet red pepper, chopped

3 tomatoes, peeled and chopped
   (see tip, page 65)

2 cloves garlic, minced

½ tablespoon chopped fresh thyme or ½ teaspoon dried thyme

½ tablespoon chopped fresh oregano or ½ teaspoon dried oregano

salt and pepper, to taste

In a bowl, combine all of the ingredients and mix well. **Makes 4 cups.**

Apple Stuffing

Add more mashed potatoes to the mixture if necessary to fill the bird's cavity.

4 apples, peeled, cored, and chopped

4 onions, chopped

½ tablespoon chopped fresh sage or
   ½ teaspoon dried sage

½ tablespoon chopped fresh thyme or
   ½ teaspoon dried thyme

¼ cup chicken stock

2 cups mashed potatoes

salt and pepper, to taste

In a saucepan over low heat, combine the apples, onions, sage, thyme, and stock and simmer until very soft. In a blender or food processor, purée the ingredients until smooth. Add the mashed potatoes, mix to incorporate, and season with salt and pepper. **Makes 5 cups.**

Sauerkraut Stuffing

2 tablespoons butter

2 onions, chopped

3 cups chopped apples

5 cups sauerkraut, drained

1 teaspoon ground cloves

salt and pepper, to taste

In a skillet over medium heat, melt the butter, add the onions, and sauté until soft. In a bowl, combine the apples and sauerkraut. Add the sautéed onions, stir, and season with the cloves and salt and pepper. Mix thoroughly. **Makes 9 cups.**

Potato Walnut Stuffing

4 cups mashed potatoes

2 tablespoons chopped fresh chives

1 cup coarsely chopped walnuts

1 teaspoon salt

½ cup heavy cream

2 tablespoons butter, melted

4 egg yolks, beaten

1 tablespoon chopped fresh basil or thyme or 1 teaspoon dried basil or thyme

In a bowl, combine all of the ingredients and mix well. **Makes 5 cups.**

Meats

Bobotie. 192

Cranberry Beef 192

Barbecued Beef 193

Vegetable Beef Casserole 194

Seven-Layer Dinner. 194

Beef Provence Pie 195

Cubaña Pie. 196

Sweet-and-Sour Pork 196

Maple Apple Pork Chops With

    Apple Rice Pilaf 197

Apples and Pork 198

Sweet Potato Casserole With Sausage 198

Lamb Shanks With Vegetables 200

Greek-Style Roast Lamb 200

Shepherd's Pie. 201

Regal Kielbasa Squares 202

Bobotie

Serve this exotic, fruity dish over rice.

2 pounds ground beef or 1 pound ground beef and 1 pound ground pork

2 onions, chopped

8 tomatoes, peeled *(see tip, page 65)* **or 1 can (16 ounces) tomatoes**

1½ tablespoons sugar

2 tablespoons curry powder

2 tablespoons cider vinegar

salt, to taste

2 firm bananas, sliced

1 apple, peeled, cored, and diced

1 tablespoon apricot jam, or 4 apricots, peeled and sliced

½ cup slivered almonds

¼ to ½ cup tomato juice (optional)

In a large skillet, brown the beef over medium heat, then drain off the fat. Add the remaining ingredients except the tomato juice and simmer gently, stirring frequently, for 30 minutes. The sauce may be thick. Add ¼ cup of tomato juice or more to thin, if desired. **Makes 8 servings.**

> ## Save 'n' Store: Apricots
>
> ■ **To freeze fresh apricots:**
> - ◆ **Cut the apricots in half.**
> - ◆ **Remove the pits.**
> - ◆ **Place the halves on a cookie sheet and put the sheet into the freezer.**
>
> **When the fruit is frozen, put it into freezer bags and return it to the freezer. Store up to 6 months.**

Cranberry Beef

Serve this dish over egg noodles.

3 tablespoons vegetable oil

2 pounds lean stew beef, cut into cubes

½ teaspoon salt

¼ teaspoon freshly ground black pepper

2 cloves garlic, chopped

1 large onion, chopped

1 cup red wine or water

1 cup beef broth

2 tablespoons cider vinegar

¼ cup tomato paste

⅓ cup brown sugar

2 tablespoons all-purpose flour

1½ cups chopped cranberries

In a large pot, warm the oil over medium heat. Add the beef and brown on all sides. Add the salt, pepper, garlic, onion, wine, broth, vinegar, and tomato paste. Bring the mixture to a boil, reduce the heat, and simmer, covered, for about 2 hours. In a medium bowl, combine the brown sugar and flour. Add the cranberries and toss to coat, then add to the stew and cook for 12 to 15 minutes, or until the berries become soft. **Makes 6 servings.**

Barbecued Beef

A zesty dish to heap on rice or serve with crusty rolls.

1 beef brisket (4½ pounds)

2 tablespoons vegetable oil

2 large onions, coarsely chopped

1 green bell pepper, coarsely chopped

2 stalks celery, coarsely chopped

2 cloves garlic, minced

1 cup ketchup

16 Italian-style plum tomatoes,
    peeled *(see tip, page 65)*, or
    1 can (35 ounces)
    Italian-style plum tomatoes,
    with liquid

¼ cup red-wine vinegar

⅓ cup light-brown sugar

½ teaspoon dried basil

½ teaspoon dried oregano

½ teaspoon cinnamon

½ teaspoon salt

½ teaspoon sweet or hot paprika

¼ teaspoon cumin

⅛ teaspoon ground cloves

⅛ teaspoon allspice

Preheat the oven to 325°F. Pat the brisket dry with paper towels. In a Dutch oven, warm the oil over medium-high heat. Add the brisket and brown, then transfer to a platter. Reduce the heat and add the onions, pepper, celery, and garlic. Stir the vegetables to coat with the oil in the Dutch oven, cover, and cook slowly until the onions are soft. Add the remaining ingredients. Return the brisket to the Dutch oven and turn to coat with the sauce. Cover and bake for 3½ to 4 hours, turning the brisket occasionally. When the brisket falls apart easily if poked with a fork, transfer it to a carving board. Set the sauce aside in the Dutch oven. Trim the fat from the brisket and break the meat into generous shreds. Skim the fat from the sauce with a shallow spoon. Warm the sauce over low heat. Return the meat to the Dutch oven and stir gently to coat with sauce. Return to the oven to warm, if necessary, before serving. **Makes 4 to 6 servings.**

MEATS

In the Kitchen: Oregano

■ **To bring out the flavor of dried oregano, crush it before adding to dishes.**

Vegetable Beef Casserole

4 medium carrots, shredded

2 medium zucchini, thinly sliced

2 medium summer squashes, thinly sliced

1 large onion, chopped

1 clove garlic, minced

1 pound lean ground beef, browned and drained

1 can (10¾ ounces) condensed cream of mushroom soup

1 cup sour cream

2 tablespoons chopped fresh basil or 2 teaspoons dried basil

¼ teaspoon salt

⅛ teaspoon freshly ground black pepper

2½ cups dry herb bread crumbs, divided

1 tomato, seeded and chopped, for garnish

Preheat the oven to 350°F. Grease a shallow 3-quart casserole. In a large bowl, combine the carrots, zucchini, squashes, onion, and garlic with the browned beef. Stir in the mushroom soup and sour cream. Add the basil, salt, and pepper. Mix all of the ingredients together. Spread 1½ cups of the bread crumbs in the bottom of the casserole. Distribute the vegetable-and-meat mixture evenly over the crumbs. Top with the remaining crumbs. Bake for 35 minutes. Cover the dish if the casserole starts to dry out. Cool slightly before garnishing with chopped tomato. **Makes 6 servings.**

Seven-Layer Dinner

A perfect one-dish, family-style meal.

4 medium potatoes, peeled and sliced

1 cup sliced onion

1 pound ground beef, browned and drained

½ cup uncooked rice

4 tomatoes, diced, or 1 can (15 ounces) diced tomatoes

1 green bell pepper, sliced

1 stalk celery, sliced

1 cup sliced mushrooms

4 slices bacon

Preheat the oven to 350°F. Line a 3- or 4-quart casserole with the potatoes. Spread the onion over the potatoes. Distribute the ground beef over the onion. Sprinkle the rice over the beef. Spread the tomatoes, then the pepper, celery, and mushrooms over the rice. Lay the bacon strips evenly across the top. Add enough cold water to just cover the casserole contents. Cover and bake for 1¾ hours. **Makes 4 to 6 servings.**

Beef Provence Pie

This dish captures the herbs and flavors of southern France. Serve with salad and toasted garlic bread slices.

2½ pounds lean stewing beef, cubed

1 cup red wine

⅓ cup olive oil

2 whole cloves

1 tablespoon chopped fresh rosemary
    or 1 teaspoon dried rosemary

3 bay leaves, divided

¼ teaspoon salt

freshly ground black pepper, to taste

1 large onion, diced

2 tablespoons minced fresh parsley

2 cups peeled and seeded Italian-style
    plum tomatoes *(see tip, page 65)*

3 cloves garlic, minced

1 cup grated zucchini

¾ teaspoon chopped fresh thyme or
    ¼ teaspoon dried thyme

¼ medium orange tied in cheesecloth
    bag

½ cup whole, pitted black olives

3 tablespoons butter (optional)

2 tablespoons all-purpose flour
    (optional)

1 unbaked 9-inch double piecrust *(see
    recipe, page 272)*

Place the beef in a large, nonmetallic bowl. Cover with the wine, olive oil, cloves, rosemary, two bay leaves, salt, and pepper. Toss to coat. Cover and refrigerate, stirring frequently, for about 24 hours. Remove the beef from the marinade. Strain the marinade and discard the herbs. Put the remaining ingredients, except the olives, flour, butter, and piecrust, into a Dutch oven. Add the beef and strained marinade, and cook over medium heat, covered, for about 45 minutes. Preheat the oven to 500°F. Remove the Dutch oven from the heat, discard the bay leaf and the cheesecloth bag with orange, stir in the olives, and taste for seasoning. If it is necessary to thicken the broth, make a roux by melting the butter in a saucepan over medium heat. Add the flour and cook, stirring, for 2 minutes. Whisk the roux into the broth. Pour the ingredients into the bottom piecrust, add the piecrust top, then pierce with a fork several times. Bake for 15 minutes, then lower the heat to 375°F and bake for 20 minutes, or until golden. **Makes 4 to 6 servings.**

In the Garden: Garlic

■ Purchase garlic heads, or bulbs, at a garden nursery. In the fall, plant each clove, pointed end up, 2 inches deep, in full sun and deep, rich soil. Harvest tender garlic greens in summer and garlic bulbs the following fall.

Cubaña Pie

Cubaña is based on a Latin American dish called piccadillo, in which raisins and olives are combined with meat to create a sweet-sour taste.

1 cup cooked white rice

1 medium onion, grated

¼ cup dark raisins

1 teaspoon chili powder

2 to 3 drops hot sauce

1½ pounds ground beef

1 clove garlic, crushed

1 jar (2 ounces) pimiento-stuffed
    olives with juice

¾ cup crushed tomatoes

⅛ teaspoon freshly ground black pepper

1 unbaked 9-inch double piecrust *(see recipe, page 272)*

Preheat the oven to 500°F. Place all of the ingredients, except the piecrust, in a medium bowl and mix to blend thoroughly. Place the mixture in the bottom piecrust, add the piecrust top, then pierce with a fork several times. Bake for 15 minutes, then lower the heat to 350°F and bake for 35 to 45 minutes, or until golden. Serve hot or at room temperature. **Makes 4 to 6 servings.**

MEATS

Sweet-and-Sour Pork

Serve this dish over white rice.

vegetable oil, for frying

2 eggs, lightly beaten

½ cup all-purpose flour

2 tablespoons soy sauce

2 pounds lean pork, cut into bite-size
    pieces

1 large green bell pepper, chopped

2 large carrots, sliced diagonally

2 cloves garlic, minced

1 cup pineapple chunks

1½ tablespoons cornstarch

2 tablespoons red-wine vinegar

½ cup maple syrup

In a large, heavy skillet over medium-high heat, warm the oil to 350°F. In a shallow bowl, combine the eggs, flour, and soy sauce and beat to make a batter. Dip the pork into the batter to coat. Deep-fry the pork for 10 minutes, then set aside to drain. In a large frying pan over medium heat, combine the pork, green pepper, carrots, garlic, pineapple, and ½ cup of water. Cover and cook for 10 minutes. In a small bowl, blend the cornstarch, vinegar, maple syrup, and ¼ cup of water. Add to the pork mixture, stir, and simmer for 5 minutes, or until the sauce thickens and the pork is tender. **Makes 6 servings.**

Save 'n' Store: Apples

■ Apples keep well for about 6 months at temperatures above freezing but below 45°F. If you don't have a root cellar, a double cardboard box in a cool mudroom or basement can approximate the conditions. Winter apples store longer than summer types.

Maple Apple Pork Chops With Apple Rice Pilaf

PORK CHOPS:

2 tablespoons butter

1 large clove garlic, minced

8 thinly sliced loin or rib pork chops

1 tablespoon Worcestershire sauce

¾ cup unsweetened apple cider

¼ cup maple syrup

2 tablespoons cider vinegar, plus
    more as needed

1 teaspoon fennel seed

¼ teaspoon freshly ground black
    pepper

PILAF:

1 tablespoon butter

½ cup tart red apple, peeled, cored,
    and diced

2 tablespoons chopped onion

1 tablespoon cider vinegar

2 tablespoons maple syrup

2 tablespoons raisins

½ teaspoon salt (optional)

¼ teaspoon allspice

⅛ teaspoon freshly ground black pepper

⅛ teaspoon turmeric

uncooked white rice (for 6 servings)

1 tablespoon chopped fresh parsley

For pork chops: In a large skillet, melt the butter over medium heat. Add the garlic, cook for 1 minute, and push to the side of the skillet. Add the pork chops and cook, turning to brown on both sides. Add the Worcestershire sauce and cover the skillet to steam for 2 minutes. Add the remaining ingredients. Cover the skillet, lower the heat to simmer, and cook for 15 to 20 minutes, or until the pork is tender. Remove the pork to a platter and keep warm. Bring the juices to a boil and cook for 1 to 2 minutes, or until smooth, satiny, and syrupy (not thick and sticky). Taste the sauce, and if more tartness is desired, add ½ to 1 tablespoon more vinegar. Pour the sauce over the pork.

For pilaf: In a 2-quart saucepan, melt the butter over medium heat. Add the apples and onion and sauté until the onion is soft. Add the amount of water specified for 6 servings of rice. Add the cider vinegar, maple syrup, raisins, and seasonings. Increase the heat and bring to a boil. Add the rice and cook as directed on the package. Fluff with a fork, then add the parsley. Serve the rice with the pork. **Makes 6 servings.**

MEATS

One-sided apples with tough skins foretell a cold winter.

Apples and Pork

This can be made in a slow cooker; simply follow the directions for cooking pork.

3 to 4 pounds lean pork (boneless is preferred, but boned chops can be used)

6 cups applesauce *(to make your own, see recipe, page 231)*

2 tablespoons apple pie spice

6 small red-skin potatoes

4 carrots, peeled and coarsely cut

2 cups white pearl onions, peeled

salt and pepper, to taste

2 firm tart apples, peeled, cored, and thinly sliced

Cut the pork into large chunks. Put the pork, applesauce, and spice into a large pot. Cover and cook on medium heat for 10 minutes. Reduce the heat to a low simmer and cook for 4 hours. One to 1½ hours before the cooking finishes, add the potatoes, carrots, and onions and stir. Season with salt and pepper. Fifteen minutes before the cooking finishes, add the apple slices and stir. Remove the pork, vegetables, and apples to a large platter and pour 1 cup of the sauce over it all. Serve the remaining sauce on the side. **Makes 6 to 8 servings.**

Sweet Potato Casserole With Sausage

6 large sweet potatoes, peeled and quartered

butter, to taste

salt and pepper, to taste

1 pound Italian sweet sausage, casings removed

2 cups fresh mushrooms, diced

1 large onion, diced

4 medium red apples, peeled, cored, and thinly sliced

1 cup shredded cheddar cheese

Preheat the oven to 350°F. Grease a 13x9-inch baking dish. Put the sweet potatoes into a saucepan, cover them with water, and bring them to a boil. Reduce the heat and simmer until the potatoes are fork-tender. Drain, then add the butter and salt and pepper. Mash the potatoes and set aside. Crumble the sausage into a skillet over medium heat and sauté until done. Drain the fat, reserving 2 tablespoons. Transfer the sausage to a bowl. Return the skillet to the heat, add the reserved fat, mushrooms, and onion, and cook until the onion is soft. In the prepared baking dish, layer half of the mashed sweet potatoes, half of the mushroom-onion mixture, half of the sausage, and all of the apple slices. Repeat (ending with the sausage). Bake uncovered for 35 minutes. Sprinkle the cheese on top and bake for 8 to 10 minutes. **Makes 6 to 8 servings.**

Apples and Pork
(recipe at left)

Lamb Shanks With Vegetables

Be sure to bake this entrée in a nonreactive pan, or the acids in the tomatoes and orange juice will react with the metal.

4 lamb shanks (2½ to 3 pounds, total)

2 tablespoons minced garlic

1 cup chopped sweet onion

1 cup chopped carrots

1 cup chopped tomatoes

½ cup orange juice

1 tablespoon butter (optional)

1 tablespoon all-purpose flour (optional)

salt and pepper, to taste (optional)

½ teaspoon tomato paste or ketchup (optional)

2 tablespoons chopped fresh parsley or 1 tablespoon chopped fresh mint, for garnish

Preheat the oven to 300°F. Place the lamb shanks, garlic, onion, carrots, and tomatoes in a baking dish just large enough to hold them. Add the orange juice and ½ to 1 cup of water to cover, then cover the dish. Bake for 3 hours. Remove from the oven and set aside for 20 minutes. Before serving, skim off the fat from the surface of the sauce.

For a thicker sauce, pour the cooked juices (1½ to 2 cups) into a measuring cup. In a saucepan over medium heat, melt the butter. Take the pan off the heat, add the flour, and stir to blend. Return the pan to medium heat, stir for 2 minutes, then add the cooked juices. Cook and stir until the sauce thickens. Add the salt and pepper and tomato paste to deepen the flavor. Pour the sauce over the lamb and vegetables.

Garnish with parsley. **Makes 4 to 6 servings.**

Greek-Style Roast Lamb

½ pound bulk breakfast sausage

1 onion, chopped

4 cloves garlic, finely chopped

1 pound fresh spinach, stemmed

1 tablespoon chopped fresh basil or 1 teaspoon dried basil

¼ pound feta cheese

1 boneless leg of lamb (3 pounds)

Preheat the oven to 325°F. In a large frying pan over medium heat, cook the sausage until almost done (almost all pink is gone). Add the onion and garlic and cook until the onion is soft. Pour off the grease. Add the spinach and basil and cook until the spinach is limp. Add the feta cheese, mix well, and set aside. Pound the lamb with a mallet to a consistent thickness. Spread the sausage mixture in the center of the lamb, roll up, and tie securely. In a roasting pan, cook the meat uncovered for 1½ hours. **Makes 6 servings.**

MEATS

Shepherd's Pie

Any type of ground meat will work well in this recipe, which is based on the traditional English leftover-meat pie.

½ cup (1 stick) plus 1 tablespoon
    butter

2 tablespoons vegetable oil

2 pounds ground veal or ground beef,
    lamb, pork, or poultry

1 large onion, grated

1 tablespoon chopped fresh thyme or
    1 teaspoon dried thyme

½ tablespoon chopped fresh dill or
    ½ teaspoon dried dill

1 cup cooked chopped spinach, drained

3 to 4 cups mashed potatoes, divided

salt and pepper, to taste

1 unbaked 9-inch single piecrust *(see recipe, page 272)*

1 tablespoon dry bread crumbs

Preheat the oven to 500°F. In a heavy saucepan, melt ½ cup of butter over medium heat. Add the vegetable oil. Add the veal, onion, and herbs and cook, stirring constantly, until the meat is almost done (almost all pink is gone). Drain off some of the fat. Add the spinach and 1 cup of mashed potatoes. Stir to blend, then add salt and pepper, to taste. Place the mixture in the piecrust. Use the remaining mashed potatoes to make a top crust, mounding it slightly in the center. Melt the remaining tablespoon of butter, then brush the potatoes with it. Sprinkle with the bread crumbs. Bake for 15 minutes, then lower the heat to 375°F and bake for 35 to 45 minutes, or until golden. **Makes 4 to 6 servings.**

MEATS

Regal Kielbasa Squares

4 potatoes, peeled and quartered

1¼ cups (2½ sticks) butter, divided

¼ cup half-and-half

1 medium onion, diced

2 cups sauerkraut, rinsed and drained

1 pound farmer's cheese

3 eggs

1 package (16 ounces) phyllo dough

1 small kielbasa, cooked and thinly
   sliced

Preheat the oven to 350°F. Grease a 13x9-inch baking dish. Put the potatoes into a saucepan, cover them with water, and bring to a boil. Reduce the heat and simmer until the potatoes are fork-tender. Drain, then add ¼ cup of the butter and the half-and-half and whip. Set the potatoes aside. In a small skillet over medium heat, melt ½ cup of the butter, add the onion, and cook until translucent. Add the sauerkraut, heat thoroughly, then set aside. In a medium bowl, mix the farmer's cheese with the eggs, then set aside. In small saucepan over medium heat, melt the remaining butter. Layer a sheet of phyllo dough in the prepared baking dish and generously brush it with the melted butter. Repeat. Layer one-quarter of the mashed potatoes, one-quarter of the cheese mixture, and one-quarter of the sauerkraut. Distribute one-quarter of the kielbasa slices on the sauerkraut. Repeat the double phyllo layers, butter, and filling layers three more times. Cover with six to eight phyllo layers, buttering between each. Bake for 30 minutes, or until golden brown. Cut into squares. **Makes 6 to 8 servings.**

How to Make Sauerkraut

■ To make sauerkraut, shred 5 pounds of cabbage. In a bowl, combine the cabbage and 3 tablespoons of sea salt. Pack the mixture into a large crock. Cover the cabbage with a plate that will fit snugly inside and weight it firmly. Cover the crock with a cloth. Over the next 24 hours, periodically push down on the weight, forcing water out of the cabbage to create the brine. Check it every day or two and remove any scum that forms, washing the plate and applying a clean cloth each time. After about a week, taste it. It will be tangy, and it will get stronger with each passing day.

When the flavor is to your liking, heat the mixture to a boil, stirring frequently. When it cools, put it into sterilized canning jars, adding enough brine to cover. Seal and process the jars in a boiling-water bath for 15 minutes.

Fish & Seafood

Flounder Fillets With Mushroom Sauce 204

Portuguese Skillet Haddock 205

Flounder With Mint Lime Sauce 205

Broiled Swordfish Kabobs 206

Mexican-Style Red Snapper 206

Applejack Fish Bake 208

Saucy Salmon Loaf 209

White Fish With Lemongrass Marinade 209

Salmon With Oregano Salsa 210

Shrimp and Creamy Spinach Feta Rice 210

Steamed Clams and Spanish Sausage 211

Sherried Shellfish With Leeks and Cream 212

Shrimp in Prosciutto al Formaggio 213

Shrimp Creole 213

Skillet Sea Scallops 214

Chicken Oyster Pie 214

Flounder Fillets With Mushroom Sauce

FISH & SEAFOOD

FISH:

6 large flounder fillets (about 2 pounds, total)

½ teaspoon salt

6 slices tomato

12 slices Gruyère or Swiss cheese

SAUCE:

2 tablespoons butter

½ cup sliced mushrooms

2 medium onions, sliced

1½ tablespoons all-purpose flour

1½ teaspoons salt

¼ cup minced fresh parsley

1 cup light cream

6 tablespoons sherry

RICE:

1½ cups long-grain rice

¾ cup snipped fresh parsley

For fish: Preheat the oven to 400°F. Grease a 13x9-inch baking dish. Sprinkle the fillets on both sides with salt and roll them up individually. Form a diagonal pattern in the baking dish with the ingredients: Place a flounder roll in the dish, then beside it a tomato slice, then beside that a pair of cheese slices. In the next row, begin with a tomato slice, then add cheese slices, then a flounder roll. Start the third row with cheese, then add flounder, then a tomato slice. Continue this pattern until all of the ingredients are used. Set aside or cover and refrigerate until the sauce is made.

For sauce: In a medium saucepan over medium heat, warm the butter and sauté the mushrooms and onions until golden. Stir in the flour, salt, and parsley. Add the cream, sherry, and ½ cup of water, stirring until they are blended. Bring the sauce to a boil, stirring constantly. Remove the pan from the heat and pour the sauce over the fish, tomato, and cheese.

Bake the fish for 15 to 20 minutes, or until the fillets are golden or the fish flakes easily with a fork.

For rice: While the fish is baking, prepare the rice according to the package directions. Stir snipped parsley into the cooked rice. Serve the rice with the fish. **Makes 6 servings.**

Portuguese Skillet Haddock

2 tablespoons olive oil

6 scallions, chopped

¼ cup finely chopped celery

½ cup sliced mushrooms

2 cloves garlic, minced

1 cup chopped tomatoes

¼ cup fresh lemon juice

3 tablespoons Madeira wine

1 tablespoon chopped fresh basil or
** 1 teaspoon dried basil**

½ tablespoon chopped fresh tarragon
** or ½ teaspoon dried tarragon**

⅛ teaspoon freshly ground black pepper

1 cup sliced zucchini

1½ pounds haddock, cut into 2-inch pieces

¼ cup sliced, pitted black olives

1½ cups cooked rice

3 tablespoons chopped fresh parsley, for garnish

In a large skillet over medium-high heat, warm the oil and sauté the scallions, celery, mushrooms, and garlic for 3 minutes, stirring constantly so that the garlic doesn't turn brown. Add the tomatoes, lemon juice, wine, basil, tarragon, and pepper. Bring the liquid to a boil, reduce the heat, and simmer for 5 minutes. Add the zucchini and cook for 5 minutes. Add the fish, cover the pan, and continue cooking until the fish flakes easily with a fork, about 10 minutes. Stir in the black olives. Serve over rice, garnished with chopped parsley. **Makes 5 servings.**

In the Kitchen: Fish

■ **To rid the kitchen of odor after cooking fish, add whole cloves, cinnamon sticks, allspice, or lemon slices to a pan of water and simmer.**

Flounder With Mint Lime Sauce

¼ cup (½ stick) butter, divided

2 tablespoons fresh lime juice

2 tablespoons fresh mint leaves,
** chopped**

½ cup heavy cream

2 flounder fillets (¼ pound each)

¼ pound lump crabmeat

2 lime slices and 2 mint leaves, for
** garnish**

In a small saucepan over medium heat, melt 2 table-spoons of butter. Add the lime juice, stir, and turn off the heat. Add the mint and cream, stir, and set the pan aside. Preheat the broiler. Spread the fillets on a lightly greased broiler pan. Spoon 3 tablespoons of crabmeat and 2 tablespoons of lime cream sauce onto each fillet. Roll the fillets and secure them with toothpicks. Dot the remaining butter on the fish and broil for approximately 2 minutes on each side. Pour the remaining sauce on the fish. When served, garnish each portion with a lime slice and mint leaf. **Makes 2 servings.**

Broiled Swordfish Kabobs

½ cup olive oil

½ cup white-wine vinegar

2 cloves garlic, minced

1 tablespoon soy sauce

½ teaspoon hot-pepper sauce

⅛ teaspoon freshly ground black
    pepper

2 pounds swordfish, cut into 1-inch
    pieces

2 red or yellow bell peppers, cut into
    1-inch pieces

24 cherry tomatoes

12 skewers

juice of 1 lemon

In a large bowl, combine the oil, vinegar, garlic, soy sauce, hot-pepper sauce, and black pepper. Marinate the swordfish in the mixture for 1 hour in the refrigerator. Remove the fish, then put the marinade into a small pan and bring to a boil for 3 to 5 minutes. Preheat the broiler. Alternate the fish, peppers, and tomatoes on the skewers. Place the skewers on a cookie sheet and broil for 10 minutes, basting with the marinade and turning several times. Before serving, sprinkle the lemon juice over the skewers. **Makes 6 servings.**

In the Garden: Cherry Tomatoes

■ Cherry tomatoes come in many hues in addition to red, including yellow, white, pink, green, black, and bicolor. A mix makes kabobs festive.

Mexican-Style Red Snapper

Lemon and orange juices brighten this dish. Serve over rice.

1 red snapper (about 2 pounds)

juice of 2 lemons

juice of 2 oranges

1 medium onion, coarsely chopped

1 clove garlic, minced

1 red bell pepper, coarsely chopped

1 tablespoon capers, nonpareille variety,
    drained and rinsed

2 tablespoons chopped fresh cilantro

2 large hard-boiled egg yolks, crumbled

½ cup pine nuts or chopped almonds

¼ teaspoon salt

freshly ground black pepper, to taste

10 pitted green olives, sliced

Rinse the cavity of the snapper under cold running water and pat dry with paper towels. In a 13x9-inch baking dish, combine the lemon juice, orange juice, onion, garlic, red pepper, capers, and cilantro to make a marinade. Add the snapper. Spoon some of the marinade into the fish's body cavity, turn the fish to coat both sides, and refrigerate for 2 to 3 hours, turning occasionally.

Preheat the oven to 375°F. Bake the fish uncovered for 35 to 45 minutes, or until it is opaque and separates easily when flaked with a fork. Transfer the fish to a warmed serving platter. In a blender or food processor, purée the marinade, egg yolks, pine nuts, salt, and black pepper. Pour the mixture over the fish, then sprinkle with the olives. **Makes 4 servings.**

Broiled Swordfish Kabobs
(recipe at left)

In the Kitchen: Fish and Seafood Freshness

- Fresh fish will have firm, elastic flesh and no smell. Beware of these signs of spoilage: odor along the backbone, pinkish color, ability to float in water.

- Refrigerate fish until ready to use. Fish that is cleaned and frozen immediately after being caught and is kept frozen until needed does not lose its flavor. Place frozen fish in the refrigerator overnight to thaw.

- Crabs, lobsters, and other shellfish must be kept alive until cooked; it is best to cook them the day they are purchased. Clams, mussels, and oysters should be wrapped in wet towels or a wet paper bag and kept refrigerated. Stored this way, they can keep for 2 to 3 days.

Applejack Fish Bake

¾ cup (1½ sticks) unsalted butter

3 to 4 carrots, julienned

1 medium onion, thinly sliced

6 ounces mushrooms, thinly sliced

juice of ½ lemon, divided

salt and pepper, to taste

4 fillets (4 to 6 ounces each) of
   firm-flesh white fish

¾ cup applejack or hard cider, divided

¼ cup apple juice

1 tablespoon arrowroot

zest of 1 lemon

nutmeg, to taste

Preheat the oven to 350°F. In a skillet over medium heat, melt the butter. Add the carrots and onion; cook until warm. Remove the vegetables and set them aside. Add the mushrooms to the skillet and sprinkle with lemon juice and salt and pepper. Cook just until warmed through. Remove the mushrooms from the skillet and set aside (separate from the carrots and onion). Place the fish in a shallow baking dish and season with salt and pepper. Spoon the carrots and onion over the fish. Pour ¼ cup of applejack and the apple juice into the skillet. Add any remaining juice from the lemon, stir to blend, and pour over the fish and vegetables. Bake for 20 minutes, or until the fish flakes easily with a fork. When the fish is done, carefully remove the carrots and onions and set them aside. Place the fillets on a warmed platter and cover to keep warm. Strain the cooking juices. In a skillet over medium heat, blend the remaining applejack with the arrowroot. Add the cooking juices and stir or whisk constantly, allowing the sauce to simmer and thicken. Add the carrots, onions, and mushrooms and cook until warm. Pour the sauce and vegetables over the fish. Sprinkle with lemon zest and a dash of nutmeg. **Makes 4 servings.**

Saucy Salmon Loaf

LOAF:

1 can (16 ounces) salmon

1½ cups mashed potatoes

1 egg

½ cup minced celery

½ cup minced onion

1 tablespoon minced fresh parsley

1½ tablespoons fresh lemon juice

⅛ teaspoon paprika

¼ teaspoon freshly ground black
    pepper

½ teaspoon salt

¾ cup milk

SAUCE:

2 tablespoons butter

2 tablespoons all-purpose flour

1 cup milk

pinch of celery salt

½ cup grated sharp cheddar cheese

For loaf: Preheat the oven to 350°F. Grease a loaf pan. Drain the salmon and flake it with a fork, removing any bones. In a large bowl, combine the salmon, potatoes, egg, celery, onion, parsley, lemon juice, paprika, pepper, and salt. Mix well and stir in the milk. Pack the mixture into the loaf pan and bake for 30 minutes.

For sauce: In a small saucepan over low heat, melt the butter. Whisk in the flour and cook for 2 minutes, stirring constantly. Scald the milk and add to the butter and flour, whisking until the sauce is thick and smooth. Add the celery salt and cheese and cook until the cheese melts. Serve over the salmon loaf. **Makes 6 servings.**

White Fish With Lemongrass Marinade

2 tablespoons vegetable or peanut oil

1 tablespoon dark sesame oil

2 tablespoons soy sauce

1½ tablespoons finely chopped fresh
    lemongrass

4 fillets (4 to 6 ounces each) of sole or
    other mild white fish

1 tablespoon sesame seeds

Combine the first four ingredients in a small bowl and whisk to blend. Rub the marinade onto the fish fillets and refrigerate, covered, for 20 to 30 minutes. Broil or bake the fish at 350°F until it flakes easily with a fork. While the fish is cooking, heat a skillet, add the sesame seeds, and toast them, stirring with a fork constantly. Sprinkle the sesame seeds onto the cooked fish. **Makes 4 servings.**

Salmon With Oregano Salsa

FISH:

4 salmon steaks (8 ounces each)

½ cup white wine

½ teaspoon freshly ground black
    pepper

SALSA:

4 scallions, trimmed

8 ounces ripe tomatoes, peeled
    (see tip, page 65)

2 tablespoons olive oil

½ teaspoon sugar

1 tablespoon tomato purée

2 teaspoons chopped fresh oregano

oregano sprigs, for garnish

For fish: Preheat the oven to 350°F. Put the salmon steaks into a greased baking dish. Pour the wine over the fish, then sprinkle with pepper. Cover and bake for 15 minutes, or until the salmon flakes easily with a fork. Set it aside to cool.

For salsa: Put all of the ingredients, except the oregano, into a blender or food processor and chop in pulses. Add the chopped oregano and pulse once.

Serve the salmon cold with the salsa, garnished with a sprig of oregano. **Makes 4 servings.**

Shrimp and Creamy Spinach Feta Rice

2 tablespoons olive oil

½ cup julienned red bell pepper

6 ounces baby spinach, washed and
    dried

½ teaspoon salt

½ teaspoon freshly ground black
    pepper

1 pound shrimp, peeled, deveined,
    and cooked

1½ cups cooked brown rice

1 cup feta cheese

⅓ to ½ cup pine nuts, toasted

In a large skillet over medium heat, warm the oil. Add the red pepper and cook for 1 minute. Add the spinach, salt, and black pepper and cook just until the spinach begins to wilt. Drain the excess liquid. Add the shrimp and cook for 30 seconds, or until the shrimp are warm. Add the rice and feta and toss until the rice is heated and the cheese is creamy. Top with pine nuts. **Makes 2 to 4 servings.**

Save 'n' Store: Spinach

- To store spinach, dry off the leaves and put them into a plastic bag. Refrigerate for up to 3 days.

In the hands of an able cook, fish can become an inexhaustible source of perpetual delight.

–Jean-Anthelme Brillat-Savarin,
French epicure and gastronome (1755–1826)

Steamed Clams and Spanish Sausage

Cherrystone clams steam open and release their juices, which intermingle with the heady flavor of sliced chorizo sausage. Serve in deep bowls with linguine or offer thick slices of crusty bread for sopping up the broth.

36 cherrystone or medium hard-shell
    clams

generous pinch of saffron threads,
    pulverized with a mortar and pestle

¼ cup boiling water

¼ cup olive oil

1 medium onion, coarsely chopped

1 green bell pepper, coarsely chopped

1 red bell pepper, coarsely chopped

2 cloves garlic, minced

1 chorizo sausage (about ¾ pound), cut
    into ½-inch slices

1 can (28 ounces) crushed tomatoes

1½ cups dry white wine

2 tablespoons fresh lemon juice

1 tablespoon chopped fresh cilantro

½ teaspoon salt

freshly ground black pepper, to taste

1 bay leaf, broken in half

1 strip (2 inches) orange zest

Scrub the clams with a stiff brush under cold running water, taking special care to dislodge any sand that may be caught in the seam between the two shells. Discard any clams that are open or have chipped shells; set the rest aside. Place the saffron in a small bowl, add the boiling water, and set it aside to steep.

In a 6-quart Dutch oven, heat the oil. Add the onion, bell peppers, and garlic, tossing to coat. Cook over medium heat, stirring slowly, until the onion is translucent. Add the sliced sausage and continue stirring until the peppers are tender. Add the tomatoes and increase the heat to high. Stir in the wine, lemon juice, saffron (including the steeping liquid), cilantro, salt, and black pepper. Submerge the bay leaf halves and orange zest in the sauce. Lightly simmer the sauce, uncovered, for 30 minutes.

Put the clams into the sauce and reduce the heat to low. Cover the pan and cook for 10 to 12 minutes, or until the clams have opened. Using a slotted spoon, transfer the clams to a serving platter or individual bowls. (Discard any that have not opened.) Stir the sauce, then retrieve and discard the orange zest and bay leaf halves. Spoon the sauce and sausage slices over the clams. **Makes 4 servings.**

FISH & SEAFOOD

Sherried Shellfish With Leeks and Cream

¾ **pound sea scallops, quartered**

¾ **pound raw shrimp, peeled and deveined**

¾ **cup all-purpose flour**

6 **tablespoons (¾ stick) butter, divided**

½ **cup dry sherry**

2 **cups chopped cooked lobster meat**

1 **can (10 ounces) whole baby clams,
    drained**

4 **ounces sliced mushrooms**

¼ **teaspoon ground fennel**

¾ **teaspoon chopped fresh tarragon or
    ¼ teaspoon dried tarragon**

4 **leeks, white part only, halved
    lengthwise, rinsed well,
    and cut into 1½-inch pieces**

1 **clove garlic, minced**

⅔ **cup heavy cream**

salt and pepper, to taste

4 **cups hot cooked rice**

1 **cup cooked green peas**

1 **jar (4¼ ounces) pimientos, diced,
    for garnish**

1 **tablespoon chopped fresh parsley,
    for garnish**

Dredge the scallops and shrimp in the flour. In a large skillet over medium heat, melt 3 tablespoons of butter. Add the scallops and shrimp and cook for 5 minutes, turning frequently. Add the sherry and cook for 3 minutes longer. Stir in the lobster meat, clams, mushrooms, fennel, and tarragon. Remove the pan from the heat, cover, and set aside.

In another large skillet over medium heat, melt the remaining butter, add the leeks, and cook for 5 minutes. Add the garlic and cook for 3 minutes longer, stirring to keep the garlic from browning. Add the shellfish mixture, cream, salt, and pepper and mix well. Lower the heat and cook, stirring, until the sauce is slightly thickened and the ingredients are heated through. Place the cooked rice and peas on a serving platter and cover with the shellfish mixture. Garnish with the pimientos and parsley. **Makes 6 servings.**

In the Kitchen: Shrimp

■ Shrimp may be cooked with or without their shells. Before cooking peeled, large shrimp, devein them with the tip of a knife or a metal pick.

Shrimp in Prosciutto al Formaggio

½ pound prosciutto, thinly sliced
1 pound raw medium shrimp, peeled
    and deveined
1 cup (2 sticks) butter
4 cloves garlic, chopped
4 shallots, chopped
1 tablespoon all-purpose flour
2 cups dry white wine
juice of 1 lemon
2 sprigs fresh basil, chopped
4 ounces sun-dried tomatoes
8 ounces mozzarella cheese, grated
4 ounces Parmesan-Romano cheese,
    grated

Preheat the oven to 375°F. Grease a casserole. Cut the prosciutto slices in half lengthwise and wrap a slice around each shrimp. In a large skillet over medium heat, melt the butter. Add the garlic and shallots and cook until soft. Add the flour, whisk to blend, and continue cooking for 2 minutes. Add the wine, lemon juice, and basil. Cook until the liquid is reduced by one-third. Put the sun-dried tomatoes into a small pan, cover with water, and bring to a boil. Cook for 3 minutes, drain, then add the tomatoes to the wine sauce. Put the prosciutto-wrapped shrimp into the casserole and bake for 20 minutes. Top with the cheeses and bake until the cheese is bubbly. Cover with the wine sauce and serve. **Makes 4 servings.**

Shrimp Creole

A dish with Southern origins; serve over a bed of fluffy white rice.

2 tablespoons butter
1 cup chopped onion
1 cup chopped green bell pepper
1 clove garlic, minced
2 cups stewed tomatoes
⅛ teaspoon paprika
salt and pepper, to taste
1 pound raw shrimp, peeled and deveined

In a large, heavy skillet, melt the butter over medium heat. Add the onion, green pepper, and garlic and sauté until the pepper is tender, about 5 minutes. Add the tomatoes and seasonings and simmer for 5 minutes. Add the shrimp and simmer for 10 minutes. Serve hot. **Makes 6 servings.**

FISH & SEAFOOD

Skillet Sea Scallops

1½ **pounds sea scallops**

¾ **cup all-purpose flour**

⅓ **cup butter**

3 **scallions, white part only, chopped**

3 **tablespoons minced fresh parsley**

1 **tablespoon chopped fresh chives**

juice of ½ **lemon**

¼ **cup dry white wine or vermouth**

½ **teaspoon salt**

Dredge the scallops lightly in the flour. In a large skillet over medium-high heat, heat the butter until it foams. Add the scallops and sauté, turning often, for about 3 minutes, or until lightly browned. Add the scallions, parsley, chives, lemon juice, wine, and salt. Toss the ingredients quickly to mix. Bring the liquid to a boil and cook the scallops uncovered for another 5 minutes. **Makes 4 servings.**

Chicken Oyster Pie

A great way to use leftover chicken and to stretch a small supply of fresh oysters. You can use less chicken if you have the oysters to spare.

2 **cups cooked chicken, diced**

2 **cups fresh oysters, drained (reserve the liquor)**

1 **unbaked double piecrust** *(see recipe, page 272)*

2 **cups chicken stock**

3 **tablespoons butter**

1 **small onion, diced**

3 **stalks celery, minced**

¾ **teaspoon chopped fresh dill or** ¼ **teaspoon dried dill**

3 **to 5 drops hot-pepper sauce**

3 **tablespoons all-purpose flour**

1½ **cups baby peas**

salt and pepper, to taste

Preheat the oven to 500°F. Mix the chicken and oysters in a medium bowl, then put them into the bottom piecrust. Measure the oyster liquor and add enough chicken stock to make 2½ cups, then set aside. In a heavy saucepan over medium heat, melt the butter. Lower the heat and add the onion, celery, and dill. Cook until the onion and celery are limp and have begun to lose their liquid. Add the hot-pepper sauce and stir in the flour. When all of the ingredients are blended, add the 2½ cups of oyster/chicken liquid. Cook over medium heat, stirring constantly, until the mixture comes to a boil. Lower the heat and cook for 5 minutes. Remove the pan from the heat. Stir in the peas and season with salt and pepper. Pour the sauce over the oyster/chicken mixture. Add the piecrust top and pierce with a fork several times. Bake for 15 minutes, then lower the heat to 375°F and bake for 20 minutes, or until golden. **Makes 4 to 6 servings.**

Pasta & Rice

Fettuccine With Mushrooms and
Clove Pinks. 217

Mediterranean Orzo 217

Thai Chicken With Linguine 218

Summertime Pasta 218

Vegetable Lasagna. 219

Pesto Lasagna 220

Spinach Fettuccine With Smoked Salmon
and Dill. 220

East Indian Spaghetti. 221

Pasta Pointers 222

Mushroom-Tomato-Spinach Spaghetti 223

Basil Rice 223

Lemon Dill Rice 224

Mexican Rice 224

Carrots Baked With Rice 225

Pakistani Rice. 225

Confetti Rice Salad. 226

Orange-Brown Rice Salad 226

Greek Rice Salad 227

Spaghetti Salad 227

Spring Risotto 228

Lamb and Rice Salad With Fresh Mint 228

Fettuccine With Mushrooms and Clove Pinks

(recipe at right)

Fettuccine With Mushrooms and Clove Pinks

The flower petals add color and spice.

- **2 tablespoons butter**
- **2 tablespoons olive oil**
- **2 shallots, finely minced**
- **1 cup sliced mushrooms**
- **¾ teaspoon chopped fresh marjoram or ¼ teaspoon dried marjoram**
- **salt and pepper, to taste**
- **¼ cup fresh clove pink petals, torn into small pieces**
- **1 tablespoon chopped fresh parsley**
- **1 pound fettuccine**
- **grated Parmesan cheese, for topping**

In a large skillet over medium heat, warm the butter and oil. Add the shallots and sauté for about a minute. Add the mushrooms and marjoram and cook, stirring, for 3 to 4 minutes. Season with salt and pepper, add the clove pinks and parsley, and toss. Cover the pan, turn the heat to low, and keep the mixture warm. Cook the fettuccine according to the package directions. Drain the pasta, add to the mushroom mixture, and toss well to coat. Add more butter or olive oil, if desired. Top with the Parmesan cheese. Serve hot. **Makes 6 servings.**

For more ideas on how to use edible flowers in recipes, see pages 242–243.

Mediterranean Orzo

- **1 cup orzo (rice-shape pasta)**
- **1 tablespoon olive oil**
- **½ cup chopped tomatoes**
- **¾ cup crumbled feta cheese**
- **2 tablespoons chopped fresh parsley**
- **¼ cup pitted and chopped Greek olives**
- **¼ teaspoon salt**
- **⅛ teaspoon freshly ground black pepper**
- **2 tablespoons grated Parmesan cheese, for topping**

Cook the orzo according to the package directions. Drain and return to the cooking pot. Stir in the olive oil, tomatoes, feta cheese, parsley, and Greek olives. Place the pan over medium heat and cook only until warmed through. Season with the salt and pepper. Top with the Parmesan cheese and serve immediately. **Makes 4 servings.**

PASTA & RICE

Thai Chicken With Linguine

1 pound linguine

1 tablespoon olive oil

1 pound skinless boneless chicken breasts, cut into 1-inch pieces

1 cup chicken broth

2 tablespoons honey

1 tablespoon soy sauce

¼ cup crunchy peanut butter

1 teaspoon cornstarch

1 teaspoon ground ginger

4 scallions, sliced

2 cloves garlic, minced

1 red bell pepper, cut into strips

Cook the linguine according to the package directions, drain, set aside, and keep warm. In a saucepan, warm the oil over medium heat. Add the chicken and cook until it loses its pink color. Remove the chicken from the pan and keep warm. Add the broth, honey, and soy sauce to the pan. Whisk in the peanut butter, cornstarch, and ginger. Add the scallions and garlic and cook over low heat, stirring constantly until blended. Add the red pepper and cooked chicken. Stir to coat and cook until the sauce has thickened. Serve over warm linguine. **Makes 6 servings.**

Summertime Pasta

2 small zucchini

1 small summer squash

¼ cup (½ stick) butter

1 tablespoon olive oil

3 to 4 cloves garlic, minced

1½ cups sliced mushrooms

6 large leaves fresh basil, thinly sliced

1 pound rotini pasta

½ cup grated Parmesan cheese

Cut the zucchini and summer squash into a neat, fine julienne and set aside. In a skillet, warm the butter and oil over medium heat. Add the garlic and sauté until opaque. Add the mushrooms and cook until they start to shrink and change color. Add the zucchini and summer squash and cook just until tender. Stir in the basil. Do not overcook. Meanwhile, cook the pasta al dente, according to the package directions. Drain the pasta and toss with the vegetables and Parmesan cheese in a serving bowl. Serve with additional Parmesan cheese. **Makes 6 servings.**

PASTA & RICE

Vegetable Lasagna

Here, a layer of garden vegetables replaces the traditional sausage. If you have space in the freezer, make two at once: Freeze one unbaked, then defrost and bake as directed.

VEGETABLE MIXTURE:

2 tablespoons olive oil

1 large onion, chopped

3 to 4 cloves garlic, finely chopped

12 ounces mushrooms, chopped

2 to 3 medium zucchini or summer
   squashes, chopped

4 cups packed, chopped Swiss chard
   or spinach

CHEESE MIXTURE:

2 cups low-fat cottage cheese

1 cup part-skim shredded mozzarella
   or other low-fat cheese

¼ cup chopped fresh basil or
   1 tablespoon dried basil

2 eggs

½ cup grated Parmesan or Romano
   cheese, divided

salt and pepper, to taste

PASTA:

9 lasagna noodles

4 cups of your favorite tomato sauce,
   divided

For vegetable mixture: In a large frying pan, warm the oil over medium heat. Add the onion, garlic, and mushrooms and sauté until soft. Add the zucchini and Swiss chard, cover, lower the heat, and cook, stirring several times, for about 10 minutes, until the chard is wilted and the zucchini is soft. Spoon the vegetables into a colander and let drain for 30 minutes.

For cheese mixture: In a mixing bowl, combine the cottage cheese, mozzarella, basil, eggs, and ¼ cup of Parmesan cheese. Season with salt and pepper.

For pasta: Cook the lasagna noodles in a large stockpot of boiling water for 5 minutes, or until just barely tender. Drain, rinse under cold water to cool, and set aside.

Preheat the oven to 375°F. Press the draining vegetables gently with a large spoon to extract as much moisture as possible. Spread ½ to 1 cup of tomato sauce on the bottom of a 13x9-inch baking dish. Place three lasagna noodles on top for the next layer; then spread half the cheese mixture over the noodles. Spread half the vegetable mixture over the cheese and dribble 1 cup of tomato sauce over this layer. Add another layer of three noodles, spread on the remaining cheese mixture and vegetables, dribble on another cup of tomato sauce, and top with the remaining noodles. Spread the top layer with the remaining tomato sauce and sprinkle with the remaining ¼ cup of Parmesan cheese. Bake for 45 minutes, or until bubbling. Let sit 15 minutes before cutting. To reheat, cover and bake at 350°F for 20 minutes. **Makes 8 servings.**

PASTA & RICE

Pesto Lasagna

PASTA:

6 lasagna noodles

PESTO:

2 cups fresh basil leaves

3 cloves garlic, minced

½ cup pine nuts

¼ cup Italian parsley

½ teaspoon salt

½ cup virgin olive oil

¼ cup grated Parmesan cheese

FILLING:

1 cup ricotta cheese

1 egg

½ cup plus 2 tablespoons grated
    Parmesan cheese

1 cup plus 2 tablespoons shredded
    mozzarella cheese

For pasta: Cook the lasagna noodles according to the package directions. Drain, rinse with cold water, and set aside.

For pesto: Put the basil, garlic, pine nuts, parsley, salt, and oil into a blender or food processor and blend into a smooth paste. Add the Parmesan cheese and pulse several times. (After making this lasagna, save any leftover pesto in a covered glass jar in the refrigerator for use within 1 week.)

For filling: In a mixing bowl, beat to blend the ricotta, egg, ½ cup of Parmesan cheese, 1 cup of mozzarella, and ½ cup of pesto.

Preheat the oven to 350°F. Grease a 13x9-inch baking dish. Place three cooked lasagna noodles in the baking dish. Cover the noodles with the ricotta-pesto mixture, then add the remaining three lasagna noodles. Sprinkle the remaining mozzarella and Parmesan cheeses on top. Bake for 25 minutes. **Makes 6 servings.**

Spinach Fettuccine With Smoked Salmon and Dill

½ **pound spinach fettuccine**

1 tablespoon butter

6 to 8 scallions, cut into ¼-inch pieces

⅓ pound smoked salmon, cut into
    ½-inch pieces

1 cup light cream

2 to 3 tablespoons chopped fresh dill

dill sprigs, for garnish

Cook the fettuccine according to the package directions, drain, and set aside. In a saucepan, melt the butter over medium heat. Add the scallions and sauté for 2 to 3 minutes. Lower the heat and add the smoked salmon and cream. Stir and heat gently (do not boil) for about 5 minutes. Add the dill. Serve immediately over the fettuccine. Garnish with dill sprigs. **Makes 4 servings.**

East Indian Spaghetti

CURRY SAUCE:

¼ cup (½ stick) butter

1 onion, minced

1 clove garlic (or more to taste), minced

1 tablespoon all-purpose flour

1 heaping tablespoon curry powder

⅓ cup coconut milk, or combine

2 tablespoons grated fresh coconut
with ⅓ cup milk, bring to boil, and
strain before using

1 tomato, chopped

¾ cup chicken broth

salt, to taste

PASTA:

1 pound spaghetti

3 tablespoons butter

1 to 1½ cups shredded cooked chicken

½ cup coarsely chopped cooked ham

salt, to taste

nutmeg, to taste

For curry sauce: In a skillet, melt the butter over medium heat. Add the onion and garlic and cook until the onion is translucent. Add the flour and curry powder and stir, warming the curry powder (be careful that the garlic does not burn). Add the coconut milk and tomato. Bring the mixture to a boil and cook for 1 to 2 minutes. Add the chicken broth, bring to a boil again, and cook, stirring occasionally, for 20 minutes. Add salt to taste.

For pasta: Cook the spaghetti according to the package directions. Drain and return to the pot. Add the butter, chicken, and ham. Season with salt and nutmeg.

Place the pasta on a serving dish and top with 1 cup of curry sauce. **Makes 6 servings.**

Save 'n' Store: Coconut

■ **To store fresh shredded coconut, place it in a plastic freezer bag and press the bag to remove the air. Allow about ½ inch of space at the top of the bag for the coconut's expansion. Seal the bag and store in the freezer for up to 6 months.**

Pasta Pointers

How Much Pasta to Cook?

- Long pasta shapes (spaghetti, linguine, fettuccine):
  2 ounces uncooked = ½-inch-diameter bundle dry
  = 1 cup cooked

- Short pasta shapes (elbows, macaroni, twists, shells,
  mostaccioli, ziti):
  2 ounces uncooked = just over ½ cup dry = 1 cup cooked

- Egg noodles:
  2 ounces uncooked = ½ cup dry = just over ½ cup cooked

Smooth Going

- To keep pasta from sticking together, add a tablespoon or two of olive oil to the boiling water before
  you add the uncooked pasta. Add the pasta slowly to the water and stir the pasta occasionally while it
  is cooking.

When Is It Done?

- Cook the pasta until "al dente," which means "to the tooth." The outside should be tender, but the
  inside should still be firm and chewy, yet not hard. If the pasta will be baked further in a recipe,
  slightly undercook it at this stage.

How to Store Pasta

- Uncooked Pasta:
  Store uncooked pasta in a cool, dry place, such as a cupboard. Unopened, it will keep for up to 1 year.
  Once opened, store it in an airtight container away from other foods with strong odors.

- Cooked Pasta:
  Mix cooked pasta with enough olive oil to coat. Refrigerate in an airtight container for up to 5 days.
  To preserve the pasta's flavor, it's best to store it separately from the sauce.

- Freezer Option:
  Baked dishes using pasta such as jumbo shells, lasagna, manicotti, and ziti work best for freezing.
  Prepare the recipe and freeze it before baking. Thaw in the refrigerator.

Mushroom–Tomato–Spinach Spaghetti

4 tablespoons olive oil

1 large onion, chopped

2½ pounds plum tomatoes, seeded
    and chopped

1½ teaspoons salt

1 tablespoon chopped fresh basil or
    1 teaspoon dried basil

1 tablespoon chopped fresh oregano
    or 1 teaspoon dried oregano

1 pound spaghetti

½ pound mushrooms, thinly sliced

1 cup chopped cooked spinach

grated Parmesan cheese, for topping

In a heavy saucepan, warm the oil over medium heat. Add the onion and sauté until soft. Add the tomatoes, salt, basil, and oregano and simmer gently for 30 minutes. Meanwhile, cook the spaghetti according to the package directions. Drain and set aside. In the final 5 minutes of cooking the sauce, add the mushrooms and spinach. Serve over the pasta with Parmesan cheese. **Makes 6 servings.**

Basil Rice

2½ cups chicken stock

2 tablespoons butter

1 tablespoon minced shallots or onion

1½ cups rice

salt, to taste

1 tablespoon finely minced fresh basil

2 tablespoons chopped fresh parsley

½ cup tomato sauce

Preheat the oven to 375°F. In a medium saucepan over medium heat, bring the chicken stock to a boil. In another saucepan over medium heat, melt the butter. Add the shallots and sauté until translucent. Add the rice and stir until the grains turn milky. Add the salt, basil, parsley, hot chicken stock, and tomato sauce and stir until blended. Transfer to a baking dish and bake for 25 minutes. **Makes 8 servings.**

PASTA & RICE

In the Kitchen: Shallots

■ Shallots grow in sections called cloves, similar to garlic. If a recipe calls for a shallot, it means one clove, not the whole bulb.

Lemon Dill Rice

3 cups chicken stock

2 tablespoons butter

1 tablespoon minced shallots or onion

1½ cups rice

salt, to taste

1½ teaspoons chopped dried lemon peel

1 tablespoon chopped fresh dill

1 teaspoon chopped fresh chives

Preheat the oven to 375°F. In a medium saucepan over medium heat, bring the chicken stock to a boil. In another saucepan over medium heat, melt the butter. Add the shallots and sauté until translucent. Add the rice and stir until the grains turn milky. Add the salt, lemon peel, dill, chives, and hot chicken stock and stir until blended. Transfer to a baking dish and bake for 25 minutes. **Makes 8 servings.**

Mexican Rice

3 cups chicken stock

2 tablespoons butter

1 tablespoon minced onion

1 clove garlic, minced

1½ cups rice

2 tomatoes, peeled, seeded, and chopped *(see tip, page 65)*

2 tablespoons finely minced mint leaves

1 cup peas

coriander leaves or parsley, finely minced, for garnish

Preheat the oven to 375°F. In a medium saucepan over medium heat, bring the chicken stock to a boil. In another saucepan over medium heat, melt the butter. Add the onion and garlic and sauté until the onion is translucent. Add the rice and stir until the grains turn milky. Add the tomatoes and cook until almost all of the moisture is gone. Add the hot chicken stock, mint, and peas and stir until blended. Transfer to a baking dish, cover, and bake for 25 minutes. Garnish the finished dish with coriander or parsley. **Makes 8 servings.**

How to Harvest: Peas

■ Pick garden peas when plump and still green. Pick snap peas just as they plump but before the seeds inside reach full size. Snow peas can be picked when the pods reach full size but the seeds inside do not yet show. To avoid damaging the plant, secure the vine with one hand and cut or pull the pods off with the other hand.

PASTA & RICE

Carrots Baked With Rice

¼ cup (½ stick) butter

3 cups grated carrots

½ cup chopped onion

1 tablespoon chopped fresh parsley

1 teaspoon salt

½ tablespoon chopped fresh summer
    savory or ½ teaspoon dried
    summer savory

⅛ teaspoon freshly ground black
    pepper

3 cups cooked rice

1 cup milk

2 eggs

Preheat the oven to 325°F. Grease a 9-inch baking dish. Prepare a slightly larger baking dish for a water bath. In a large skillet over medium heat, melt the butter. Add the carrots and onion and sauté for 10 minutes. Add the parsley, salt, savory, and pepper. Stir and cook for 5 minutes. Add the rice, toss to combine, and remove the pan from the heat. In a bowl, combine the milk and eggs and beat until foamy. Add the liquid to the carrot-rice mixture, stirring until well mixed. Spoon the ingredients into the prepared baking dish and set in the larger baking dish. Add ½ inch of hot water to the larger dish. Cover with foil and bake for 1 hour. **Makes 6 servings.**

In the Garden: Summer Savory

■ Summer savory is an annual herb that grows 4 to 15 inches tall. Start seeds indoors, but do not cover them with soil, as they need light to germinate. Harden off seedlings before planting outdoors, where they will thrive in poor but well-drained soil in full sun.

Pakistani Rice

5 whole cloves

5 coriander seeds

¼ teaspoon cumin seeds

¼ teaspoon whole peppercorns

2 cinnamon sticks (each 3 inches long)

2 bay leaves

3 cups chicken stock

1½ cups rice

2 cups peas

1 tablespoon butter

1 tablespoon fresh lemon juice

¼ cup minced fresh parsley, for garnish

Grind the cloves, coriander seeds, cumin seeds, peppercorns, cinnamon sticks, and bay leaves with a mortar and pestle (or with a rolling pin) and place in a 4-inch-square piece of cheesecloth. Tie shut.

In a medium saucepan over medium heat, bring the chicken stock to a boil. Add the rice and the cheesecloth of herbs and spices; reduce the heat to low, stir, and cook for about 18 minutes. Meanwhile, in another saucepan, cook the peas with the butter. When the rice is soft, remove the cheesecloth and add the peas. Toss with the lemon juice and garnish with the parsley. **Makes 8 servings.**

Confetti Rice Salad

1 box long-grain or wild rice mix with
   herbs
1 cup walnut pieces
1 cup sweetened dried cranberries
¾ cup chopped yellow bell pepper
¾ cup chopped red bell pepper
½ cup finely chopped red or Vidalia
   onion
¾ cup raspberry walnut vinaigrette
1 cup mandarin orange slices, drained

Prepare the rice according to the package directions. Preheat the oven to 325°F. Place the walnuts on a cookie sheet and toast them in the oven for 6 to 8 minutes, stirring once or twice to toast evenly. Set aside. When the rice is cooked, place it in a large bowl and fluff with a fork. Add the cranberries, peppers, onion, and vinaigrette and toss well. Set the rice mixture aside for 1 hour. Just before serving, adjust the flavor, adding more vinaigrette if necessary. Add the oranges and walnuts, saving a few to garnish the top, and toss to mix. **Makes 6 to 8 servings.**

Orange–Brown Rice Salad

The brown rice should be firm so that the salad can be mixed and stored without becoming mushy.

2 cups cooked brown rice
½ pound baby shrimp, cooked and
   peeled
1 to 2 stalks celery, finely chopped
1 to 2 carrots, finely chopped
1 tablespoon chopped fresh dill or
   1 teaspoon dried dill
¼ cup olive oil
zest from 1 large orange, divided
juice from 1 large orange
salt and pepper, to taste
½ cup slivered almonds, for garnish

In a large bowl, combine the rice, shrimp, celery, and carrots. In another bowl, combine the dill, olive oil, half of the zest, and the orange juice (be sure to zest the orange before juicing). Season with salt and pepper and whisk to blend. Add the dressing to the rice mixture, stirring gently to coat. Taste, then add more zest if you wish. Garnish with slivered almonds. **Makes 6 to 8 servings.**

Save 'n' Store: Dill

■ Fresh dill will keep for up
   to 2 weeks if the stems are
   immersed in a glass of water
   tented with a plastic bag in
   the refrigerator.

PASTA & RICE

Greek Rice Salad

3 cups cooked rice

2 tablespoons olive oil

3 tablespoons fresh lemon juice

¾ teaspoon salt

¼ teaspoon freshly ground black
   pepper

1 tablespoon chopped fresh chives

1 tablespoon chopped fresh parsley

1 clove garlic, minced

1 teaspoon chopped fresh dill

¾ cup chopped cucumber

½ cup chopped fresh tomato

¼ cup finely chopped black olives

spinach leaves

1 avocado, pitted, peeled, and sliced,
   for garnish

1 tomato, sliced, for garnish

Place the rice in a large bowl. In a separate bowl, combine the olive oil, lemon juice, salt, pepper, chives, parsley, garlic, and dill and whisk to blend. Pour the dressing over the rice and stir to coat thoroughly. Add the cucumber, tomato, and black olives and mix to combine. Refrigerate for several hours. To serve, place on a bed of spinach leaves, then garnish with avocado and tomato slices. **Makes 6 servings.**

Spaghetti Salad

Essentially a "potato salad" with pasta instead!

8 ounces thin spaghetti

4 hard-boiled eggs, chopped

1 green pepper, finely chopped

1 stalk celery, finely chopped

1 teaspoon finely chopped onion

salt and pepper, to taste

1 cup whipped salad dressing
   (not mayonnaise)

½ of 5-ounce jar green olives, finely chopped,
   plus a few slices for garnish

Cook the spaghetti according to the package directions. Drain, then rinse with cold water and put into a large bowl. Add the remaining ingredients (except the olive slices for garnish) and mix thoroughly. Chill in the refrigerator for a few hours before serving to allow flavors to blend. **Makes 6 to 8 servings.**

Spring Risotto

1 small bunch asparagus, trimmed and
    cut into 2-inch pieces
½ pound bay or sea scallops
6 to 8 cups chicken broth
3 tablespoons butter
1 yellow onion, chopped
1½ cups arborio rice
2 tablespoons heavy cream
½ cup grated Parmesan cheese
salt and pepper, to taste

Steam the asparagus briefly, drain, and set aside. In a medium saucepan, bring 3 cups of lightly salted water to a boil. Add the scallops to the water and cook (poach) until white and firm. Drain, set aside, and keep warm. In a separate saucepan, heat the broth. In a skillet, melt the butter over medium heat. Add the onion and sauté until soft. Add the rice to the onion, reduce the heat, and stir for 3 minutes. Add the hot broth, ½ cup at a time, stirring until the liquid is absorbed before adding more. Continue cooking and stirring for about 20 minutes, or until the rice is tender. Remove the rice from the heat. Add the cream, Parmesan, scallops, and asparagus. Season with salt and pepper. **Makes 8 servings.**

Lamb and Rice Salad With Fresh Mint

¾ cup olive oil
⅓ cup fresh lemon juice
¾ cup finely chopped mint
1½ cups cubed or shredded cooked
    lamb
½ pound mushrooms, sliced
2 cups cherry tomatoes, halved
1 cup cooked rice
½ head Bibb lettuce

In a small bowl or jar, mix the olive oil, lemon juice, and mint. Put the lamb, mushrooms, cherry tomatoes, and rice into a large mixing bowl. Pour half of the oil–lemon juice dressing over the lamb, rice, and vegetables and toss well. Cover and refrigerate for up to 1 hour. When ready to serve, toss with the remaining dressing and arrange portions on beds of Bibb lettuce. **Makes 6 servings.**

Spring Risotto
(recipe at left)

CHAPTER 11

Sauces & Condiments

Indian Summer Applesauce 231

Cranberry Sauce 231

Béarnaise Sauce. 232

Cucumber Sauce 232

Remoulade Sauce 233

Peanut Sauce 234

Sour Cream Herb Sauce. 234

Watermelon Barbecue Marinade 235

Barbecue Sauce 235

Peachy Glaze 236

Peach Mint Sauce. 236

Herb Marinade. 237

Lemon Marinade 237

Orange Marinade. 237

Sweet Onion Watermelon Salsa 238

Fruit Salsa With Thai Basil 238

Salsa Verde. 239

Chive Mustard 240

Curry Mayonnaise 240

Cilantro and Mint Sauce 241

Horseradish Butter 241

Indian Summer Applesauce

Process this sauce in canning jars (see tips, page 150), freeze in freezer bags, or refrigerate until used.

5 pounds apples, quartered

3 or 4 purple plums, pitted and quartered

2 cups sugar

juice from 1 lemon

cinnamon, to taste

nutmeg, to taste

In a large pot over medium-high heat, combine the apples, plums, and 2 cups of water. Bring to a boil, then lower heat to medium. Cover and cook until the apples are soft and the peels fall off easily. Add the sugar and simmer for 2 to 5 minutes, or until the sugar dissolves. Pour the fruit and liquid into a food mill or sieve, in batches, and press out the applesauce, discarding the peels, seeds, and cores. Add the lemon juice, cinnamon, and nutmeg to the applesauce and stir to incorporate. **Makes about 2 quarts.**

Cranberry Sauce

This sauce is the perfect accompaniment to any poultry dish.

1 pound whole cranberries

½ to 2 cups sugar

1 stick (2 inches) cinnamon

Put the cranberries into a saucepan, add 2 cups of water, cover, and bring to a boil. Reduce the heat and cook until the berries' skins burst. In a blender or food processor, purée the mixture. Return the sauce to the saucepan and sweeten with sugar, to taste. Bring to a boil. Remove the saucepan from the heat and add the cinnamon stick. Set the sauce aside to cool, then refrigerate. Before serving, remove the cinnamon stick. **Makes 2½ cups.**

CRANBERRY JELLY: Prepare as above, but boil for 5 to 10 minutes before cooling. Pour into a mold and chill.

Crazy Cranberry Facts

■ The name "cranberry" probably came about because the flower looked like the head of a crane, a bird familiar to early Dutch and German settlers.

■ Ripe cranberries bounce— hence their alternate name, "bounceberry."

Béarnaise Sauce

This classic sauce, usually served with beef tenderloin, also goes well with fish.

½ cup white wine

2 tablespoons tarragon vinegar

1 tablespoon chopped shallots

2 teaspoons chopped fresh tarragon

2 crushed peppercorns

pinch of salt

3 egg yolks

¾ cup (1½ sticks) butter, melted

pinch of cayenne pepper

1 teaspoon minced fresh tarragon

In a saucepan over low heat, combine the wine, vinegar, shallots, chopped tarragon, peppercorns, and salt. Simmer until the liquid is reduced by half. Remove the saucepan from the heat and set aside until the ingredients cool. Add the egg yolks to the mixture and beat briskly with a whisk. Cook over low heat and slowly add the butter, whisking until the sauce thickens. Strain the sauce. Add the cayenne pepper and minced tarragon and stir to incorporate. **Makes 1½ cups.**

Cucumber Sauce

Serve with cold chicken or turkey.

½ cup sour cream

½ cup mayonnaise

2 medium cucumbers, peeled, seeded, and diced

1 tablespoon chopped fresh chives

1 tablespoon chopped fresh dill

salt and pepper, to taste

In a medium bowl, combine all of the ingredients and stir to blend. **Makes 2 cups.**

In the Kitchen: Tarragon

■ The slender leaves of tarragon have a delicate, anise flavor. It is the defining ingredient of béarnaise sauce and fines herbes (an equal blend of finely chopped chervil, chives, parsley, and tarragon) and one of the best herbs for flavoring vinegar.

Remoulade Sauce

Enjoy with shellfish and cold veal.

1 egg
½ teaspoon salt
1 teaspoon dry mustard
dash of freshly ground black pepper
2 teaspoons fresh lemon juice or
    vinegar, divided
1 cup oil, divided
1 tablespoon chopped fresh parsley
1 tablespoon chopped fresh chervil
1 teaspoon minced fresh tarragon
½ teaspoon anchovy paste
1 tablespoon finely chopped pickles
1 teaspoon prepared mustard
capers, to taste

In a blender or food processor, combine the egg, salt, dry mustard, pepper, 1 teaspoon of lemon juice, ¼ cup of oil, parsley, chervil, tarragon, anchovy paste, pickles, prepared mustard, and capers. Cover and blend on high. Slowly pour in ¾ cup of oil and blend until thick. Add 1 teaspoon more lemon juice and blend again. **Makes 1¼ cups.**

SAUCES & CONDIMENTS

Peanut Sauce

A nutty complement to steamed vegetables, pasta, or grilled fish or chicken.

1 cup unsweetened, chunky peanut butter

3 tablespoons tamari or soy sauce

2 tablespoons sugar

8 cloves garlic

1 tablespoon hot chili oil (optional)

1 cup chopped fresh cilantro

In a blender or food processor, combine all of the ingredients except the cilantro, add 2 tablespoons of water, and blend until smooth. Remove from the blender and fold in the chopped cilantro. (If you process the cilantro, the sauce will turn an odd shade of green.) **Makes about 2 cups.**

MAKE AHEAD: *This peanut sauce keeps for months in an airtight container in the refrigerator. To use, dilute to the desired consistency with near-boiling water, adding ½ teaspoon at a time and stirring.*

Sour Cream Herb Sauce

Use with fish, egg dishes, and cucumber or tomato salads.

1 egg

½ teaspoon salt

1 teaspoon dry mustard

½ cup sour cream

2 tablespoons minced fresh chives

2 tablespoons minced fresh parsley

2 tablespoons minced fresh dill

2 teaspoons lemon juice or vinegar, divided

1 cup oil, divided

salt and pepper, to taste

In a blender or food processor, combine the egg, salt, dry mustard, sour cream, chives, parsley, dill, 1 teaspoon of lemon juice, ¼ cup of oil, and salt and pepper. Blend on high. Slowly pour in ¾ cup of oil and blend until thick. Add 1 teaspoon more lemon juice and blend again. **Makes 1¾ cups.**

In the Garden: Dill

■ **In early or midspring, plant dill seeds ¼-inch deep, or start indoors and transplant when all danger of frost has passed.**

Watermelon Barbecue Marinade

An all-around, all-American favorite for marinating chicken, pork, fish, or shellfish.

½ cup watermelon juice*
½ cup balsamic vinegar
¼ cup brown sugar
¼ cup soy sauce
2 tablespoons vegetable oil
2 tablespoons Dijon-style mustard
2 cloves garlic, minced
2 teaspoons red pepper flakes

To make watermelon juice, see tip, page 301.

In a glass, stainless steel, or ceramic bowl, combine the watermelon juice with the rest of the ingredients. Whisk vigorously to blend. Pour to cover meat or fish, seal with plastic or foil, and refrigerate for several hours or overnight. **Makes 1½ cups.**

Barbecue Sauce

Use as a marinade or for basting meats.

1½ cups maple syrup
2 tablespoons chili sauce
2 tablespoons cider vinegar
1½ tablespoons finely chopped onion
⅛ teaspoon freshly ground black pepper
½ tablespoon soy sauce
½ teaspoon salt
½ teaspoon dry mustard

In a medium bowl, combine all of the ingredients and whisk vigorously. **Makes 1¾ cups.**

Before cooking outdoors, coat the undersides of pans with soap; soot will wash off more easily afterward.

In the Kitchen: Peaches

- White peaches have a more delicate, less acidic, flavor than yellow peaches and therefore are good for eating fresh.

- Ripen peaches in a paper bag. Refrigerate only to prolong storage.

Peachy Glaze

This is a delicious glaze for grilled spareribs, pork chops, or chicken. Add it only during the last 10 minutes of grilling or the subtle peach flavor will be lost.

3 to 4 medium ripe peaches, peeled, pitted, and sliced

2 tablespoons butter

2 tablespoons minced onion

1 large clove garlic, minced

½ teaspoon freshly ground black pepper

½ teaspoon dry mustard

1 tablespoon brown sugar

2 teaspoons soy sauce

2 tablespoons frozen orange juice concentrate

juice of 1 lemon

Put the peach slices into a blender or food processor and purée until smooth. Set aside 1 cup of puréed peaches. In a saucepan over medium heat, melt the butter. Add the onion and garlic and sauté until soft. Add the pepper, mustard, sugar, and soy sauce. Stir, and heat only until well blended. In a small bowl, mix together the peach purée, orange juice, and lemon juice. Add the fruit to the onion mixture. **Makes 1½ cups.**

Peach Mint Sauce

This sauce is the perfect accompaniment to sliced cold chicken.

1 cup chicken stock

¾ cup fresh mint leaves

½ cup peach jam

In a saucepan over medium heat, bring the stock to a simmer. Add the mint leaves, then cover and remove the saucepan from the heat. Set aside until the ingredients cool. Strain to remove the leaves and return the liquid to the saucepan. Add the jam and stir to combine. **Makes 1½ cups.**

SAUCES & CONDIMENTS

Marvelous Marinades

■ Marinades can add flavor to foods, and some help to tenderize meat, poultry, and fish. For either use, place the food and marinade in a nonmetallic container (cover with foil or plastic wrap) or resealable plastic bag. Marinate the food for the time specified in the recipe, turning it occasionally so that all food surfaces are coated. For safety reasons, discard the marinade after use.

The following marinades go well with chicken and small game birds.

Herb Marinade

½ cup oil
½ cup wine vinegar
2 cloves garlic, minced
1 teaspoon chopped fresh thyme or basil
salt and pepper, to taste

Combine all of the ingredients in a blender or food processor and mix well. **Makes 1 cup.**

Lemon Marinade

⅔ cup fresh lemon juice
⅓ cup oil
⅓ cup cider vinegar
3 tablespoons chopped shallots
salt and pepper, to taste

Combine all of the ingredients in a blender or food processor and mix well. **Makes 1⅓ cups.**

Orange Marinade

1 cup orange juice
1 teaspoon chopped fresh tarragon
1 sprig parsley
1 clove garlic, crushed

Combine all of the ingredients in a blender or food processor and mix well. **Makes 1 cup.**

SAUCES & CONDIMENTS

Sweet Onion Watermelon Salsa

Serve this tangy mixture with tortilla chips or alongside chicken or fish.

¼ cup orange marmalade

¼ cup chopped fresh cilantro

¼ cup finely chopped jalapeño

2 tablespoons white vinegar

1 clove garlic, minced

½ teaspoon salt

2 cups seeded and chopped watermelon

1 cup chopped sweet onion

1 cup peeled, seeded, and chopped orange sections

In a large bowl, add the orange marmalade, cilantro, jalapeño, vinegar, garlic, and salt and stir to coat. Add the watermelon, onion, and orange sections and toss gently. Refrigerate for at least 30 minutes before serving. **Makes 4½ cups.**

Fruit Salsa With Thai Basil

Serve atop chicken or seafood or as tortilla chip dip. Instead of mango, you can use cantaloupe or pineapple.

10 to 12 Thai basil leaves

2 cups diced mango

¼ cup finely chopped sweet onion, such as Vidalia

1 small hot chile, such as serrano or jalapeño, seeded and chopped

1 tablespoon fresh lime juice

¼ teaspoon salt

Stack the basil leaves, then roll them up together along their length. Thinly slice the leaves across the width of the roll. Put all of the ingredients into a medium bowl and toss to mingle. Cover and refrigerate for at least 10 minutes before serving. **Makes 2 cups.**

Salsa Verde

For more heat, add some of the chile seeds.

20 tomatillos

2 chiles, such as serrano or jalapeño,
   halved and seeded

1 medium onion, quartered

1 clove garlic, quartered

2 tablespoons minced fresh cilantro

¼ teaspoon sugar

salt, to taste

2 tablespoons olive oil

Husk the tomatillos, then gently put them into a large pot of boiling water and blanch for 10 minutes, or until tender. Drain. In a blender or food processor, chop the chiles to medium fine. Add the onion and garlic and chop again to medium fine. Add the cilantro, tomatillos, sugar, and salt and pulse until the ingredients are saucy. In a large skillet over medium heat, warm the oil. Add the salsa and stir for 5 minutes. Cool and serve. **Makes 2 to 3 cups.**

In the Garden: Tomatillos

■ Tomatillos are related to tomatoes and can be grown the same way. In cold regions, start seeds indoors 6 to 8 weeks before the first spring frost.

How to Harvest

■ Harvest tomatillos when the paper husks turn tan and begin to split open. Green fruit is the tangiest and best; near or fully ripe yellow or purple fruit are sweeter and less desirable. Before using, remove the husks and wash off the sticky coating.

SAUCES & CONDIMENTS

In the Garden: Chive

■ Chive is a perennial bulb that can be invasive. If the flowers are left to mature, they'll scatter vigorous seeds. For more about growing chives, see page 36.

Chive Mustard

This mustard has zing!

¼ cup mustard seeds, any type
1 tablespoon dry mustard
⅓ cup white-wine vinegar
1 tablespoon corn syrup
1 to 1¼ teaspoons sugar
1 to 1¼ teaspoons salt
pinch of ground cloves
3 tablespoons freshly snipped chives

Grind the mustard seeds with a mortar and pestle. In a small bowl, mix the ground mustard seeds, dry mustard, and ⅓ cup of water. Let stand, uncovered, at room temperature for 1 to 4 hours, stirring occasionally. In a blender or food processor, combine the mustard mixture with the remaining ingredients, except the chives, and process until smooth. Bring 1 cup of water to boil. Put the chives into a bowl and cover with the boiling water. Set the chives aside for 30 seconds, then drain. Add the chives to the mustard and season to taste, with more salt or sugar. Put the mustard into an airtight jar and refrigerate for 2 to 3 days before using. **Makes 1 cup.**

Curry Mayonnaise

1 egg
½ teaspoon salt
1 teaspoon dry mustard
dash of freshly ground black pepper
2 teaspoons lemon juice or vinegar, divided
1 cup oil, divided
2 tablespoons curry powder
1 tablespoon each minced fresh parsley, chives, and scallions

In a blender, combine the egg, salt, dry mustard, pepper, 1 teaspoon of lemon juice, ¼ cup of oil, curry, parsley, chives, and scallions. Blend on high. Slowly pour in ¾ cup of oil and blend until thick. Add 1 teaspoon more lemon juice and blend again. **Makes 1¼ cups.**

SAUCES & CONDIMENTS

Cilantro and Mint Sauce

Great with grilled fish.

½ cup plain yogurt
1 small onion, coarsely chopped
1 or 2 jalapeños, to taste, seeded and
    coarsely chopped
½ cup tightly packed cilantro leaves
½ cup tightly packed mint leaves
salt and pepper, to taste

In a blender or food processor, combine all of the ingredients except the salt and pepper. Process, scraping down the sides every 15 seconds, for 1 minute, or until the ingredients are finely chopped and the mixture is smooth. Season with salt and pepper. **Makes ¾ cup.**

Horseradish Butter

½ cup (1 stick) butter, softened
2 tablespoons grated horseradish
2 teaspoons vinegar
1 teaspoon sugar

In a mixing bowl, combine all of the ingredients and cream until smooth. **Makes ½ cup.**

In the Garden: Horseradish

■ Horseradish can be invasive when grown in the ground. Instead, use a deep container, such as a wooden half-barrel, filled with a mixture of compost and potting soil. Place the container in full sun. Plant the root sections at a 45-degree angle and water well.

Pick young horseradish leaves throughout the growing season to toss in salads. In late fall, after the leaves have died back and a few frosts have occurred, gently dig up the crown of roots. Harvest any roots greater than 1 inch thick and replant the remaining crown.

AN EDIBLE
Flower Garden

How many flowers there are that only serve to produce essences, which could have been made into savory dishes.

—Charles Pierre Monselet,
French writer (1825–88)

Many flowers that are valued for their appearance also add color and exotic flavors to food. Gather blossoms early in the day, wash them gently in cool water, and then pat dry. Refrigerate until you are ready to use.

—Nancy Dougherty

—Marissa Rose

1 CALENDULA (POT MARIGOLD). Cut the flower head when it's fully open, then pluck the spicy petals. Use them fresh in soups and salads and fish and poultry dishes or dried as a salad and beverage garnish. Grind them and use in place of saffron or to add color to foods. Or try them in Confetti Salad, page 91.

2 CLOVE PINK (CARNATION). Cut the spicy, clove-flavor petals away from the flower's bitter-tasting white base. Dry them in the oven on low heat (200°F) and then add to cake batter. Sprinkle minced fresh petals over a bowl of berries or use them in Fettuccine With Mushrooms and Clove Pinks, page 217.

3 NASTURTIUM. The yellow, orange, or red blossoms have a slightly peppery taste. Harvest as needed to float in a soup or punch bowl. Use the flowers and leaves in salads, as a garnish, or in Nasturtium and Shrimp Salad Appetizer, page 30. Pickle the fresh seedpods (see the recipe on page 159) and substitute for capers.

4 PANSY. The mildly mint-tasting flowers look dramatic when set into a gelatin mold for a salad or frozen into ice cubes or a ring for punch. Fresh blossoms also add vibrant color to green salads, desserts, and soups.

Picking Precautions

- **AVOID** harvesting flowers growing by the roadside, as they have been exposed to road dirt, car exhaust, and/or herbicides.

- **AVOID** eating flowers from florists, nurseries, or garden centers. Often these flowers have been treated with pesticides.

- **AVOID** eating flowers if you have hay fever, asthma, or allergies.

- To learn about other edible flowers, consult a guide book. Some flowers taste terrible and a few are poisonous.

PINEAPPLE SAGE. The delicately fruit-flavored red petals are best used fresh or added at the end of cooking time. Toss blossoms in salads such as Fruit Salad, page 20; add to desserts or fruit sorbets; or use as a garnish for iced tea and other beverages.

ROSE. All roses are edible; the flavor is more pronounced in the darker varieties. Rose petals are sweet, with subtle undertones ranging from fruit to mint to spice. Sprinkle petals onto salads, ice cream, or desserts; use them in syrups and jellies; or steep them in hot water to make tea.

SWEET VIOLET. Use leaves and flowers in salads or decorate cakes with the blossoms. The flowers are ideal for candying *(see recipe, right)*.

Candied Flowers

Candied flowers and petals can be used to decorate cakes, ice cream, fruit salads, and cocktails. Good choices include clove pinks, pansies, rose petals, and sweet violets.

powdered egg whites
warm water
edible flowers
superfine granulated
sugar

In a small bowl, mix the powdered egg whites and water, following package directions for creating the equivalent of 1 raw egg white. Using tweezers, dip each flower or petal carefully into the egg white to coat. Sprinkle with the sugar and place on wax paper to dry. Flowers are completely dry when stiff to the touch. Store the candied flowers in an airtight container in the refrigerator or put them into the freezer for later use.

Note: You can use unflavored gelatin instead of powdered egg whites.

CHAPTER 12

Breads

Apple Cheese Bread 245

Pear Bread With Ginger 246

Blueberry–Maple Walnut Bread. 246

Marbled Rhubarb Orange Bread 247

Strawberry Crunch Muffins. 248

The Best Fruit Muffins 248

Breakfast Muffins 250

Squash and Blueberry Muffins 250

Fresh Raspberry Muffins. 251

Spicy Pumpkin Muffins 252

Sweet Potato and Pecan Muffins 253

Zucchini Oatmeal Muffins 253

Granny's Blueberry Muffins 254

Cheese Herb Biscuits. 254

Lavender Scones 255

Herbed Popovers. 256

Corn Bread With Pine Nuts and
  Rosemary. 256

Martha Washington's Potato Rolls 258

Sour Cream Cranberry Rye Bread 259

Dill Bread. 259

Mexican Hot-Pepper Bread. 260

Good bread is the most fundamentally satisfying of all foods; and good bread with fresh butter, the greatest of feasts.

–James Beard, American author (1903–85)

Apple Cheese Bread

2¾ cups all-purpose flour

1 tablespoon baking powder

½ teaspoon salt

½ teaspoon nutmeg

¼ teaspoon cinnamon

⅓ cup sugar

¼ cup (½ stick) butter, melted

1 egg, beaten

1 cup milk

1½ cups grated cheddar cheese

2 medium apples, peeled, cored, and grated, tossed with 2 tablespoons sugar

⅔ cup apple jelly

Preheat the oven to 350°F. Grease a 9x5-inch loaf pan. Into a large bowl, sift together the flour, baking powder, salt, nutmeg, cinnamon, and sugar. In a small bowl, combine the melted butter, beaten egg, and milk; set aside. Mix the cheese and apples into the dry ingredients. Add the milk mixture and stir only until the batter is evenly moistened. Pour into the prepared pan. Bake for 35 minutes, then lower the heat to 325°F. Continue baking until a toothpick inserted into the center comes out clean, about another 20 minutes. Meanwhile, in a small pan over low heat, melt the apple jelly. When the bread is done, remove it from the oven and pour the melted jelly over the top. Let cool in the pan until the jelly sets, then remove to a wire rack to cool completely. **Makes 1 loaf.**

BREADS

Pear Bread With Ginger

This bread has a cakelike texture, in part because the butter and sugar are creamed together.

½ cup (1 stick) butter or shortening,
    softened

2 cups all-purpose flour

1 teaspoon baking powder

½ teaspoon baking soda

½ teaspoon salt

½ teaspoon ground ginger

1 cup sugar

2 large eggs

1 teaspoon vanilla extract

¼ cup sour cream, divided

1 cup peeled, cored, and coarsely
    chopped pears (about 2 medium)

Preheat the oven to 350°F. Grease a 9x5-inch loaf pan. Place the butter in a large mixing bowl. In a separate bowl, sift together the flour, baking powder, baking soda, salt, and ginger. Beat the butter until creamy. Gradually sprinkle in the sugar, beating continuously until the mixture is light and fluffy. Add the eggs, one at a time, beating after each. Beat in the vanilla. Add half of the dry ingredients, then stir in 2 tablespoons of sour cream. Repeat with the remaining dry ingredients followed by the rest of the sour cream. Gently stir in the chopped pears. Pour into the prepared pan and bake for 50 to 60 minutes, or until a toothpick inserted into the center comes out clean. Cool on a rack for 10 minutes, then turn out. Cool completely before slicing. **Makes 1 loaf.**

Blueberry–Maple Walnut Bread

2 eggs

1 cup sour cream

½ cup maple syrup

½ cup sugar

1 teaspoon vanilla extract

½ cup wheat bran or bran cereal

1½ cups all-purpose flour

½ teaspoon salt

1 teaspoon baking soda

1 cup blueberries

1 cup walnuts, chopped

Preheat the oven to 350°F. Lightly grease a 9x5-inch loaf pan. In a mixing bowl, beat the eggs, sour cream, maple syrup, sugar, and vanilla until smooth. Stir in the bran. In a separate bowl, sift together the flour, salt, and baking soda. Add the flour mixture to the wet ingredients, gently stirring to combine. Add the blueberries and walnuts and stir to blend. Spoon the batter into the prepared pan. Bake for 45 to 50 minutes, or until a toothpick inserted into the center comes out clean. **Makes 1 loaf.**

Marbled Rhubarb Orange Bread

1¾ cups diced rhubarb

2½ cups plus 2 tablespoons all-purpose flour

¼ cup wheat germ

¼ cup finely chopped pecans

¼ cup light-brown sugar

½ teaspoon cinnamon

zest and juice of 1 orange

¾ cup sugar

2 tablespoons shortening

1 egg

2 teaspoons baking powder

¼ teaspoon baking soda

¼ teaspoon salt

1 cup buttermilk

Preheat the oven to 350°F. Grease and flour a 9x5-inch loaf pan. In a small bowl, toss the rhubarb pieces with 2 tablespoons of flour to coat. Set aside. In a separate bowl, combine the wheat germ, pecans, brown sugar, and cinnamon. Set aside. In a large bowl, combine the orange zest and sugar. Add the shortening and mix thoroughly. To this mixture, add the orange juice and egg. Mix well. Sift together the remaining flour, baking powder, baking soda, and salt. Add these dry ingredients to the orange mixture alternately with the buttermilk, stirring between each addition until the batter is smooth. Fold in the rhubarb pieces. Spoon half of the batter into the prepared loaf pan. Sprinkle three-quarters of the wheat germ–pecan mixture on top. Spoon the remaining batter into the loaf pan. Top with remaining wheat germ–pecan mixture. Swirl a knife through the batter several times to create marbling. Bake for about 60 minutes, or until a toothpick inserted into the center comes out clean. Remove from the oven, cool in the pan for 10 minutes, then remove from the pan and cool completely on a wire rack before slicing. **Makes 1 large loaf.**

How to Harvest: Rhubarb

■ To harvest rhubarb, cut the stalks at ground level and remove and discard the leaves. Avoid any frostbitten stalks, which may contain toxins from the leaves.

Strawberry Crunch Muffins

TOPPING:

½ cup brown sugar

¼ cup all-purpose flour

½ cup chopped pecans

¼ cup oatmeal

3 tablespoons unsalted butter, melted

MUFFINS:

¾ cup all-purpose flour

¾ cup whole wheat flour

½ cup sugar

2 teaspoons baking powder

¼ teaspoon salt

1 teaspoon cinnamon

1 egg, lightly beaten

½ cup (1 stick) unsalted butter, melted

1 teaspoon vanilla extract

½ cup milk

1 cup sliced strawberries

1 teaspoon lemon zest

For topping: Combine all of the topping ingredients in one bowl and mix well. Set aside.

For muffins: Preheat the oven to 350°F. Grease a standard 12-cup muffin pan or line with paper baking cups. Sift the flours, sugar, baking powder, salt, and cinnamon into a mixing bowl. In a separate bowl, mix the beaten egg, melted butter, vanilla, and milk. Add the wet ingredients to the dry all at once and stir until just combined. Quickly stir in the strawberries and lemon zest. Pour into the prepared muffin cups, filling them two-thirds full. Sprinkle the topping evenly over the muffins. Bake for 20 to 25 minutes, or until a toothpick inserted into the center of a muffin comes out clean. **Makes 12 muffins.**

In the Kitchen: Strawberries

■ A 9-inch pie will hold 1½ quarts of strawberries.

■ 1 cup of sliced, fresh strawberries is the equivalent of one 10-ounce package of frozen, sweetened strawberries.

The Best Fruit Muffins

1 cup sugar

1 egg

1 cup sour cream

¼ cup vegetable oil

1¾ cups all-purpose flour

1 teaspoon baking soda

½ teaspoon salt

1 cup diced fruit, such as apples,
    peaches, or mangoes

Preheat the oven to 400°F. Grease a standard 12-cup muffin pan or line with paper baking cups. In a blender or food processor, combine the sugar, egg, sour cream, and oil. Pulse until the ingredients are well blended. In a separate bowl, combine the flour, baking soda, and salt. Add the dry ingredients to the blender and pulse just to combine. Remove the batter to a bowl and stir in the fruit. Spoon into the prepared muffin cups, filling them three-quarters full. Bake for 20 minutes, or until a toothpick inserted into the center of a muffin comes out clean. **Makes 12 muffins.**

Strawberry Crunch Muffins

(recipe at left)

Breakfast Muffins

These muffins are delightful served with cream cheese.

2 cups shredded apples

1⅓ cups sugar

1 cup chopped cranberries

1 cup shredded carrots

1 cup chopped walnuts

2½ cups all-purpose flour

1 tablespoon baking powder

2 teaspoons baking soda

½ teaspoon salt

2 teaspoons cinnamon

2 teaspoons coriander

2 large eggs, beaten

½ cup safflower oil

Preheat the oven to 375°F. Grease a standard 12-cup muffin pan or line with paper baking cups. In a large bowl, mix the apples and sugar. Add the cranberries, carrots, and nuts and stir well. In a separate bowl, combine the dry ingredients. Add these to the apple mixture. Stir in the eggs and oil, mixing gently but thoroughly. Divide the batter evenly among the prepared muffin cups. Bake for 25 to 30 minutes, or until a toothpick inserted into the center of a muffin comes out clean. **Makes 12 muffins.**

Squash and Blueberry Muffins

1½ cups all-purpose flour

1 tablespoon baking powder

1 teaspoon salt

½ cup sugar

1¼ cups yellow cornmeal

½ teaspoon freshly grated nutmeg

1 teaspoon cinnamon

¼ cup melted butter

2 eggs

¾ cup mashed squash or pumpkin

⅔ cup milk

1 cup blueberries

½ cup coarsely chopped sliced almonds

Preheat the oven to 425°F. Grease a standard 12-cup muffin pan or line with paper baking cups. In a large bowl, mix the flour, baking powder, salt, sugar, cornmeal, nutmeg, and cinnamon. Put the melted butter, eggs, squash, and milk into a medium bowl and stir to blend. Add these ingredients to the flour mixture and stir until blended. Do not overmix. Gently stir in the blueberries and almonds. Pour into the prepared muffin cups. Bake for 20 minutes, or until a toothpick inserted into the center of a muffin comes out clean. **Makes 12 muffins.**

BREADS

Mm-mm! Crustier Muffins!

■ You can make crusty muffins by using a preheated cast-iron muffin pan. Grease the cups with solid shortening and then preheat the pan by placing it in a cold oven and setting the dial to 400°F. When the oven reaches that temperature, remove the pan and fill with batter. Then set the oven temperature according to recipe directions before baking.

Fresh Raspberry Muffins

1½ cups all-purpose flour, sifted

½ cup sugar

2 teaspoons baking powder

¼ teaspoon salt

1 large egg

½ cup milk

¼ cup (½ stick) butter, melted and cooled

1 cup raspberries

Preheat the oven to 400°F. Grease a standard 12-cup muffin pan or line with paper baking cups. In a large mixing bowl, combine the flour, sugar, baking powder, and salt with a whisk or fork. In a separate bowl, whisk the egg and milk until well blended. Stir in the cooled melted butter. Make a well in the dry ingredients and pour in the egg mixture. Stir until the dry ingredients are moistened. The batter will be lumpy. Fold in the berries, being careful not to break them. Spoon the batter into the prepared muffin cups, filling them two-thirds full. Bake for 20 to 25 minutes, or until the tops are browned. Muffins baked directly in the pan will show signs of pulling away from the sides when they are done. **Makes 12 muffins.**

In the Garden: Raspberries

■ Raspberries will not ripen further once picked.

Save 'n' Store: Pumpkins and Winter Squashes

- Harvested pumpkins and winter squashes keep well at temperatures of 50° to 65°F. If you have a cool bedroom, stash them under the bed.

Spicy Pumpkin Muffins

These crunchy, spicy muffins complement a roast turkey.

2 cups all-purpose flour

2 teaspoons baking powder

3 tablespoons brown sugar

½ teaspoon salt

½ teaspoon cinnamon

¼ teaspoon ground cloves

¼ teaspoon ground ginger

2 eggs

¾ cup milk

¼ cup melted shortening

½ cup mashed pumpkin

½ cup Grape-Nuts breakfast cereal

Preheat the oven to 400°F. Grease a standard 12-cup muffin pan or line with paper baking cups. Sift together the flour, baking powder, brown sugar, salt, and spices. In a separate bowl, beat the eggs, then add the milk and shortening. Beat briefly to blend. Stir in the pumpkin and Grape-Nuts. Add this mixture to dry ingredients all at once, stirring only until the flour is moistened. Fill the prepared muffin cups two-thirds full and bake for 20 to 25 minutes, or until a toothpick inserted into the center of a muffin comes out clean. **Makes 12 muffins.**

How to Harvest: Pumpkin

- A pumpkin is ready to harvest when its color is rich and its rind is firm. Watch for the vines to begin to wither. Cut the stem, leaving about 4 inches on the pumpkin. Pick and store the entire crop before a hard frost.

BREADS

Sweet Potato and Pecan Muffins

1¾ cups sifted all-purpose flour

¾ teaspoon salt

½ cup sugar

2 teaspoons baking powder

1 teaspoon cinnamon

1 teaspoon nutmeg

2 eggs

3 tablespoons melted butter

¾ cup milk

1 cup mashed sweet potato

1 cup chopped pecans

2 teaspoons grated orange zest

Preheat the oven to 400°F. Grease a standard 12-cup muffin pan or line with paper baking cups. Into a large bowl, sift together the flour, salt, sugar, baking powder, cinnamon, and nutmeg. In a separate bowl, beat the eggs, then add the melted butter, milk, and sweet potato. Combine the wet ingredients with the dry ingredients in a few quick strokes, then fold in the nuts and orange zest. Pour into the prepared muffin cups and bake for 20 to 25 minutes, or until a toothpick inserted into the center of a muffin comes out clean. **Makes 12 muffins.**

Zucchini Oatmeal Muffins

2 eggs, beaten

1 medium zucchini, shredded

¼ cup vegetable oil

1 cup plain yogurt

2½ cups all-purpose flour

1 cup sugar

½ cup rolled oats (not instant)

1 tablespoon baking powder

1 teaspoon salt

1 teaspoon cinnamon

1 cup chopped pecans

Preheat the oven to 400°F. Grease a standard 12-cup muffin pan or line with paper baking cups. In a large bowl, mix together the eggs, zucchini, oil, and yogurt. Set aside. In a separate bowl, whisk together the flour, sugar, oats, baking powder, salt, and cinnamon. Add the dry ingredients to the zucchini mixture and stir just to moisten. Fold in the pecans. The batter will be lumpy. Spoon the batter into the prepared muffin cups and bake for 20 minutes, or until a toothpick inserted into the center of a muffin comes out clean. Do not overbake. **Makes 12 muffins.**

Granny's Blueberry Muffins

3 cups all-purpose flour

½ teaspoon salt

½ cup sugar

2½ teaspoons baking powder

2 eggs

1 cup milk

½ cup melted butter or vegetable oil

1½ cups blueberries

Preheat the oven to 400°F. Grease a standard 12-cup muffin pan or line with paper baking cups. In a mixing bowl, combine the flour, salt, sugar, and baking powder and stir. In a separate bowl, combine the eggs, milk, and butter and stir until smooth. Add the dry ingredients to the wet, stirring until well blended. Gently mix in the blueberries. Spoon the batter into the prepared muffin cups and bake for 20 to 25 minutes, or until a toothpick inserted into the center of a muffin comes out clean. **Makes 12 muffins.**

Cheese Herb Biscuits

2 cups all-purpose flour

2 teaspoons baking powder

1 teaspoon salt

5 tablespoons butter, cut into small
    pieces

¼ cup shredded cheddar cheese

1 tablespoon chopped fresh thyme or
    1 teaspoon dried thyme

1 teaspoon powdered sage

⅔ cup milk or light cream

Preheat the oven to 425°F. In a large bowl, sift together the flour, baking powder, and salt. Add the butter to the flour mixture. Cut in the butter until the mixture resembles cornmeal. Add the cheese, herbs, and milk and stir with a fork. Turn the dough onto a floured surface and roll out. Use a biscuit cutter to cut out each biscuit. Place the biscuits on an ungreased cookie sheet. Bake for 15 minutes, or until golden brown. **Makes about 20 biscuits.**

VARIATIONS:
Omit the thyme and sage for these versions:

CARAWAY CHEESE BISCUITS
Sprinkle caraway seeds over the biscuits before baking.

DILL AND CHIVE BISCUITS
Omit the cheese. Use ¾ cup of sour cream in place of the butter. Add 2 tablespoons each of finely chopped fresh chives and dill (or 2 teaspoons each of dried chives and dill).

BREADS

If thou tastest a crust of bread, thou tastest all the stars and all the heavens.

–Robert Browning, English poet (1812–89)

Lavender Scones

2 cups all-purpose flour

2½ teaspoons baking powder

¼ teaspoon baking soda

2 tablespoons sugar

½ teaspoon salt

1 teaspoon orange zest

2 teaspoons fresh lavender flowers or
**   1 teaspoon dried lavender**

¼ cup (½ stick) butter

1 egg, slightly beaten

⅔ cup buttermilk

Preheat the oven to 400°F. In a large bowl, combine the flour, baking powder, baking soda, sugar, salt, zest, and lavender. Cut in the butter until the mixture resembles cornmeal. Stir in the egg and buttermilk with a fork. Turn the dough onto a floured surface and briefly knead gently (don't overknead). Divide the dough in half and pat each portion into a ¾-inch-thick round. Cut each round into six wedges and place the wedges 1 inch apart on an ungreased cookie sheet. Bake for 20 minutes, or until golden. Serve warm or at room temperature. **Makes 12 scones.**

VARIATION:

Substitute four fresh rose-scented geranium leaves, finely minced, for the lavender flowers.

In the Kitchen: Lavender

- Lavender has a sweet flavor; some find its perfume pungent. English lavender is sweeter than other types. The flowers, buds, and leaves are used in jellies, cakes, cookies, sorbets, lemonades, and savory dishes such as stews.

Herbed Popovers

Serve warm with whipped butter.

1 cup all-purpose flour

½ teaspoon salt

1 cup milk

3 large eggs

2 tablespoons butter, melted and
    cooled

½ tablespoon chopped fresh thyme
    or ½ teaspoon dried thyme

½ tablespoon chopped fresh
    oregano or ½ teaspoon dried
    oregano

Position a rack in the center of the oven. Preheat the oven to 400°F. Grease 12 popover or custard cups. In a large mixing bowl, combine the flour and salt. Stir with a whisk or fork to blend thoroughly. Whisk the milk, eggs, and butter in a small bowl. Make a well in the center of the dry ingredients. Slowly pour the milk mixture into the well while beating the batter. Continue beating for 2½ to 3 minutes, or until the mixture is smooth and free of lumps. Fold in the herbs. Pour into the prepared cups, filling only halfway. Place the cups in the oven on the center rack and immediately lower the heat to 375°F. Bake for 35 to 45 minutes, or until puffed and browned. **Makes 12 popovers.**

Corn Bread With Pine Nuts and Rosemary

1¼ cups cornmeal

¾ cup all-purpose flour

2 teaspoons baking powder

½ teaspoon baking soda

½ teaspoon salt

2 large eggs

⅔ cup milk

⅔ cup buttermilk

2 tablespoons honey

½ cup corn (optional)

2 to 3 tablespoons warm, melted,
    unsalted butter or vegetable oil

½ cup pine nuts, lightly toasted

½ tablespoon chopped fresh rosemary or ½ teaspoon dried rosemary

Preheat the oven to 425°F. Grease a 9x9-inch baking dish. In a large bowl, combine the cornmeal, flour, baking powder, baking soda, and salt. In a separate bowl, whisk the eggs, milk, buttermilk, honey, and corn if using. Add the wet ingredients to the dry ingredients and stir just until moistened. Fold in the butter, pine nuts, and rosemary. Spread the batter evenly in the prepared baking dish. Bake for 20 to 25 minutes, or until a toothpick inserted into the center comes out clean. Serve warm. **Makes 10 to 12 servings.**

Herbed Popovers

(recipe at left)

How to Scald Milk

1. Use a double boiler or a heavy saucepan with a thick bottom. Pour the milk into the pan.
2. Turn the heat to medium low.
3. Stir occasionally, until you see tiny bubbles forming where the milk meets the edge of the pan and steam starts to rise. (Do not let the milk boil.)
4. Remove the pan from the heat.
5. Cool the milk to lukewarm (about 105° to 115°F) before using, unless the recipe calls for otherwise.

- Scalding was used in the past to kill bacteria that may have spoiled unpasteurized milk. With pasteurized milk, this is no longer a worry. Occasionally, scalded milk is used in recipes to help the performance of other ingredients and/or to increase their flavor. In breads, scalded milk provides warmth for the yeast, encouraging higher rising and a lighter texture.

Martha Washington's Potato Rolls

2 large potatoes, peeled and halved

1 teaspoon salt

2 tablespoons sugar

6 tablespoons (¾ stick) butter, melted, divided

¾ cup scalded milk

1 package (¼ ounce) active dry yeast

7 cups sifted all-purpose flour, divided

In a large saucepan of boiling water, cook the potatoes for about 30 minutes, or until they are tender. Grease a large bowl and set it aside. Grease a cookie sheet and set it aside. Drain the potatoes and save 1½ cups of the cooking water. Mash the hot potatoes. Add the salt, sugar, and 3 tablespoons of melted butter and beat well. Add the potato water and milk, stir to blend, and set aside to cool until lukewarm. Add the yeast and stir in 4 cups of flour, beating well. Add enough of the remaining flour to make a stiff dough. Knead the dough on a floured surface until it is smooth and elastic. Place in the greased bowl, turning to grease all sides. Brush the top with melted butter. Cover and let rise in a warm place until it has doubled in size (this may take several hours). Place on a floured surface and pat out to a thickness of about ½ inch; do not knead again. Pinch off small pieces and shape into small rolls. Place on the prepared cookie sheet and let rise until more than doubled in size. Bake at 400°F for 20 minutes, or until lightly browned. **Makes about 48 small rolls.**

BREADS

Sour Cream Cranberry Rye Bread

2 packages (¼ ounce each) active dry yeast

1 cup sour cream

1 tablespoon salt

½ cup molasses

¼ cup sugar

¼ teaspoon allspice

¼ teaspoon ground cloves

2 cups cranberries, finely chopped

3 cups rye flour

4½ to 5 cups all-purpose flour

Grease a large bowl and set aside. Grease two 9x5-inch loaf pans. In a large mixing bowl, dissolve the yeast in 1 cup of lukewarm (105° to 115°F) water. After the yeast proofs, add the sour cream, salt, molasses, sugar, allspice, cloves, cranberries, and rye flour. Beat on low speed to blend the ingredients, then beat at medium speed for 5 minutes. Add enough flour to make a soft dough. Turn onto a floured surface and knead for 5 minutes. Place in the greased bowl, turning to grease all sides. Cover with a towel and let rise until doubled in size. Punch down. Remove from the bowl, divide in half, and let rest, covered, for 10 minutes. Shape each half into a loaf and place in a prepared pan. Cover and let rise until doubled in size. Bake at 375°F for 35 to 40 minutes, until deep golden brown. If the loaves brown too quickly, cover them loosely with foil during the last 10 minutes of baking. Remove the loaves from the pans immediately and cool on wire racks. **Makes 2 loaves.**

Dill Bread

1 package (¼ ounce) active dry yeast

1 cup creamed cottage cheese

2 tablespoons honey

1 tablespoon chopped onion

1 tablespoon butter plus 1 tablespoon melted butter

⅓ cup chopped fresh dill or 3 tablespoons dried dill, dill seed, or a combination of both

1 teaspoon baking soda

1 egg, slightly beaten

2½ cups all-purpose flour

Grease a large bowl and set aside. Grease an 8x4-inch loaf pan. Combine the yeast with ¼ cup of lukewarm (105° to 115°F) water and set aside. In a saucepan over low heat, combine the cottage cheese, honey, onion, unmelted butter, dill, baking soda, and egg. When the butter is melted, remove the saucepan from the heat. Stir in the yeast mixture. Transfer the ingredients to a large mixing bowl and add the flour gradually to form a stiff dough. Turn onto a lightly floured surface and knead for 5 to 10 minutes. Place in the greased bowl, turn to grease all sides, cover, and let rise until doubled in size, about 1 hour. Punch down, shape into a loaf, and place in the prepared pan. Let rise until doubled again, about 40 minutes. Bake at 350°F for 40 to 50 minutes. Brush the top with the melted butter while the bread is still warm. **Makes 1 loaf.**

Mexican Hot-Pepper Bread

5 to 6 cups all-purpose flour, divided

1 cup finely crushed corn flakes

1 tablespoon sugar

1 tablespoon salt

2 packages (¼ ounce each) active dry yeast

1½ cups milk

⅓ cup vegetable oil

2 eggs

1½ cups shredded sharp cheddar cheese

½ cup finely chopped onion

¼ to ½ cup finely chopped hot chiles

2 tablespoons melted butter

Grease a large bowl and set aside. Grease two 1½-quart round casseroles and set aside. In a separate large bowl, stir together 2 cups of flour and the corn flakes, sugar, salt, and yeast. Set aside. In a small saucepan, combine the milk and vegetable oil. Place the pan over low heat until the liquids are warm (120°F). Gradually add the liquid to the flour mixture and beat until well combined. Add the eggs and stir in the cheese, onion, and peppers. Beat in enough remaining flour to make a stiff dough. On a floured surface, knead for about 5 minutes, or until smooth and elastic. Place in the greased bowl, turning to grease all sides. Cover lightly and let rise in a warm place until doubled in size (about 1 hour). Punch down. Remove from the bowl and divide the dough in half. Put each portion into a prepared casserole. Cover and let rise in a warm place until doubled again. Bake at 350°F for 25 to 35 minutes, or until the bread sounds hollow when tapped. To prevent overbrowning, cover loosely with foil during the last few minutes of cooking. Remove from the casseroles and cool on wire racks. Brush with the melted butter. **Makes 2 loaves.**

Chili vs. Chile

- "Chili" is a prepared dish usually made with "chili powder."

- A "chile" is a hot pepper that is red or green, fresh or dried.

CHAPTER 13

Desserts

PUDDINGS:

Strawberry Mousse 263

Minted Fruit Mold 265

Summer Pudding. 266

Blueberry Slog 267

Apple Pudding 268

FRUIT DESSERTS:

Grilled Fresh Fruit Kabobs. 269

Cranberry Pears. 271

PIECRUSTS:

Mom's Flaky Pastry 272

Graham Cracker Crust 273

Gingersnap Crust 273

PIES:

French Strawberry Pie. 274

Rhubarb Pie 274

Cherry Cheese Pie 275

Grape Pie 275

Ginger Peach Pie 276

Praline Peach Pie. 276

(continued on next page)

Desserts *(continued)*

Pear Custard Pie 277

Pumpkin Chiffon Pie 277

Apple Pie With Cider Pecan Crust. 278

Apple Cranberry Pie 280

Apple Squash Pie. 280

The Best Baking and Cooking Apples in

    North America 281

CHEESECAKES:

Cranberry-Crowned Pumpkin

    Cheesecake. 282

Fresh Rhubarb Cheesecake 283

Apple Spiced Cheesecake 284

COOKIES:

Cranberry Cookies. 285

Pumpkin Cookies. 285

Caraway Applesauce Cookies 286

Cheesy Apple Squares. 286

Ten Secrets to Making Great Cookies 287

CAKES:

Raspberry Honey Cake With Raspberry

    Sauce 288

Fresh Tomato Cake With Cream Cheese

    Frosting. 290

Hawaiian Carrot Cake With Coconut

    Frosting. 291

Chocolate Berry Torte 292

Vegetables are a must on a diet. I suggest carrot cake,
zucchini bread, and pumpkin pie.

–Garfield, cartoon character created by Jim Davis,
American cartoonist (b. 1945)

Puddings

Strawberry Mousse

Maximum flavor with minimum calories.

2 tablespoons unflavored gelatin

3 cups strawberries

1 tablespoon plus 2 teaspoons sugar

1½ cups plain yogurt

1 medium banana, peeled

¼ teaspoon cinnamon

Lightly oil a 4-cup mold. In a small bowl, combine the gelatin with 2 tablespoons of water and soften for 5 minutes. Halve a few more than half of the strawberries, then sprinkle the cut sides with 1 tablespoon of sugar and set aside. In a blender or food processor, purée the yogurt, remaining strawberries, banana, cinnamon, and 2 teaspoons of sugar. In a small saucepan, bring ¼ cup of water to a boil. Add the gelatin, stir, and heat until the gelatin is completely dissolved. In a separate saucepan over medium heat, warm the strawberry purée until it is hot to the touch but not boiling. Add the gelatin mixture and stir to combine. Place half of the sweetened strawberries in the mold, cut side up. Pour half of the yogurt mixture over the berries. Add the remaining strawberries and top with the remaining yogurt mixture. Refrigerate for at least 4 hours, or overnight. Unmold before serving. **Makes 8 servings.**

DESSERTS

Minted Fruit Mold
(recipe at right)

Minted Fruit Mold

Use your favorite fruit in season. Refrigerated, the fruit mold will keep well for a day.

2 tablespoons unflavored gelatin

1 cup orange juice

1 teaspoon fresh lemon juice

⅛ teaspoon ground ginger

1 tablespoon sugar

¾ teaspoon chopped fresh mint or
   ¼ teaspoon dried mint

1 cup ginger ale

2 cups fresh fruit (such as berries, melon, or peaches, singly or in combination), cut into bite-size pieces*

*If using apples, peaches, or pears, cut them just before using so that they don't turn brown.

Lightly oil a 4-cup mold or small individual molds. In the top of a double boiler, sprinkle the gelatin over the orange juice, then set aside for 5 minutes. Add the lemon juice, ginger, sugar, and mint and stir to blend. Place the top saucepan over simmering water in the bottom of the double boiler and cook until the gelatin is dissolved. Remove from the heat, add the ginger ale, and stir. (Strain the mixture to eliminate the mint leaves, if desired.) Pour a thin coating of the mixture into the mold. Arrange the best-looking pieces of fruit decoratively in the thin coat of gelatin. (The fruit will appear on top when the dish is unmolded.) By tablespoonfuls, coat each piece of fruit with a portion of the gelatin mixture. Refrigerate for 15 minutes, or until the gelatin sets. Mix the remaining fruit into the remaining gelatin mixture and pour the combination into the mold. Refrigerate for 3 hours, or until the gelatin is firm. Unmold before serving. **Makes 4 to 6 servings.**

In the Garden: Mint

■ **Pick mint leaves and sprigs in the morning, after any dew dries. Their oils are strongest at this time.**

Summer Pudding

This classic English dessert can be made with firm leftover or day-old bread. For an authentic version, include currants.

PUDDING:

2 quarts mixed fruit (strawberries, blueberries, raspberries, blackberries, or currants)

1 cup sugar

8 to 10 slices white bread, crusts removed

SAUCE:

1 tablespoon all-purpose flour

¼ cup sugar

½ teaspoon salt

3 egg yolks

1 cup milk

1 teaspoon vanilla extract

½ cup heavy cream

For pudding: In a large saucepan, combine the fruit and sugar, then crush gently with a masher. Over medium heat, bring the mixture to a boil and cook, stirring for 5 minutes, or until the fruit softens. Remove the saucepan from the heat and cool slightly. Line a 2-quart mold with plastic wrap, letting the edges of the wrap hang over the rim of the mold. Cover the bottom and sides of the mold with some of the bread slices, leaving no spaces in between. Spoon the warm fruit mixture over the bread. (The bread will absorb the juice and lose its shape.) Layer the remaining bread slices on the fruit. Put a plate that fits just inside the rim of the mold on top and weight it (a canned good works well). Refrigerate for at least 10 hours, or overnight.

For sauce: In the top saucepan of a double boiler, combine the flour, sugar, and salt. Add the egg yolks and milk and stir to blend. Place the pan over simmering water and whisk constantly, until the sauce becomes thick and smooth (do not boil). Remove the pan from the heat and set aside to cool slightly. Add the vanilla and stir to incorporate. Refrigerate until ready to serve.

Unmold the pudding and cut into slices. In a chilled bowl, whip the heavy cream and fold it gently into the sauce. Serve the sauce with the pudding. **Makes 6 to 8 servings.**

DESSERTS

Pastries are believed to be better when they come from a pink box or are served on a pink plate.

Blueberry Slog

An American cousin of English summer pudding, this version uses only one fruit. Try this when you don't have the time or energy to make a pie (or a summer pudding).

3½ cups blueberries

1 cup plus 1 teaspoon sugar

1 cinnamon stick

1 slice (2 inches long) lemon peel

1 loaf slightly stale homemade or old-fashioned white bread, sliced

1 pint heavy cream

In a large saucepan, combine the berries with 1 cup of the sugar, the cinnamon stick, and lemon peel. Add water to barely cover and simmer over low heat for 15 minutes, or until the berries' skins burst and the mixture turns syrupy. Remove the saucepan from the heat. Discard the cinnamon stick and lemon peel. Cover the bottom of a 2-quart mold with a layer of bread cut to fit the dish. Spoon some berries and liquid on the bread until it is soaked and purple. Add another layer of bread, soak with berries, and repeat, until the dish is filled. Cover with plastic wrap, place a dish that fits just inside the rim of the mold on top, and weight it (a canned good works well). Refrigerate for 12 to 18 hours. In a large, chilled bowl, beat the heavy cream until foamy. Sprinkle with 1 teaspoon of sugar and beat into soft peaks. Unmold the pudding and cover with the cream. **Makes 6 to 8 servings.**

Apple Pudding

Delicious with a scoop of vanilla ice cream!

9 tablespoons butter, divided

8 medium apples, peeled, cored, and sliced

¾ cup plum jam

2 tablespoons rum or ½ teaspoon rum extract

½ cup plus 1 tablespoon sugar

1 teaspoon all-purpose flour

½ teaspoon cinnamon

3 eggs, separated

1 cup soft bread crumbs

⅛ teaspoon salt

Preheat the oven to 325°F. Grease a 13x9-inch glass baking dish. In a large saucepan over medium heat, melt 5 tablespoons of butter. Add the apple slices and sauté for 5 minutes, or until just soft. Add the plum jam and rum and stir. Spread the mixture in the baking dish. Put the remaining butter and ½ cup of sugar into a mixing bowl and mix until creamy. Add the flour, cinnamon, egg yolks, and bread crumbs, mix to incorporate, then set aside. In a separate bowl, beat the egg whites until foamy. Sprinkle with the salt and 1 tablespoon of sugar, while beating constantly. Continue beating until stiff. Fold the egg whites into the bread crumb mixture, then spread over the apple slices. Bake for 20 to 25 minutes. **Makes 10 servings.**

Gardening With Fruit Trees

When choosing a fruit tree, consider your climate, your available space, your time, and your use of the tree.

- **Dwarf types take up the least space and are low-maintenance, but fruit production is minimal.**

- **Semidwarfs can be very productive and are a manageable size.**

- **Standards grow to full size, provide good yields, and can act as landscape accents. However, they require the most maintenance.**

After choosing a type of fruit tree, consult your local nursery or state's cooperative extension for local varieties and plant care. Ask about the need for more than one variety for successful pollination. If space allows, choose varieties that ripen at different times for a longer harvest.

Plant trees in the fall or spring. Be prepared to wait 3 years for fruit. Depending on your climate, some trees to consider are . . .

Apple	**Cherry**	**Grapefruit**	**Lime**	**Peach**
Apricot	**Crab apple**	**Lemon**	**Orange**	**Pear**

DESSERTS

Fruit Desserts

Grilled Fresh Fruit Kabobs

You'll need 12 wooden skewers about 15 inches long. Before using, soak them in water for 3 to 4 hours to prevent burning.

SAUCE:

2 tablespoons fresh orange juice

1 teaspoon cornstarch

½ cup dry white wine

½ cup honey

2 tablespoons butter

¼ teaspoon dry mustard

¼ teaspoon ground ginger

1 teaspoon coarsely cracked black pepper

KABOBS:

3 firm, ripe peaches, peeled, pitted, and quartered

3 firm, ripe pears, peeled, cored, and quartered

12 large, firm strawberries, hulled

1 large ripe, firm papaya, peeled, seeded, and cut into eighths

For sauce: In a medium saucepan over medium heat, combine the orange juice and cornstarch. Stir in the remaining ingredients and bring to a boil. Lower the heat, stir constantly, and cook for 6 to 8 minutes, or until the mixture is slightly thickened. Set it aside to cool.

For kabobs: Light the grill or preheat the broiler. Arrange the fruit on a serving plate and brush with the sauce. Warm the remaining sauce on the grill or stovetop. Skewer the fruit, alternating kinds, and brush again with the sauce.

Grill on high heat for about 10 minutes, turning often and brushing with the sauce. Eat as is or spoon over ice cream. **Makes 6 servings.**

In the Kitchen: Papaya

■ To ripen a green papaya, place it in a paper bag with an apple. The ethylene gas in the apple will speed the process and turn the fruit yellow.

DESSERTS

Cranberry Pears
(recipe at right)

Cranberry Pears

2½ cups cranberries

1 cup sugar

⅓ cup plus 1 tablespoon almond-flavor
    liqueur (such as Amaretto)

6 firm, ripe pears, stems attached

½ cup heavy cream

6 sprigs fresh mint, for garnish

toasted blanched slivered almonds,
    for garnish

In a large saucepan, bring the cranberries and 1½ cups of water to a boil. Simmer for 15 minutes, stirring occasionally. In a blender or food processor, purée the mixture, in batches. Return it to the saucepan, add the sugar and ⅓ cup of liqueur, then stir. Peel the pears carefully, leaving the stem attached. Cut a small slice from the bottom of each pear so that it can stand upright. Place the pears in the cranberry-liqueur mixture, bring to a simmer, then cook for 15 minutes. Transfer the pears to a bowl and set them aside. Bring the cranberry-liqueur mixture to a boil, then reduce the heat and simmer for 10 to 15 minutes, or until thickened. Pour the cranberry-liqueur syrup over the pears, cover, and refrigerate. Turn the pears occasionally. To serve, remove the pears from the syrup and blot lightly. Spoon the sauce into serving dishes and place a pear on each one. In a large, chilled bowl, whip the cream with 1 tablespoon of liqueur. Serve with the pears. Garnish pears with mint sprigs and a sprinkling of toasted almonds. **Makes 6 servings.**

Piecrusts

Mom's Flaky Pastry

Use for any type of pie, sweet or savory.

2 cups all-purpose flour
½ teaspoon salt
1 cup (2 sticks) vegetable shortening
¼ cup ice water, approximately, divided

Note: This piecrust may be frozen unbaked for up to 6 months.

In a bowl, mix together the flour and salt. Using two knives or a pastry blender, cut the shortening into the flour until the mixture resembles coarse meal. Sprinkle water on the dough, a tablespoon at a time, mixing quickly with a fork after each. Add only enough water for the dough to hold together and be formed into a ball. Handling the dough as little as possible, divide it into two equal portions and form into two smooth balls. To use later, wrap separately in plastic and refrigerate or freeze. To use now, roll each portion out onto a lightly floured surface until it forms a circle about ⅛-inch thick and 2 inches wider than a 9-inch pie plate. **Makes two 9-inch piecrusts.**

Unless otherwise directed, follow these instructions to complete the pie . . .

For a single-crust pie: Line the pie plate with the dough, pressing it firmly against the sides. Trim the dough so that 1 inch extends beyond the rim; turn the excess under along the rim of the plate. Use a fork or your fingers to press the edges every inch or so to make a fluted design. Fill as desired.

For a double-crust pie: Line the pie plate with the bottom piecrust, pressing it firmly against the sides. Trim the dough so that ½ inch extends beyond the rim. Fill as desired. Roll out the top piecrust and lay it over the pie filling. Trim the overhang to 1 inch beyond the rim. Fold the edge of the top crust under the bottom crust and press to seal the crusts together. Use a fork or your fingers to pinch the dough along the rim every inch or so to make a fluted design. Pierce holes in the top crust with a fork to allow steam to escape.

For a double-crust pie with a lattice top: Line the pie plate with the bottom piecrust, pressing it firmly against the sides; trim so that ½ inch extends beyond the rim. Fill as desired. Roll out the top piecrust and then cut it into ½- to ¾-inch-wide strips. Lay the strips lattice-like over the pie filling. Trim the ends of the strips to slightly shorter than the edge of the bottom crust; press the strips' ends to the bottom crust. Fold the overhanging edge of the bottom crust over the strip ends until the bottom crust's edge meets the plate's rim. To seal, flute the edges of the pie, using a fork or your fingers.

Graham Cracker Crust

Use this piecrust for any cream, chiffon, or cheese pie.

2 cups graham cracker crumbs

2 to 4 tablespoons sugar, to taste

¼ teaspoon cinnamon, nutmeg, or ground ginger, or ½ teaspoon grated lemon or orange zest (optional)

⅓ cup unsalted butter, melted

Preheat the oven to 375°F. Butter the bottom only of a 9-inch pie plate. In a mixing bowl, combine the crumbs and sugar (and optional flavoring, if desired). Pour the melted butter over the crumb mixture and work with your fingers to coat until the crumbs begin to hold together. Distribute the graham cracker mixture into the prepared plate and gently and evenly press the mixture over the bottom and up the sides of the plate. Neatly finish off the rim. Bake for 8 minutes, or until the edge is just light brown. Cool before filling. **Makes one 9-inch piecrust.**

Note: This piecrust may be frozen unbaked or used unbaked if it is thoroughly chilled before filling.

Gingersnap Crust

2 cups gingersnap crumbs

3 tablespoons butter, melted

1 egg white

Preheat the oven to 350°F. In a large bowl, combine the gingersnap crumbs, melted butter, and egg white and mix with a fork. Set the bowl aside for 5 minutes. Distribute the mixture into a 9-inch pie plate and, using your fingers, gently and evenly press the mixture over the bottom and up the sides of the plate. Bake for 5 minutes, then check the crust and smooth the edges up if sagging. Bake for 5 minutes more. **Makes one 9-inch piecrust.**

Pies

French Strawberry Pie

This elegant and light dessert tastes best on the day that it is made. Whole strawberries look the best, but sliced berries are easier to cut and eat.

¾ package (6 ounces) cream cheese, softened
1 teaspoon vanilla extract
¾ cup heavy cream, at room temperature
½ cup sugar
1 baked 9-inch graham cracker crust (see recipe, page 273)
2 cups strawberries, hulled
4 square (4 ounces total) bittersweet chocolate, melted

In a small bowl, beat the cream cheese and vanilla until blended and light. Set aside. In a separate chilled bowl, whip the cream until it doubles in volume. Continue beating on high speed while adding the sugar a little at a time. Add the cream cheese mixture and beat briefly, or just until combined. Pour the mixture into the piecrust and cover with the berries. Drizzle with the melted chocolate. Refrigerate, uncovered, for at least 4 hours before serving. **Makes 6 to 8 servings.**

Rhubarb Pie

Tart, pink rhubarb stalks are sure signs of spring.

1 unbaked 9-inch double piecrust (see recipe, page 272)
5 cups diced rhubarb
⅓ cup all-purpose flour
1 cup sugar (for young, tender stalks; older stalks may require more)
1 teaspoon orange juice
2 tablespoons unsalted butter, cut into bits
1 tablespoon grated orange zest

Preheat the oven to 450°F. Place the bottom piecrust in a 9-inch pie plate; trim the dough so that ½ inch extends beyond the rim. In a large bowl, combine the rhubarb, flour, sugar, orange juice, butter, and orange zest and toss to mix. Transfer the rhubarb mixture to the pie plate. Finish with a lattice top *(see tip, page 272)*. Bake for 10 minutes at 450°F, then lower the temperature to 350°F and bake for 35 minutes, or until the pie bubbles and the pastry is golden. **Makes 6 to 8 servings.**

DESSERTS

Cherry Cheese Pie

A fresh cherry pie is a labor of love but worth every bite.

1 package (8 ounces) cream cheese, softened

¼ cup sour cream

½ teaspoon grated lemon zest

1 baked 9-inch graham cracker crust (see recipe, page 273)

2 cups Bing cherries, pitted

½ cup sugar

2 tablespoons fresh lemon juice

3 tablespoons cornstarch

In a large bowl, combine the cream cheese, sour cream, and lemon zest and beat to blend. Pour the mixture into the piecrust, cover with wax paper, and refrigerate. In a heavy saucepan over medium heat, combine the cherries, sugar, lemon juice, and 1 cup of water and bring to a boil. Remove the saucepan from the heat, drain and reserve the liquid, and set the cherries aside. Measure 1¼ cups of the cherry liquid into a separate saucepan. Sprinkle the liquid with the cornstarch, whisk to blend, and bring to a boil over medium heat, whisking constantly until the liquid has thickened. Remove the saucepan from the heat. Add the drained cherries, stir to blend, and set aside to cool. Pour the cherry mixture over the chilled cheese filling. Return the pie to the refrigerator for 1 hour, or until the pie is set. **Makes 6 to 8 servings.**

In the Kitchen: Lemon Juice

■ If you need just a few drops of lemon juice, poke a lemon with a toothpick and squeeze. Store the lemon in the refrigerator. It will keep longer than if you had cut it open.

Grape Pie

1 unbaked 9-inch double piecrust (see recipe, page 272)

6 cups seedless Concord grapes

6 tablespoons honey

3 tablespoons tapioca

1 tablespoon butter, cut into bits

1 teaspoon fresh lemon juice

pinch of salt

Preheat the oven to 375° F. Place the bottom piecrust in a 9-inch pie plate; trim the dough so that ½ inch extends beyond the rim. In a mixing bowl, stir together the remaining ingredients. Pour the mixture into the piecrust, then add the piecrust top. Pierce the top crust with a fork several times. Bake for 40 minutes, or until golden brown. Cool for at least 10 minutes before serving. **Makes 6 to 8 servings.**

DESSERTS

Ginger Peach Pie

This pie looks and tastes like something that's been fussed over. (It's actually easy to make.)

3 tablespoons all-purpose flour

1½ cups half-and-half, divided

⅓ cup sugar

1 egg yolk

3 tablespoons finely chopped candied ginger or 1 tablespoon grated fresh ginger

1 teaspoon vanilla extract

1 baked 9-inch gingersnap crust
(see recipe, page 273)

4 medium peaches, peeled, pitted, and sliced

⅓ cup seedless raspberry jam or jelly

In a heavy saucepan, combine the flour and ¼ cup of the half-and-half and whisk until smooth. Place the saucepan over medium-low heat and add the remaining half-and-half in a thin stream, whisking constantly. Add the sugar and continue to cook, whisking constantly, until the mixture is as thick as pudding (do not boil). In a small bowl, combine the egg yolk and 1 to 2 tablespoons of the heated sauce. Whisk to combine, then add to the saucepan. Cook for a few more minutes, whisking steadily to incorporate (do not boil). Remove the saucepan from the heat, add the ginger and vanilla, and stir. Set the ingredients aside to cool for 10 minutes. Pour the mixture into the piecrust and chill until the custard is set. Arrange the sliced peaches on the custard. In a small saucepan over medium-low heat, melt the jam, then brush it over the peaches. Refrigerate for 2 to 3 hours. **Makes 6 to 8 servings.**

Praline Peach Pie

Top with a scoop of peach ice cream, because you can never have too much of a good thing.

1 unbaked 9-inch single piecrust
(see recipe, page 272)

3 eggs

½ cup heavy cream

1 cup dark corn syrup

1 teaspoon vanilla extract

¾ cup sugar

3 tablespoons all-purpose flour

1½ cups chopped peaches

1 cup chopped pecans

Preheat the oven to 375°F. Place the piecrust in a 9-inch pie plate; finish the edges *(see tip, page 272)*. In a large bowl, combine the eggs, heavy cream, and corn syrup and beat to blend. Add the vanilla, sugar, and flour and beat until smooth. Gently fold in the peaches and pecans, then pour into the piecrust. Bake for 10 minutes at 375°F, then lower the temperature to 325°F and bake for 40 minutes, or until the pie is set. **Makes 6 to 8 servings.**

DESSERTS

Pear Custard Pie

More like a tart, this pie should be eaten soon after baking because pears often darken as they sit.

1 unbaked 9-inch single piecrust
   (see recipe, page 272)
4 cups sliced pears
1 tablespoon fresh lemon juice
½ teaspoon nutmeg
½ teaspoon grated orange zest
¼ cup (½ stick) unsalted butter, melted
½ cup brown sugar
½ cup granulated sugar
½ cup all-purpose flour
3 eggs
confectioners' sugar, for sprinkling

Preheat the oven to 400°F. Place the piecrust in a 9-inch pie plate; finish the edges *(see tip, page 272)*. In a large bowl, mix the pear slices with the lemon juice, nutmeg, and orange zest. Arrange the fruit in the piecrust. In a large bowl, combine the butter, brown and granulated sugars, flour, and eggs and beat or whisk to blend. Pour the custard on top of the pears. Bake for 10 minutes at 400°F, then lower the temperature to 350°F and bake for 30 minutes, or until the custard is set. Sprinkle the top with confectioners' sugar while still warm. Serve immediately. **Makes 6 to 8 servings.**

Pumpkin Chiffon Pie

Lighter than the traditional pumpkin pie, this is a perfect finish to a holiday meal.

1 envelope unflavored gelatin
2 cups mashed or canned pumpkin
¾ cup granulated sugar, divided
4 egg yolks, lightly beaten
1 cup heavy cream, divided
½ teaspoon ground ginger
½ teaspoon cinnamon
¼ teaspoon nutmeg
3 egg whites
1 baked 9-inch gingersnap crust
   (see recipe, page 273)
1 teaspoon confectioners' sugar

Dissolve the gelatin in 1 tablespoon of water. In a saucepan, combine the pumpkin and ½ cup of granulated sugar. Add the softened gelatin and stir. Add the egg yolks, ½ cup of heavy cream, and spices and whisk to blend. Cook over medium heat until the mixture thickens, stirring frequently. Remove the saucepan from the heat and set it aside to cool slightly. In a large bowl, beat the egg whites until foamy, then sprinkle with ¼ cup of granulated sugar, beating constantly until stiff. Fold the whites into the pumpkin mixture. Pour the filling into the prepared crust and refrigerate until set. In a large, chilled bowl, beat the remaining ½ cup of heavy cream until foamy. Sprinkle with the confectioners' sugar, beating constantly, until soft peaks form. Serve with the pie, or put some of the whipped cream into a pastry bag fitted with a decorative tip and pipe rosettes on the pie. Refrigerate until ready to serve. **Makes 6 to 8 servings.**

DESSERTS

Apple Pie With Cider Pecan Crust

CRUST:

2 cups all-purpose flour

1 teaspoon salt

⅔ cup shortening

½ cup finely crushed pecans

¼ cup cold cider

FILLING:

7 firm, juicy, tart apples, peeled, cored, and sliced

½ teaspoon nutmeg

½ teaspoon cinnamon

¼ cup sugar

½ cup raisins

½ cup diced candied fruit

1 tablespoon fresh lemon juice

1 tablespoon cold butter, cut into bits

TOPPING:

1 egg yolk

cinnamon, to taste

sugar, to taste

For crust: In a large bowl, combine the flour and salt. Add the shortening and cut it in until the dough resembles giant peas. Add the pecans and mix to blend. Sprinkle cider on the dough a drop at a time and mix gently until the dough holds together. Divide the dough into two balls. Roll out each ball on a lightly floured surface until it forms a circle about ⅛-inch thick and 2 inches wider than a 9-inch pie plate. Place the bottom piecrust in the pie plate; trim the dough so that ½ inch extends beyond the rim.

For filling: Preheat the oven to 425°F. In a large bowl, combine the apples with the spices, sugar, raisins, candied fruit, and lemon juice and toss gently to coat. Spoon the filling into the piecrust. Distribute the butter on the filling, then add the piecrust top. Pierce the top crust with a fork several times.

For topping: In a small bowl, whisk the egg yolk, then brush it on the piecrust. In a small bowl or jar with a lid, combine the cinnamon and sugar, mix or shake, then sprinkle it on the pie.

Bake for 50 to 60 minutes, or until golden. **Makes 6 to 8 servings.**

Save 'n' Store: Pecans

■ Pecans have a high oil content and may spoil if not stored properly. Keep them in an airtight container to prevent them from absorbing odors or other flavors. Store them in the refrigerator for up to 9 months or in the freezer for 1½ to 2 years.

DESSERTS

Apple Pie With Cider Pecan Crust

(recipe at left)

An apple pie without some cheese
Is like a kiss without a squeeze.

Apple Cranberry Pie

A favorite for Thanksgiving.

- 1 unbaked 9-inch double piecrust
    (*see recipe, page 272*)
- 3 cups peeled, cored, and sliced tart
    cooking apples
- 2 cups whole cranberries
- 1 teaspoon grated lemon zest
- 2 tablespoons orange juice
- ⅔ cup sugar, or to taste
- 3 tablespoons all-purpose flour
- ¼ teaspoon cinnamon
- ¼ teaspoon nutmeg
- 2 tablespoons unsalted butter, melted

Preheat the oven to 450°F. Place the bottom piecrust in a 9-inch pie plate; trim the dough so that ½ inch extends beyond the rim. In a large bowl, combine the remaining ingredients and toss to coat. Pour the filling into the piecrust. Finish with a lattice top (*see tip, page 272*). Bake for 15 minutes at 450°F, then lower the temperature to 350°F and bake for 30 minutes, or until golden. **Makes 6 to 8 servings.**

In the Kitchen: Brown Sugar

■ To soften brown sugar that has turned hard, put it into an airtight container with a piece of fresh bread or slice of apple. Seal and leave for a day.

Apple Squash Pie

If preferred, substitute sweet potatoes for squash.

- 1 unbaked 9-inch double piecrust
    (*see recipe, page 272*)
- 2 cups peeled, cored, and sliced tart
    cooking apples
- 2 cups peeled and sliced winter squash
- ½ cup honey
- ¼ cup brown sugar
- 3 tablespoons unsalted butter, melted
- ¼ cup all-purpose flour
- 1 teaspoon cinnamon
- 1 teaspoon nutmeg

Preheat the oven to 450°F. Place the bottom piecrust in a 9-inch pie plate; trim the dough so that ½ inch extends beyond the rim. In a large bowl, combine the remaining ingredients and toss to coat. Pour the filling into the piecrust, then add the piecrust top. Pierce the top crust with a fork several times. Bake for 15 minutes at 450°F, then lower the temperature to 350°F and bake for 40 minutes, or until golden. **Makes 6 to 8 servings.**

DESSERTS

The Best Baking and Cooking Apples in North America

■ Almost any apple can be enjoyed when eaten fresh. When faced with how to use apples in the kitchen, consider these recommendations:

VARIETY	APPEARANCE	FLAVOR CHARACTERISTICS	BEST USES
'Braeburn'	bright color, firm	sweet-tart, aromatic, crisp	pie, salad, sauce
'Cortland'	larger than 'McIntosh'	tart, crisp	pie, salad, sauce
'Fuji'	red skin, firm	sweet, juicy	baking
'Gala'	yellow-orange skin with red striping (resembles a peach)	mild, sweet, juicy, crisp	cider, dried
'Granny Smith'	green skin	tart, moderately sweet, crisp	baking
'Jonagold'	yellow top, red bottom	tangy-sweet	pie, sauce
'Jonathan'	bright-red on yellow	mild to tart, juicy, crisp	sauce
'McIntosh'	red skin	spicy, sweet, aromatic, juicy	sauce
'Newtown Pippin'	greenish-yellow skin	sweet-tart, crisp	cider, pie, sauce
'Rhode Island Greening'	grass-green skin, tending toward yellow/orange	very tart	pie
'Rome Beauty'	thick skin	mildly tart, crisp	baking, cider
'Winesap'	sturdy, red skin	sweet-sour, winey, very juicy, aromatic	cider, pie, sauce

How Much Is Enough?

■ 1 pound of apples = 2 large, 3 medium, or 4 to 5 small apples = 3 cups peeled, cored, and sliced apples

Cheesecakes

Cranberry-Crowned Pumpkin Cheesecake

To prevent cheesecake from cracking while baking, place a pan of water in the oven.

CRUST:

2 cups gingersnap crumbs

¼ cup (½ stick) butter, softened

CAKE:

4 packages (8 ounces each) cream cheese, softened

1¼ cups light-brown sugar

5 large eggs

¼ cup cornstarch

1 teaspoon ground ginger

¼ teaspoon allspice

2 teaspoons cinnamon

2 cups mashed or canned pumpkin

TOPPING:

2 cups cranberries

¾ cup sugar

1 cup cranberry juice, divided

½ cup coarsely chopped walnuts

1 envelope unflavored gelatin

whipped cream, for garnish

For crust: In a bowl, mix the crumbs and butter to blend. Using your fingers, press the crumb mixture evenly into the bottom and 1 inch up the sides of a 9- or 10-inch springform pan.

For cake: Preheat the oven to 325°F. In a large bowl, beat the cream cheese until it is light and fluffy. Add the brown sugar gradually, beating constantly, until blended. Add the eggs, one at a time, beating after each. Sift in the cornstarch, followed by the spices. Stir to blend after each. Add the pumpkin and beat to blend. Pour the mixture over the prepared crust. Bake in the center of the oven for 1½ hours, or until the cake begins to pull away from the sides of the pan. Cool completely, then refrigerate for at least 1 hour before adding the topping.

For topping: In a large saucepan over high heat, combine the cranberries, sugar, and ¾ cup of cranberry juice and cook to boiling, stirring occasionally. Reduce the heat to medium. Cook for 5 minutes, or until the berries' skins burst, stirring occasionally. Remove from the heat. Add the walnuts and stir. In a small bowl, sprinkle the gelatin over the remaining ¼ cup of cranberry juice and let stand for 1 minute to soften slightly. Stir the gelatin mixture into cranberry nut mixture. Cook over medium heat until the gelatin is dissolved, stirring frequently. Cover and refrigerate until a teaspoon of the mixture mounds slightly when dropped. Spoon the topping over the cheesecake.

Cover and refrigerate until set, for at least 45 minutes. Remove the sides of the pan. Garnish the cake with dollops or rosettes of whipped cream. **Makes 12 servings.**

DESSERTS

Fresh Rhubarb Cheesecake

CRUST:

⅓ cup butter, softened

½ cup chopped walnuts

1¼ cups all-purpose flour

½ cup brown sugar

1 teaspoon vanilla extract

FILLING:

2 packages (8 ounces each) plus
    1 package (3 ounces) cream
    cheese, softened

3 eggs

¾ cup sugar

2 teaspoons vanilla extract

TOPPING:

3 cups finely chopped rhubarb

⅔ cup sliced strawberries

½ teaspoon cinnamon

¾ cup sugar

1 tablespoon cornstarch

For crust: Preheat the oven to 375°F. Grease a 13x9-inch baking pan. In a large bowl, combine all of the crust ingredients, stirring to blend. Using your fingers, press the mixture into the bottom of the prepared pan. Bake for 15 minutes. Remove from the oven and set the crust aside.

For filling: In a large bowl, combine all of the filling ingredients and beat until smooth. Pour the filling over the crust. Bake for 15 to 20 minutes.

For topping: In a large saucepan, combine the rhubarb, strawberries, cinnamon, sugar, and ¼ cup of water and stir to coat. In a small bowl, combine the cornstarch with 2 tablespoons of water and stir. Add the dissolved cornstarch to the saucepan and cook over medium heat until the rhubarb is tender. Cool. Spread the fruit mixture over the cheesecake. Refrigerate until ready to serve. **Makes 12 servings.**

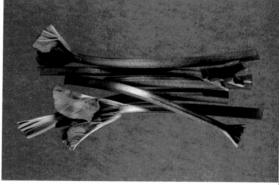

Save 'n' Store: Rhubarb

■ To freeze rhubarb, choose firm, tender, well-colored stalks. Wash, trim, and cut into 1- to 2-inch pieces. Blanch the rhubarb pieces in boiling water for 1 minute. Cool promptly in cold water to retain color and flavor. Drain well, then pack in a container or plastic freezer bag before freezing.

In the Kitchen: Cut Fruit

▪ Fresh fruit, such as apples, can quickly turn brown as you peel it and cut it into sections. One way to prevent this is to fill a large bowl with 2 quarts of cold water and stir in 1 tablespoon of white vinegar. As you prepare the fruit, place the finished sections in the bowl to soak. When you are ready to use them, drain the water, place the fruit in a colander, and rinse the sections in cold water.

Apple Spiced Cheesecake

CRUST:

1½ cups graham cracker crumbs

¼ cup brown sugar

½ teaspoon ground cardamom

¼ teaspoon cinnamon

⅓ cup butter, melted

APPLE LAYER:

6 cooking apples, peeled and cored

¼ cup sugar

¼ cup (½ stick) butter, cut into bits

¼ teaspoon cinnamon

¼ teaspoon ground cardamom

¼ teaspoon nutmeg

¼ teaspoon ground cloves

CHEESE LAYER:

2 packages (8 ounces each) cream cheese, softened

⅔ cup sugar

2 teaspoons vanilla extract

1 teaspoon grated lemon zest

4 extra-large or 5 large eggs

For crust: In a large bowl, combine all of the crust ingredients and mix to blend. Using your fingers, press the crumb mixture over the bottom and 1 inch up the sides of a 9-inch springform pan. Set aside.

For apple layer: Cut the apples into eighths. In a large, heavy skillet over medium heat, combine the apples with the sugar, butter, and spices and cook, stirring frequently, until the apples just start to caramelize. Arrange the apples over the crust.

For cheese layer: Preheat the oven to 325°F. In a large mixing bowl, beat the cream cheese until fluffy. Add the sugar gradually, beating constantly. Add the vanilla and lemon zest and beat to blend. Add the eggs, one at a time, beating after each, until smooth. Pour the cheese mixture over the apples.

Bake the cheesecake for 65 minutes, or until lightly browned. Turn off the oven and leave the cheesecake inside, with the door ajar, for 1 hour. Cool in the pan on a rack. Refrigerate for several hours before serving. Remove from the pan to serve. **Makes 12 servings.**

DESSERTS

Cookies

Cranberry Cookies

Try this recipe for a holiday cookie exchange. It makes a large quantity, and the taste is a welcome change from the familiar holiday selections.

½ cup (1 stick) butter, softened

1 cup sugar

¾ cup brown sugar

¼ cup milk

2 tablespoons orange juice

1 egg

3 cups all-purpose flour

1 teaspoon baking powder

½ teaspoon salt

¼ teaspoon baking soda

1 cup chopped walnuts

2½ cups coarsely chopped cranberries

Preheat the oven to 375°F. Grease one or two cookie sheets. In a large bowl, combine the butter and sugars and beat to cream them together. Add the milk, orange juice, and egg, beating after each to blend. In a medium bowl, combine the flour, baking powder, salt, and baking soda and sift them into the butter-sugar mixture. Stir to blend. Add the walnuts and cranberries and stir to blend. Drop the dough by spoonfuls onto the prepared cookie sheet. Bake for 10 to 15 minutes. **Makes 10 dozen cookies.**

Pumpkin Cookies

½ cup (1 stick) butter, softened

1¼ cups brown sugar

2 eggs, beaten

1½ cups mashed or canned pumpkin

1½ cups all-purpose flour

1 tablespoon baking powder

1 teaspoon cinnamon

½ teaspoon nutmeg

½ teaspoon salt

¼ teaspoon ground ginger

1 cup walnuts, chopped

Preheat the oven to 400°F. In a large bowl, combine the butter and sugar and mix until creamy. Add the eggs and pumpkin and mix to blend. In a separate bowl, combine the dry ingredients, then sift them into the pumpkin mixture. Stir to blend, add the nuts, and stir again. Drop the batter by spoonfuls onto a cookie sheet. Bake for 15 minutes, or until lightly browned. **Makes about 5 dozen cookies.**

Caraway Applesauce Cookies

COOKIES:

1 cup (2 sticks) butter, softened

¾ cup sugar

1 egg

1 cup unsweetened applesauce*

2 cups all-purpose flour

2 teaspoons baking powder

½ teaspoon salt

1 tablespoon caraway seeds or cumin seeds

1 teaspoon vanilla extract

GLAZE:

juice and grated zest of ½ lemon

juice and grated zest of ½ orange

confectioners' sugar

For cookies: Preheat the oven to 375°F. Grease one or two cookie sheets. In a large bowl, combine the butter and sugar and beat to cream them together. Add the egg and beat to blend. Add the applesauce and stir. In a separate bowl, combine the flour, baking powder, and salt and sift together into the butter-sugar mixture. Add the caraway seeds and vanilla and stir to incorporate. Drop the batter by spoonfuls onto the prepared cookie sheet and bake for 10 to 12 minutes.

For glaze: In a small bowl, combine the lemon and orange juices and grated zests. Add confectioners' sugar, 1 teaspoon at a time, stirring to blend to a desired consistency. Glaze the cookies while they are still warm. **Makes about 5 dozen cookies.**

*To make your own applesauce, peel, core, and slice two McIntosh apples. Place them in a microwave-safe bowl, cover loosely, and cook for 5 to 8 minutes on high, or until mushy. Mash. Set aside to cool.

Cheesy Apple Squares

1½ cups all-purpose flour

1½ cups graham cracker crumbs

1 cup brown sugar

½ teaspoon baking soda

¾ cup (1½ sticks) butter, softened

½ cup walnuts, chopped

6 ounces of cheddar cheese, thinly sliced

2½ cups peeled, cored, and sliced apples

¾ cup sugar

Preheat the oven to 350°F. In a large bowl, mix together the flour, cracker crumbs, brown sugar, baking soda, and butter. Transfer 1½ cups of the crumb mixture to a separate small bowl, add the nuts, and mix. Set this aside. Using your fingers, spread the remaining crumbs in an ungreased, 13x9-inch baking dish. Place the cheese slices over the crumbs. In a large bowl, combine the apples with the sugar and toss to coat. Spread the apples over the cheese. Spread the crumb-nut mixture over the apples. Bake for 35 to 40 minutes, or until golden brown. **Makes 12 servings.**

DESSERTS

Ten Secrets to Making Great Cookies

Crazy about cookies? These morsels of advice will ensure that your batches come out perfectly.

- Read the recipe through before you do anything. Check your supply of staples (flour, sugar, butter) and watch for any unusual or time-consuming steps. For example, if the dough has to chill for 12 hours, be prepared.

- Use good, fresh ingredients. Spices lose their flavor over time; if they are more than a year old, replace them. Unsalted ("sweet") butter is preferable to salted; the taste is usually cleaner and sweeter.

- Use good cookie sheets. Thin, flimsy sheets don't diffuse heat well or evenly and can result in scorched cookie bottoms. Tinned steel and anodized aluminum are two good material choices that will last.

- Invest in a heavy-duty, stainless steel cooling rack that's large enough to hold two to three dozen cookies.

- If you forget to soften your butter, cut the stick(s) into thin pats and place them on a plate. Leave in a warm spot for 10 minutes or so, until the butter yields to gentle finger pressure.

- Don't overmix the dough, or you could end up with tough cookies.

- Bake only one sheet of cookies at a time, on the center rack. This allows for the most even baking.

- If you own only one cookie sheet, cool it to room temperature between batches. This prevents the butter from melting out of the dough and puddling on the sheet.

- Let cookies cool on the cookie sheet for 1 to 2 minutes, just long enough to firm them slightly and make it easier to slide them off the sheet and onto a cooling rack.

- When baking cookies to ship, choose a relatively firm or dense type of cookie. Wrap cookies individually in waxed paper and pack them snugly in a tin. Pack the tin inside a bigger box, cushioned on all sides with newspaper.

DESSERTS

Cakes

Raspberry Honey Cake With Raspberry Sauce

*If using a Bundt pan, bake at a lower temperature and for a longer time. Test for
doneness periodically.*

CAKE:

1 cup (2 sticks) unsalted butter, softened

2 cups honey

2 teaspoons vanilla extract

6 large eggs

2 cups whole wheat flour

1 cup all-purpose flour

½ teaspoon baking soda

½ teaspoon salt

½ cup plain yogurt

½ cup sour cream

1 tablespoon grated lemon zest

2 cups raspberries

¼ cup chopped blanched almonds

SAUCE:

⅓ cup sugar

1 tablespoon cornstarch

2 cups raspberries

For cake: Preheat the oven to 350°F. Grease and flour a
10-inch tube pan. In a large bowl, cream the butter and
honey until light. Add the vanilla and eggs, beating
well after each addition. In a separate bowl, combine
the flours, baking soda, and salt. Sift the dry ingredients into the creamed mixture alternately with yogurt
and sour cream, beating after each addition. Fold in
the lemon zest, raspberries, and almonds. Pour into
the prepared pan. Bake for 45 to 55 minutes, or until
the cake pulls away from the side of the pan. Cool on
a rack for 10 minutes before inverting the cake onto a
serving plate.

For sauce: In a saucepan, combine the sugar, cornstarch, and raspberries with ⅓ cup of water. Boil and
stir until the sauce is smooth and thickened. If desired,
strain through a sieve or cheesecloth to remove the
seeds.

Serve the cake with the raspberry sauce. **Makes 10
servings.**

DESSERTS

**Raspberry Honey Cake
With Raspberry Sauce**
(recipe at left)

Fresh Tomato Cake With Cream Cheese Frosting

In the 1930s, tomato soup cakes were all the rage, yet they were a mystery because they did not taste like tomato soup. Make your tomato cake with ripe tomatoes from your own garden!

CAKE:

1 cup dark-brown sugar

½ cup shortening

2 eggs

3 cups all-purpose flour

2 teaspoons baking powder

1 teaspoon baking soda

1 teaspoon nutmeg

1 teaspoon salt

2 cups peeled, seeded, and chopped ripe
   tomatoes *(see tip, page 65)*

½ cup chopped nuts

½ cup chopped dates

½ cup chopped raisins

FROSTING:

½ cup (1 stick) butter, softened

1 package (8 ounces) cream cheese,
   softened

2 teaspoons vanilla extract

1 package (1 pound) confectioners' sugar

milk, as needed

For cake: Preheat the oven to 350°F. Grease and flour a 13x9-inch baking pan. In a large bowl, combine the sugar and shortening and mix until creamy. Add the eggs, beating after each. In a separate bowl, combine the flour, baking powder, baking soda, nutmeg, and salt. Sift the dry ingredients into the creamed mixture and stir to blend. Add the tomatoes, nuts, dates, and raisins and stir thoroughly. Pour the batter into the prepared pan. Bake for 35 minutes, or until a toothpick inserted into the center comes out clean. Cool.

For frosting: In a large bowl, combine the butter, cream cheese, and vanilla and mix until creamy. Gradually beat in the sugar. If the mixture becomes too thick, add a little milk. Frost when the cake is cool. **Makes 12 servings.**

In the Kitchen: Drying Grapes

■ Summertime is perfect for making raisins. Rinse and dry a bunch of seedless grapes. Separate the grapes from their stems. Line a cookie sheet with paper towels and arrange the grapes in a single layer, with none touching. Cover the sheet with cheesecloth to protect from dust and insects. Place the sheet outdoors in the sun for 3 to 6 days. (Bring them indoors each night.) Check the grapes occasionally. When they are dried but still plump, store them in an airtight container.

Hawaiian Carrot Cake With Coconut Frosting

CAKE:

3 eggs

2 cups sugar

1½ cups vegetable oil

2 teaspoons vanilla extract

1 cup crushed pineapple in juice

2 cups peeled, coarsely grated carrots

2½ cups cake flour or 2½ cups less 3
   tablespoons all-purpose flour

1 teaspoon baking powder

1 teaspoon baking soda

1 teaspoon salt

1 teaspoon cinnamon

1 teaspoon nutmeg

1 cup coarsely chopped macadamia nuts

½ cup shredded coconut

FROSTING:

¼ cup (½ stick) butter, softened

4 tablespoons cream cheese, softened

1 teaspoon vanilla extract

1½ cups sifted confectioners' sugar

⅛ teaspoon salt

¼ cup shredded coconut

For cake: Preheat the oven to 350°F. Grease a tube or large Bundt pan. In a large bowl, combine the eggs, sugar, and oil and beat to blend. Add the vanilla, pineapple in juice, and carrots and stir to blend. In a separate bowl, combine the flour, baking powder, baking soda, salt, cinnamon, and nutmeg and sift them together three times. Sift the dry ingredients into the batter, in batches, stirring after each. Add the chopped nuts and coconut and stir well. Pour the batter into the prepared pan and bake for 1 hour, 15 minutes. Cool in the pan on a rack for 10 minutes. Invert the cake onto the rack to cool completely.

For frosting: In a large bowl, cream the butter and cream cheese until light. Add the vanilla, sugar, and salt, beating well after each addition. Stir in the coconut. Frost when the cake is cool. **Makes 10 servings.**

Start Out Right

■ Before making a cake, bring
   the ingredients to room
   temperature (unless otherwise
   instructed). You'll get better
   results than if you use them
   straight from the refrigerator.

Chocolate Berry Torte

CAKE:

⅔ cup all-purpose flour

⅓ cup unsweetened cocoa

6 eggs, at room temperature

¾ cup sugar

1 teaspoon vanilla extract

6 tablespoons (¾ stick) butter, melted
   and cooled slightly

FILLING:

½ cup granulated sugar

1 cup fresh cranberries

1 cup raspberries

3 tablespoons raspberry-flavor liqueur,
   such as Chambord (optional)

3 cups heavy cream

½ cup confectioners' sugar

1½ teaspoons vanilla extract

¼ cup unsweetened cocoa

GARNISH:

3½ ounces semisweet chocolate,
   made into leaves, chilled
   (see tip, right)

fresh mint leaves

raspberries

For cake: Preheat the oven to 350°F. Grease two 9-inch round cake pans. Sift the flour and cocoa into a small bowl and set it aside. Fill a large baking pan with very hot or boiling water and set aside. In a mixing bowl, combine the eggs, sugar, and vanilla. Set the bowl into the pan of hot water for 3 minutes. Remove from the water and beat the egg mixture on medium-high speed for 10 minutes. Sift the flour and cocoa (again) over the beaten eggs and fold to combine. Fold in the melted butter. Pour the batter into the prepared pans. Bake for 20 to 25 minutes, or until a toothpick inserted into the center comes out clean. Cool completely on racks.

For filling: In a saucepan over medium heat, combine the granulated sugar and ¼ cup of water. Bring the mixture to a boil, stirring frequently. Add the cranberries and cook for 8 minutes, or until the berries' skins burst. Remove the pan from the heat and strain the fruit, reserving the syrup. Set the cranberries aside to cool. Add the raspberries to the cranberries and stir to combine. Add the liqueur, if desired, to the syrup, and set aside. In a large, chilled bowl, beat the cream until peaks form. Sprinkle with the confectioners' sugar, beating constantly. Add the vanilla and beat. Place about two-thirds of the whipped cream in a separate bowl. Sift the cocoa over the remaining whipped cream and beat to incorporate. Strain the berries and add any liquid to the syrup.

Slice the cake layers in half horizontally, making four layers. Place one layer, cut side up, on a serving plate and brush generously with syrup. Spread half of the cocoa whipped cream on top. Cover with a second cake layer. Spread the berries on the cake and cover them completely with plain whipped cream. Cover with a third cake layer and brush it with syrup. Spread the remaining cocoa whipped cream on the cake. Place the last cake layer on top. Cover the top and sides of the cake with plain whipped cream. (Put some in a pastry bag fitted with a decorative tip, if desired, and pipe rosettes on top of the torte.)

Garnish with chocolate leaves *(see below)*, fresh mint leaves, and raspberries. Refrigerate until ready to serve. **Makes 10 to 12 servings.**

How to Make Chocolate Leaves

- Collect 12 fresh, nontoxic leaves (such as from roses) about 1½ inches long. Keep a bit of the stem attached. Wash them thoroughly with warm soapy water, rinse completely, and pat dry between two paper towels.

  Over low heat, melt about 3½ ounces of good-quality chocolate. Use a pastry brush to brush the melted chocolate to a thickness of about ⅛ inch onto the underside of each leaf. Place each leaf chocolate side up on a cookie sheet lined with waxed paper. Place the cookie sheet in the refrigerator for 15 to 20 minutes, or until the chocolate is firm. Then, with the chocolate side down, hold the leaf stem and carefully peel the leaf away from the chocolate, working quickly so that the chocolate doesn't melt.

  Place the chocolate leaves in a waxed-paper–lined container and keep refrigerated until ready to use. Makes 12 chocolate leaves.

A Berry Garden

The time, how beautiful and dear,
When early fruits begin to blush.

–Lucy Larcom, American poet (1824–93)

Homegrown berries are a treat. To be sure that birds don't get the entire harvest, cover the plants with netting before the fruit ripen.

BLUEBERRIES. A particular requirement of blueberry bushes is acidic soil (pH of 4.0 to 5.0). Test your soil; if necessary, add limestone to raise the pH; ground sulfur to lower it. For larger berries and a greater yield, plant two or more varieties. Ripe berries are blue and come off the stem easily when gently twisted.

- Highbush varieties are 6- to 12-foot-tall shrubs that typically produce large, plump berries.

- Lowbush types are cold-tolerant. The 1- to 2-foot-tall creeping plants form small, sweet fruit every other year.

Ground Rules

- Plant bush berries, cane berries, and strawberries in spring in full sun and well-drained soil amended with aged organic matter and other ingredients as noted here.

- Half-high blueberries are hybrids that contain qualities of both highbush and lowbush types.

- Rabbiteye blueberries are native to the southeastern United States and grow up to 15 feet tall. The berry's thick skin helps it to tolerate heat.

RASPBERRIES. Choose from red, yellow, black, or purple varieties.

Harvest when the berries reach full color and release easily from the stem. It's best to use them on the same day that they are picked.

Each cane lives for 2 years; most varieties produce fruit in the second year. Pruning increases productivity.

Fair Warning

- **Do not plant raspberries, blackberries, and strawberries where tomatoes, eggplants, peppers, or potatoes have been grown within 3 years. All of these plants are susceptible to the same pests and diseases.**

- **Summer bearers produce a crop every summer on new shoots from last year's canes.**

–Wendy Strang-Frost

- **Everbearers form fruit at the tips of first-year canes in fall and at the base of those canes in the following summer.**

BLACKBERRIES. The canes of most blackberry varieties form black to dark red berries in their second year, after which the canes die. Some newer varieties fruit on first-year canes. Blackberries can have upright, semi-upright, or trailing habits.

Harvest when the berries' black color becomes dull and they release easily when gently twisted.

–Jurvetson

STRAWBERRIES. A particular requirement of strawberries is sandy soil; amend as necessary. Apply 1 to 2 inches of straw mulch to keep the berries clean, conserve water, and control weeds. The plants spread by runners; some varieties are perfect for containers or hanging baskets. Water well. Harvest a day or so after they reach full red color. Gently pinch off the stem above the berry, taking the cap and stem stub with the fruit.

- **June-bearing types produce large fruit from June into July.**

- **Day-neutral strawberries flower and fruit continuously when temperatures are moderate. Plant in small gardens; they produce few runners.**

- **Everbearing varieties provide about three crops per year. Runners are few, so they are also good in small spaces.**

CHAPTER 14

Beverages

Spiced Peach Shake 297

Raspberry Shrub 297

Strawberry Lemonade 299

Ginger Lemonade 299

Ginger Splash 300

Melon, Ginger, and Borage Drink 300

Watermelon Punch 301

Mint Mango Smoothie 302

Mint Chiller 302

Calming Chamomile Tea 303

Peach Basil Iced Tea 303

Spiced Peach Shake

1 large peach, peeled, pitted, and quartered

½ cup vanilla frozen yogurt

1 teaspoon honey

pinch of cinnamon

pinch of ground ginger

sprig of mint, for garnish

Place all of the ingredients except the mint in a blender or food processor and process until smooth. Pour into a tall, chilled glass. Garnish with mint and serve. **Makes 1 serving.**

Raspberry Shrub

Shrubs made from currants, gooseberries, and other fruit were popular summer refreshments during the 19th and early 20th centuries. This version was a legendary thirst-quencher.

3 cups raspberries

2 cups white-wine vinegar

sugar

Combine the raspberries and vinegar in a glass or ceramic bowl. Cover and let stand for 24 hours, stirring once or twice. Strain the berry juice into a bowl, pressing down on the fruit with the back of a spatula or spoon (or squeezing in cheesecloth) to remove as much juice as possible. Leave the berries to strain over the bowl for at least 1 hour to catch the remaining juice. Measure the strained juice and combine it with an equal amount of sugar in a nonreactive saucepan. Bring the mixture to a boil, reduce the heat, and simmer for 10 minutes. Cool. Pour the mixture into a jar, cover, and refrigerate. When ready to serve, add 2 to 3 tablespoons of shrub to an 8-ounce glass of ice water. **Makes about 3 cups.**

BEVERAGES

Strawberry Lemonade

(recipe at right)

Strawberry Lemonade

1 cup strawberries, hulled and sliced
½ cup sugar
1 cup fresh lemon juice
1¼ to 1½ cups cold sparkling water

Put the strawberries into a blender or food processor and purée. Add the sugar to the lemon juice and stir to blend. Add the lemon juice and sparkling water to the puréed berries. Stir or process for a few seconds to blend, then pour into ice-filled glasses. **Makes 3 servings.**

Ginger Lemonade

1 piece (2 inches) fresh ginger, peeled
⅓ cup sugar
¾ cup fresh lemon juice
1¼ cups sparkling water

Cut the ginger into four or five pieces and put them into a small saucepan with ½ cup of water. Bring to a boil, remove from the heat, cover, and let steep for 30 minutes. Remove the cover and refrigerate the liquid until it is cold. Put the sugar and the lemon juice into a pitcher and stir to blend. Remove and discard the ginger pieces. Stir the ginger water into the sugar mixture. Add the sparkling water, stir, and pour into ice-filled glasses. **Makes 2 servings.**

In the Kitchen: Lemons

- **To nearly double the amount of juice collected from a lemon, submerge it in hot water for 15 minutes before squeezing. Or, microwave the uncut fruit on high for 20 seconds, then roll it on the counter under the palm of your hand. Cut in half and press it on a handheld wooden lemon reamer or a glass juicer.**

BEVERAGES

Ginger Splash

2 lemons

12 whole cloves

1 or 2 pieces (4 inches total) fresh
  ginger, peeled and grated

2 sticks cinnamon, broken into 2-inch
  pieces

¼ cup sugar, or more to taste

lemon slices, for garnish

Cut the lemons in half, then squeeze out and reserve the juice. Stud the rinds of the lemon halves with three cloves each. Place the lemons in a large saucepan with the lemon juice, grated ginger, cinnamon sticks, sugar, and 6 cups of water. Bring the mixture to a boil, reduce the heat, cover, and simmer for 15 minutes. Remove the pan from the heat and let the liquid steep for 30 minutes. Strain the liquid into a large jar or pitcher and chill. Add more sugar, if needed. Pour into ice-filled glasses. Garnish with lemon slices. **Makes 6 to 8 servings.**

Melon, Ginger, and Borage Drink

½ large honeydew melon

1 quart nonalcoholic ginger beer

1 teaspoon ground ginger, or to taste

borage sprigs with flowers, for garnish

borage leaves (optional)

Discard the seeds from the melon and scoop out the flesh. Place it in a blender or food processor and purée. Pour the purée into a large pitcher and add the ginger beer. Add the ground ginger to taste and stir. Pour into ice-filled glasses and garnish with borage sprigs. For enhanced flavor, crush some borage leaves and stir them into the drink. **Makes 6 to 8 servings.**

In the Kitchen: Ginger

■ To remove the thin peel from ginger, scrape it with a spoon, which works more easily than a knife when maneuvering around the bumpy parts.

Watermelon Punch

6 cups watermelon juice *(see tip, below)*

2 cups pineapple juice

1 can (12 ounces) frozen raspberry juice
   blend

1 small can (6 ounces) frozen orange
   juice concentrate

¼ cup fresh lemon juice

Put all of the ingredients into a large jar or pitcher and stir to blend. Refrigerate until ready to serve. **Makes 12 to 14 servings.**

■ **TO MAKE WATERMELON JUICE,** process small chunks of watermelon flesh in a blender or food processor until they turn to liquid. Make more than you need for this punch, freeze the extra in ice cube trays, and use the watermelon cubes to chill the punch. (You can also use watermelon juice instead of water when preparing frozen lemonade or limeade.)

BEVERAGES

Mint Mango Smoothie

1 small ripe mango, peeled, pitted, and
    coarsely chopped
1 banana, coarsely chopped
½ cup vanilla frozen yogurt
8 spearmint leaves
½ cup or more fresh orange juice, as
    needed for consistency

Put the mango and banana into a blender or food processor. Add the frozen yogurt, spearmint, and orange juice and blend until smooth. Add more juice as necessary for a smooth consistency. **Makes 2 servings.**

Mint Chiller

1 cup sugar
2 cups fresh mint leaves, with stems
1 cup fresh lemon juice
1 cup fresh orange juice
1 cup ginger ale

In a small saucepan, combine the sugar with 3 cups of water. Bring to a boil over high heat, reduce the heat, and simmer for 5 minutes. Add the mint, remove the pan from the heat, cover, and let the liquid steep for 1 hour. Strain the liquid into a bowl. In a large pitcher, combine the mint syrup, lemon juice, orange juice, and ginger ale. Stir until well blended. Serve over crushed ice. **Makes 6 to 8 servings.**

After-Dinner Mint

- **Mint is recommended for relieving heartburn, but avoid it if you have acid reflux; it stimulates digestive juices, possibly worsening the condition.**

Calming Chamomile Tea

chamomile flowers

honey, to taste

Fill a kettle with 1 cup of water for each serving and bring to a boil. Warm a ceramic teapot by filling it with hot tap water. For each cup of tea, place 1 tablespoon of fresh chamomile flowers or 1 teaspoon of dried flowers into a tea ball or strainer. Empty the teapot and place the tea ball in the pot. Pour the boiling water over the tea ball. Steep the tea, covered, for 5 to 10 minutes. Remove the herbs and sweeten the tea with honey.

How to Harvest: Chamomile

■ The apple-scented flowers of both perennial Roman and annual German chamomile can be harvested and dried for tea. Pick the flowers when the petals are fully open and dry them immediately on screens for 7 to 10 days. Store in an airtight container.

–Horváth Dénes Péter

Peach Basil Iced Tea

3 orange pekoe tea bags

1 cup basil leaves, loosely packed

3⅓ cups chilled peach nectar

¼ cup simple syrup,* or to taste

Put the tea bags and basil into a 1-quart glass or heat-resistant bowl. Bring 4 cups of water just to a boil and pour over the tea bags. Steep the liquid for 5 minutes, strain into a pitcher, and let cool. Chill in the refrigerator, covered, for at least 1 hour. Stir in the peach nectar and syrup. Pour into ice-filled glasses. **Makes 6 to 8 servings.**

Simple syrup is a mixture of equal parts water and sugar, fully dissolved. To make: In a small saucepan, bring to a boil 1 cup of water mixed with 1 cup of sugar. Simmer until the sugar is completely dissolved. Remove the saucepan from the heat and cool to room temperature. The syrup will keep in a glass jar in the refrigerator for up to 1 month.

Reference

IN THE GARDEN:

Frosts and Growing Days 305

USDA Plant Hardiness Zone Map 306

When to Plant Second-Season Crops 307

FOR YOUR HEALTH:

Why Garden-Fresh Foods Are Good for You 308

How Long Will It Keep? 309

Facts About Fiber 310

IN THE KITCHEN:

How to Know What's Ripe 312

How to Dry Herbs 316

Weights, Measures, and Equivalents 317

Substitutions for Common Ingredients 318

Pan Sizes and Equivalents 319

Frosts and Growing Days

- Dates given are normal averages for a light freeze (29° to 32°F, or −2° to 0°C); local weather and topography may cause considerable variations. The possibility of frost occurring after the spring dates and before the fall dates is 50 percent. The classification of freeze temperatures is usually based on their effect on plants. A light freeze kills only tender plants, with little destructive effect on other vegetation. For local data, go to Almanac.com/FrostDates.

City	Number of Growing Days	Last Spring Frost	First Fall Frost	City	Number of Growing Days	Last Spring Frost	First Fall Frost
UNITED STATES (alphabetical by state)				**CANADA (alphabetical by province)**			
Juneau, AK	148	May 8	Oct. 4	Calgary, AB	114	May 23	Sept. 15
Pine Bluff, AR	240	Mar. 16	Nov. 12	Edmonton, AB	138	May 7	Sept. 23
Denver, CO	157	Apr. 30	Oct. 4	Red Deer, AB	106	May 25	Sept. 9
Hartford, CT	166	Apr. 26	Oct. 9	Dawson Creek, BC	84	June 5	Aug. 29
Wilmington, DE	202	Apr. 10	Oct. 30	Kelowna, BC	123	May 19	Sept. 20
Athens, GA	227	Mar. 24	Nov. 7	Nelson, BC	159	May 4	Oct. 13
Boise, ID	147	May 10	Oct. 6	Vancouver, BC	221	Mar. 28	Nov. 5
Chicago, IL	187	Apr. 20	Oct. 24	Victoria, BC	200	Apr. 19	Nov. 5
Indianapolis, IN	181	Apr. 17	Oct. 16	Brandon, MB	105	May 27	Sept. 10
Cedar Rapids, IA	163	Apr. 25	Oct. 6	Lynn Lake, MB	89	June 8	Sept. 6
Topeka, KS	174	Apr. 19	Oct. 11	Thompson, MB	61	June 15	Aug. 16
Lexington, KY	192	Apr. 15	Oct. 25	Winnipeg, MB	119	May 25	Sept. 22
Portland, ME	156	May 2	Oct. 6	Edmundston, NB	112	May 28	Sept. 18
Baltimore, MD	200	Apr. 11	Oct. 29	Saint John, NB	139	May 18	Oct. 4
Worcester, MA	170	Apr. 26	Oct. 14	Gander, NL	123	June 3	Oct. 5
Lansing, MI	145	May 10	Oct. 3	St. John's, NL	131	June 2	Oct. 12
Willmar, MN	154	Apr. 30	Oct. 1	Aklavik, NT	76	June 13	Aug. 31
Jefferson City, MO	188	Apr. 13	Oct. 18	Yellowknife, NT	110	May 27	Sept. 15
Helena, MT	121	May 19	Sept. 18	Halifax, NS	166	May 6	Oct. 20
North Platte, NE	137	May 9	Sept. 24	Sydney, NS	141	May 24	Oct. 13
Concord, NH	124	May 20	Sept. 21	Truro, NS	113	May 30	Sept. 21
Newark, NJ	217	Apr. 3	Nov. 7	Kapuskasing, ON	87	June 12	Sept. 8
Albany, NY	153	May 2	Oct. 3	Kingston, ON	160	May 2	Oct. 10
Bismarck, ND	129	May 14	Sept. 21	Ottawa, ON	151	May 6	Oct. 5
Cincinnati, OH	192	Apr. 13	Oct. 23	Sudbury, ON	130	May 17	Sept. 25
Tulsa, OK	225	Mar. 27	Nov. 7	Thunder Bay, ON	105	June 1	Sept. 15
Portland, OR	236	Mar. 23	Nov. 15	Toronto, ON	149	May 9	Oct. 6
Williamsport, PA	168	Apr. 30	Oct. 15	Charlottetown, PE	150	May 17	Oct. 14
Kingston, RI	147	May 8	Oct. 3	Tignish, PE	138	May 23	Oct. 9
Rapid City, SD	140	May 9	Sept. 27	Montreal, QC	156	May 3	Oct. 7
Memphis, TN	235	Mar. 22	Nov. 13	Quebec, QC	139	May 13	Sept. 29
Amarillo, TX	185	Apr. 18	Oct. 20	Sherbrooke, QC	100	June 1	Sept. 10
Cedar City, UT	133	May 21	Oct. 1	Trois-Rivières, QC	124	May 19	Sept. 23
Richmond, VA	206	Apr. 6	Oct. 30	Prince Albert, SK	93	June 2	Sept. 4
Burlington, VT	147	May 8	Oct. 3	Regina, SK	111	May 21	Sept. 10
Seattle, WA	251	Mar. 10	Nov. 17	Yorkton, SK	110	May 23	Sept. 11
Parkersburg, WV	183	Apr. 21	Oct. 22	Watson Lake, YT	91	June 2	Sept. 4
Casper, WY	120	May 22	Sept. 19	Whitehorse, YT	74	June 11	Aug. 25

USDA Plant Hardiness Zone Map

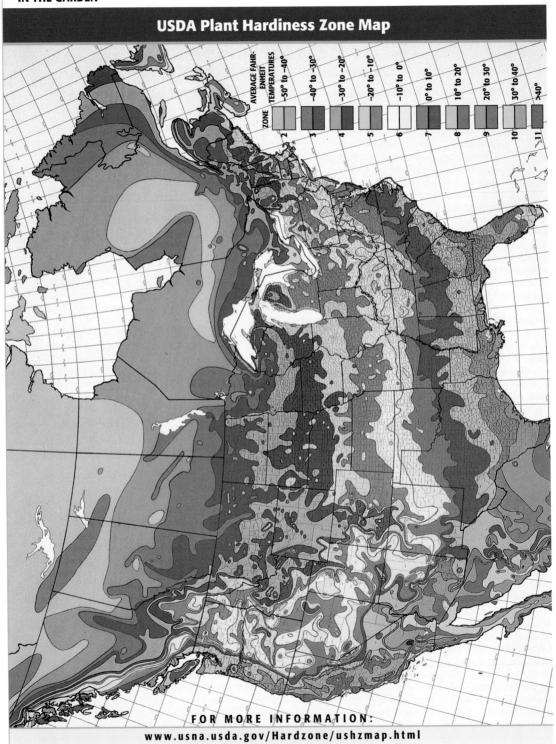

AVERAGE FAHRENHEIT TEMPERATURES										
−50° to −40°	−40° to −30°	−30° to −20°	−20° to −10°	−10° to 0°	0° to 10°	10° to 20°	20° to 30°	30° to 40°	>40°	
ZONE 2	3	4	5	6	7	8	9	10	11	

FOR MORE INFORMATION:
www.usna.usda.gov/Hardzone/ushzmap.html

When to Plant Second-Season Crops

■ To calculate the best time to plant your second vegetable crops, use the chart below. Choose the date that comes closest to the expected first fall frost in your area. (If you do not know the frost date, see page 305 or go to Almanac.com/FrostDates.)

IF THE EXPECTED FIRST FROST IS . . .

	SEPT. 10	SEPT. 20	SEPT. 30	OCT. 10	OCT. 20	OCT. 30
PLANT A SECOND CROP OF THESE VEGETABLES BY . . .						
Beets	June 25	July 5	July 15	July 25	August 5	August 20
Broccoli (transplants)	*	June 15	June 25	July 10	July 25	August 10
Bush beans	*	*	June 15	July 1	July 15	July 30
Cabbage (transplants)	*	June 15	June 25	July 10	July 25	August 10
Carrots	June 25	July 5	July 15	July 25	August 5	August 15
Chard	June 25	July 5	July 10	July 20	July 30	August 15
Corn	*	*	June 15	June 25	July 10	July 20
Cucumbers	*	*	June 15	June 30	July 15	August 1
Leaf lettuce	July 20	August 1	August 10	August 20	September 1	September 10
Peas	June 25	July 10	July 20	August 1	August 10	August 20
Peppers (transplants)	*	June 20	June 30	July 7	July 15	July 25
Radishes	August 1	August 15	September 1	September 10	September 20	September 30
Spinach	July 15	July 25	August 5	August 15	August 25	September 5
Tomatoes (transplants)	June 15	June 20	June 25	June 30	July 5	July 15
Winter squashes/ pumpkins	*	*	June 15	June 25	July 5	July 15

*indicates a vegetable that probably will not survive as a second crop in your garden

Why Garden-Fresh Foods Are Good for You

■ **People who eat more fruit and vegetables, particularly the more deeply colored varieties, may have less heart disease, cancer, diabetes, osteoporosis, and age-related neurological decline. This is partly due to plant pigments. Plant pigments deliver a variety of benefits to the plants that produce them and to the people who eat them, too.**

PIGMENT CLASS: Chlorophylls
Indicative color: green
Plants rich in these: deep-green leafy greens
In plants, these pigments harvest light and initiate photosynthesis.
In people, these pigments help to deactivate carcinogens.
Surprise! Chlorophylls may deactivate colon and liver cancer carcinogens.

PIGMENT CLASS: Carotenoids
Indicative colors: yellow, orange to red
Plants rich in these: apricots, cantaloupes, carrots, leafy greens, pumpkins, sweet potatoes, tomatoes, winter squashes
In plants, these pigments aid in photosynthesis, protect from solar radiation, act as antioxidants, and attract pollinators and seed dispersers.
In people, these pigments protect the immune system, skin, and epithelial cells and may prevent heart disease, cancer, and macular degeneration.
Surprise! Eating carotenoids with a little fat can help the body to absorb them.

PIGMENT CLASS: Anthocyanins
Indicative colors: blue, purple-burgundy
Plants rich in these: black turtle beans; purple cabbage, eggplant, potatoes; red onions; red and purple grapes and berries
In plants, these pigments attract pollinators and seed dispersers, repel predators, resist disease, and prevent oxidative damage to cells.
In people, these pigments may prevent or reverse age-related cognitive decline and/or neuro-degenerative disease; improve vision; help to prevent cancer, heart disease, insulin resistance, and obesity; promote wound healing.
Surprise! Anthocyanins are water-soluble and never occur with betalains.

PIGMENT CLASS: Betalains
Indicative colors: red-violet, yellow-orange
Plants rich in these: beets, Swiss chard, prickly pear cactus fruit, spinach
In plants, these pigments protect against excess photoradiation.
In people, these pigments may protect against cancer, heart disease, liver damage, and ulcers.
Surprise! Betalains are water-soluble and never occur with anthocyanins.

How Long Will It Keep?

■ Almost any food can be frozen. Exceptions are eggs in shells and food in certain containers. (Once food has been removed from its storage container, it may be frozen.) To retain vitamin content, color, flavor, and texture, freeze items at peak freshness and store at a constant 0°F or lower. If this is done, food will always be safe to thaw and eat; only quality suffers with lengthy freezer storage.

PRODUCT	MONTHS IN FREEZER
FRESH VEGETABLES (PREPARED FOR FREEZING)	
Artichokes, eggplant	6 to 8
Asparagus, rutabagas, turnips	8 to 10
Avocados	3
Bamboo shoots, cabbage, celery, cucumbers, endive, radishes, salad greens, watercress	Not recommended
Beans, beets, bok choy, broccoli, brussels sprouts, carrots, cauliflower, corn, greens, kohlrabi, leeks, mushrooms, okra, onions, parsnips, peas, peppers, soybeans, spinach, summer squashes	10 to 12
Tomatoes (overripe or sliced)	2
FRESH FRUIT (PREPARED FOR FREEZING)	
All fruit except those listed below	10 to 12
Bananas	3
Citrus fruit	4 to 6
Juices	8 to 12
MISCELLANEOUS	
Cakes	4 to 6
Casseroles	2 to 3
Cookie dough	2
Cookies	3
Fruit pies, baked	2 to 4
Fruit pies, unbaked	8
Pastry, unbaked	2
Pumpkin or chiffon pies	1
Quick breads	2
Raw egg yolks, whites	12
Soups and stews	2 to 3
Yeast breads	6
Yeast dough	2 weeks

Note: When freezing liquids or foods with liquid, be sure to leave space in the container for expansion.

–*adapted from the USDA Food Safety and Inspection Service*

Facts About Fiber

Fiber is an indigestible material that is found only in plants, such as fruit, vegetables, legumes, nuts, seeds, and grains. It is essential for digestive health and takes two forms:

- **Soluble fiber** dissolves in water, forming a gelatinous texture. It helps to lower cholesterol and to regulate blood sugar by slowing digestion. Good sources are apples, barley, legumes, oats, and strawberries.

- **Insoluble fiber** absorbs water. It speeds digestion and promotes regularity and overall health. Good sources are whole wheat breads and cereals, brussels sprouts, carrots, celery, and the edible skins of fruit and vegetables.

Adults should consume between 20 and 35 grams of fiber per day. The following chart shows the fiber content in a variety of common foods.

	SERVING SIZE / FIBER CONTENT (g)
FRUIT	
Apples	1 apple, with skin 3.3
Apricots	1 apricot 0.7
Bananas	1 banana 3.1
Blackberries	1 cup, raw 7.6
Blueberries	1 cup, raw 4.0
Grapefruit, red	½ grapefruit 2.0
Grapefruit, white	½ grapefruit 1.3
Grapes	1 cup, raw 1.4
Kiwifruit	1 kiwifruit 2.3
Lemons	1 lemon 1.6
Mangoes	1 cup, raw 3.0
Melons, cantaloupe & honeydew	1 cup, raw 1.4
Nectarines	1 nectarine 2.3
Oranges	1 orange 3.1
Papayas	1 cup, raw 2.5
Peaches	1 peach 1.5
Pears	1 pear 5.1
Pineapples	1 cup, raw 2.2
Plums	1 plum 1.0
Raisins	1 cup 5.4
Raspberries	1 cup, raw 8.0
Strawberries	1 cup, raw 3.3

	SERVING SIZE / FIBER CONTENT (g)
VEGETABLE	
Artichokes	1 cup, cooked 14.4
Asparagus	4 spears, cooked 1.2
Avocados, California	1 avocado 9.0
Beets	1 cup, cooked 3.4
Broccoli	1 cup, chopped, raw 2.3
Brussels sprouts	1 cup, cooked 4.1
Cabbage, green	1 cup, shredded, raw 1.8
Cabbage, red	1 cup, shredded, raw 1.5
Carrots	1 cup, chopped, raw 3.1
Cauliflower	1 cup, chopped, raw 2.0
Celery	1 cup, chopped, raw 1.9
Collards	1 cup, cooked 5.3
Corn, sweet white	1 ear, cooked 2.1
Corn, sweet yellow	1 ear, cooked 1.8
Eggplants	1 cup, cooked 2.5
Endive	1 cup, raw 1.6
Kale	1 cup, cooked 2.6
Leeks	1 cup, bulb and lower leaves, cooked 1.0
Mushrooms, shiitake	1 cup, cooked 3.0
Mushrooms, white	1 cup, sliced, raw 0.8
Okra	1 cup, cooked 4.0
Onions	1 cup, raw 2.7

	SERVING SIZE / FIBER CONTENT (g)		SERVING SIZE / FIBER CONTENT (g)
Parsnips	1 cup, cooked 5.6	Sunflower seeds	1 ounce 2.6
Peppers, green	1 cup, chopped, raw 2.5	Walnuts	1 ounce 1.9
Peppers, red	1 cup, chopped, raw 3.1	**GRAIN**	
Potatoes	1 baked, with skin 4.6	Barley, pearled	1 cup cooked 6.0
Potatoes, sweet	1 baked, with skin 4.8	Bread, pumpernickel	1 slice 2.1
Pumpkins	1 cup, cooked 2.7	Bread, rye	1 slice 1.9
Spinach	1 cup, raw 0.7	Bread, white	1 slice 0.6
Squashes, summer	1 cup, cooked 2.5	Bread, whole wheat	1 slice 1.9
Squashes, winter	1 cup, cooked 5.7	Buckwheat flour, whole groat	1 cup 12.0
Tomatoes	1 tomato 1.5	Bulgur	1 cup, cooked 8.2
Turnips	1 cup, cooked 3.1	Cornmeal, whole grain	1 cup 8.9
LEGUME		Couscous	1 cup, cooked 2.2
Beans, black	1 cup, cooked 15.0	Oat bran	1 cup, cooked 5.7
Beans, garbanzo (chickpeas)	1 cup, cooked 12.5	Oatmeal	1 cup, cooked 4.0
Beans, kidney (red)	1 cup, cooked 13.1	Pasta, whole wheat	1 cup, cooked 5.4
Beans, lima	1 cup, cooked 13.2	Rice, brown	1 cup, cooked 3.5
Beans, navy	1 cup, cooked 19.1	Rice, white	1 cup, cooked 0.6
Beans, pinto	1 cup, cooked 15.4	Rice, wild	1 cup, cooked 3.0
Beans, snap	1 cup, cooked 4.0	Wheat bran	1 cup 24.0
Beans, string	1 cup, cooked 4.0	Wheat germ	1 cup 16.0
Lentils	1 cup, cooked 15.6	Wheat flour, white, all-purpose, enriched	1 cup 3.4
Peas, edible-podded	1 cup, cooked 4.5	Wheat flour, whole grain	1 cup 14.6
Peas, green	1 cup, cooked 8.8		
Peas, split	1 cup, cooked 16.3		

–adapted from the USDA National Nutrient Database

NUT/SEED

Almonds	1 ounce 3.5
Hazelnuts/ filberts	1 ounce 2.7
Peanuts, dry-roasted	1 ounce 2.3
Pecans	1 ounce 2.7
Pine nuts	1 ounce, dried 1.0
Pistachios	1 ounce 2.9
Popcorn	1 cup, air-popped 1.2
Pumpkin seeds	1 ounce 1.8

How to Know What's Ripe

Farmers' markets, small farm stands, and pick-your-own farms are great places to buy fresh fruit and vegetables. To make the best selections . . .

- Choose produce that is displayed in the shade; when exposed to sunlight, fresh produce tends to deteriorate rapidly.

- Avoid produce that shows signs of age, poor storage, or inferior quality—bruises, wrinkles, cuts or nicks, and soft spots.

- After purchasing, store fresh produce properly and use as soon as possible.

For specific foods, use the following guidelines.

FRUIT

APPLES
Look for: Firm body, heavy for size, rich color, smooth skin
Avoid: Blemishes, soft spots

APRICOTS
Look for: Orange-yellow color, hint of softness
Tip: To ripen, put apricots in a paper bag, close, and store at room temperature until soft and juicy.
Avoid: Blemishes, greenish tinge or pale color, mushy spots

BANANAS
Look for: Firm body; bright, mostly yellow color
Tip: If peel is greenish, sauté or ripen in a bowl; if peel is brown-speckled, use for blender drinks or baking.
Avoid: Dull color, bruises, broken peel

BLACKBERRIES
Look for: Plump fruit; uniform black, shiny color with a hint of dullness; no juice stains on container
Avoid: Crushed fruit, mold, reddish color, stems attached

BLUEBERRIES
Look for: Plump, firm fruit; uniform dark blue color with powdery white coating (called bloom); free movement in package when gently shaken, no juice stains on container
Avoid: Dull, green or red color; mold; mushy or shriveled fruit

CANTALOUPES (muskmelons)
Look for: Fragrant aroma, heavy for size, no stem parts, blossom end slightly springy when pressed, hollow sound when thumped, yellow or cream color under skin's netting
Avoid: Dull or high-pitched sound when thumped, green color under skin's netting, soft spots

CHERRIES
Look for: Fragrant aroma; firm body; large, plump fruit; glossy, uniform, dark color for the variety; green, flexible stems
Avoid: Blemishes, dull color, dry stems, shriveled or spongy fruit, small size

GRAPES
Look for: Plump, firm fruit; tight attachment to stems; green tinged with yellow, if green variety; dark red, no green if red variety; almost black, no green, if purple variety
Avoid: Mushy or shriveled fruit, off- or pale color, shriveled stems

LEMONS

Look for: Heavy for size, bright yellow color

Tip: Lemons with thin, fine-grained skins are best for juice; thick, bumpy skins are good for zest.

Avoid: Dull or greenish color, wrinkles, soft spots

PEACHES

Look for: Fragrant aroma, body that yields easily when gently squeezed, golden color

Tip: To ripen, store in a paper bag at room temperature for 2 to 3 days; for canning, use firmer clingstone, not freestone types.

Avoid: Greenish tinge, hard or mushy fruit, wrinkles

PEARS

Look for: Fragrant aroma, stem area that yields slightly to pressure, consistent color. Most varieties do not change color when ripe; 'Bartlett' turns yellow.

Tip: To ripen, select firm, almost hard, pears.

with smooth, unblemished skins and store in a bowl at room temperature.

Avoid: Softness around the middle

PINEAPPLES

Look for: Heavy for size, pleasing aroma near stem, plump fruit, bright shell color, shell that yields slightly when pressed, healthy leaves

Tip: Pineapples do not ripen after they are harvested.

Avoid: Dried leaf tips, dull color, mushy shell, strong or sour odor

RASPBERRIES

Look for: Fragrant aroma; plump, fairly firm fruit; bright, uniform color; no juice stains on container

Avoid: Crushed or mushy fruit, hulls attached, mold

STRAWBERRIES

Look for: Fragrant aroma; plump fruit; shiny, red color; green caps and stems; no juice stains on container

Avoid: Green or white tips, mold, mushy or shriveled fruit, no caps, odd shape

WATERMELONS

Look for: Symmetrical body shape, heavy for size, buttery yellow underbelly, neither too dull nor shiny skin

Avoid: Soft spots

VEGETABLES

ARTICHOKES

Look for: Plump, compact globes, heavy for size, tightly closed, green bracts ("leaves" of the bud) that squeak if gently squeezed

Avoid: Blemishes, mold, "off" color, wilted bracts

ASPARAGUS

Look for: Fresh spears with tightly closed tips and firm stalks, tender stalks (whether thick or thin)

Tip: White asparagus (grown underground) has the mildest flavor.

Avoid: Shriveled, twisted, or woody spears

BEANS, GREEN

Look for: Pods that snap when bent

Tip: Small, young beans taste best.

Avoid: Large pods with bumps at seeds

BEETS

Look for: Small to medium-size roots, smooth skin, firm flesh, rich color, healthy green leaves

Avoid: Cracks, shriveled or soft roots, wilted leaves
(continued)

How to Know What's Ripe *(continued)*

BROCCOLI
Look for: Firm stalks, compact florets tightly closed buds, dark green to greenish purple heads, fresh green leaves
Avoid: Limp or woody stalks, opening flowers, strong odor, yellow spots

CABBAGE
Look for: Firm body; heavy for size; crisp, richly colored leaves
Avoid: Cracked head, moldy stem, pale color, wilted leaves

CARROTS
Look for: Firm, plump body; smooth skin; bright color; healthy, crisp, green leaves
Tip: Young carrots are usually sweetest. "Baby" carrots might be large carrots cut to size; check with seller.
Avoid: Blemishes, cracks, limp or shriveled body, odd shape, rootlets

CAULIFLOWER
Look for: Firm head; tightly clustered florets; uniform color; crisp, bright green leaves firmly attached
Avoid: Flowering heads; loosely clustered florets; yellow, brown, or black spots

CELERY
Look for: Fresh aroma; straight, green, glossy, firm stalks; heavy for size; healthy green leaves
Avoid: Limp stalks, wilted leaves, "off" color

CORN, SWEET
Look for: Just-picked ears; tightly attached, pliable, healthy, green husks; plump kernels arranged in tight rows that extend to the tip of the ear; milky liquid that oozes out from a punctured kernel
Avoid: Dry husks, kernels that ooze clear liquid or none at all, missing kernels, worms or signs of them (holes, excrement)

CUCUMBERS
Look for: Heavy, firm body; rich, dark green skin
Tip: Small cukes are sweetest and have the softest seeds.
Avoid: Blemishes, oversize body, rubberiness, soft spots, wrinkles, yellowing (unless the cuke is a yellow variety)

EGGPLANT
Look for: Small to medium size for the variety; heavy, firm body; smooth, shiny, richly colored skin; green stem
Avoid: Brown or dry stems, dull or "off" color, oversize for the variety, shriveled or spongy body

FENNEL, FLORENCE
Look for: Fresh aroma; white, firm, tight bulb; bright green stalks, healthy, feathery leaves
Avoid: Blemishes, cracks, wilted leaves or stalks

GARLIC
Look for: Firm, plump bulb; unbroken, tight, dry skin ("paper")
Avoid: Dark or soft spots, shriveled or spongy bulbs, sprouts

GREENS (such as arugula, kale, or leaf lettuce)
Look for: Crisp leaves, good color
Avoid: Wilted leaves, brown or yellow areas

LEEKS
Look for: Small to medium size for the variety; firm but pliable stalks; a few inches of white flesh; roots attached and healthy; crisp, dark green leaves
Avoid: Blemishes, cracks, dry or wilted leaves, dry roots, limp or yellow stalks

LETTUCE, HEADING
Look for: Compact head; slight yield when squeezed; clean, crisp leaves with healthy color
Avoid: Odd shape; brown, slimy, or wilted leaves; spongy head

MUSHROOMS

Look for: Woodsy aroma, firm body, fresh appearance, uniform color; caps that are tightly closed in button and like varieties; gills that are intact and dry (not dried) in open-cap types (portobello or shiitake)

Avoid: Odd shape or color, slimy or shriveled body

ONIONS

Look for: Firm body; shiny, healthy, dry, bright-color skin; layers adhere tightly to bulb

Avoid: Loose, peeling skin; mold; "off" color; soft spots; sprouts; strong odor

PEAS

Look for: Freshly picked, crisp pods; bright green color; green pea and sugar snap pods that are plump with developing seeds; sugar snap peas that "snap" when bent; snow peas pods that are thin and shiny

Avoid: Large or thick pods, "off" color, shriveled pods, pre-shelled peas

PEPPERS

Look for: Crisp, firm body with thick walls; smooth skin; shiny, bright color

Avoid: Blemishes, cracks, pale color, pitted or shriveled skin, soft spots

POTATOES, SWEET POTATOES

Look for: Firm body; heavy for size; unwashed, but free of dirt

Avoid: Black or soft spots, greenish tinge, sprouts, wrinkles

RADISHES

Look for: Firm, smooth, well-shaped body; bright color; healthy green leaves

Avoid: Blemishes, cracks, soft spots, wilted leaves

RHUBARB

Look for: Crisp, firm, medium-size stalks with bright color; leaves removed

Tip: Leaves are toxic; greenish rhubarb is tarter than all-red varieties.

Avoid: Blemishes, limp or shriveled stalks, oversize or tough stalks, dry or split ends

SPINACH

Look for: Healthy, dark green leaves

Avoid: Blemishes, wilted or yellowing leaves

SQUASHES, SUMMER, AND ZUCCHINI

Look for: Small, firm body; heavy for size; bright, shiny skin; healthy stem

Avoid: Blemishes, dry stem, dull or hard skin, oversize body, soft spots

SQUASHES, WINTER

Look for: Firm, heavy body; dull (nonglossy), hard skin; rich color; dry, firm stem

Avoid: Blemishes, cracks, glossy skin, mold, soft spots

TOMATOES

Look for: Fragrant aroma; firm, plump body; heavy for variety; smooth, glossy skin; rich color

Avoid: Cracks, dark or soft spots, poor color, shriveled body

TURNIPS

Look for: Small, firm body; heavy for size; smooth skin; rich color; crisp, green leaves

Avoid: Blemishes, soft spots, wilted or yellowing leaves

Garden and cook with us at Almanac.com/GardenFresh.

How to Dry Herbs

Cut herbs just as the dew does dry.
Tie them loosely and hang them high.
If you plan to store away,
Stir the leaves a bit each day.
—American Farmer, *1842*

■ **Homegrown dried herbs, when properly prepared and stored, can be more colorful, aromatic, and flavorful than store-bought ones.**

Harvest the herbs and remove any dead or diseased leaves or stems. Wash the herbs under cool water to rinse away insects or dirt. Shake off any excess water and put the herbs on a towel to dry completely.

Air drying preserves an herb's essential oils. Use this method for sturdy herbs such as bay, dill, marjoram, oregano, parsley, rosemary, sage, summer savory, and thyme. An oven, food dehydrator, or microwave dries herbs more quickly, so mold is less likely to develop. Use these methods for moist, tender herbs, such as basil, lemon balm, mint, and tarragon.

Herbs are sufficiently dry when the stems snap and leaves are crisp and crumble easily. Store them in a labeled, airtight container in a cool, dry, dark place. For best results, use within 1 year.

IN THE AIR

Hanging Method

Gather four to six stems of fresh herbs in a bunch and tie with string, leaving a loop for hanging. Or, use a rubber band with a paper clip attached to it. Hang the herbs in a warm, well-ventilated area, out of direct sunlight, until dry. For herbs that have full seed heads, such as dill or coriander, use a paper bag. Punch holes in the bag for ventilation, label it, and put the herb bunch into the bag before you tie a string around the top of the bag. The average drying time is 1 to 3 weeks.

Window Screen Method

Set a clean window screen on bricks or cinder blocks in a dry, well-ventilated area out of direct sunlight. Lay fresh herbs on the screen. Turn the herbs every few days while they dry; check for mold, too. Remove any diseased pieces.

IN AN OVEN

Preheat the oven to 140°F. Place a layer of cheese-cloth on a cookie sheet to prevent the herbs from reacting to the metal and affecting the flavor. Arrange the herbs in a single layer and put the sheet into the oven. Prop open the oven door. Check every 15 minutes or so for doneness and turn the herbs as needed. Average drying time is 2 to 4 hours.

IN AN ELECTRIC FOOD DEHYDRATOR

Lay the herbs in a single layer, not touching each other, on the dehydrator trays. Follow the manufacturer's directions about the temperature setting. Most herbs will dry in 1 to 4 hours.

IN A MICROWAVE

This method is better for small quantities, such as a cup or two at a time. Arrange a single layer of herbs between two paper towels and put them in the microwave for 1 to 2 minutes on high power. Let the leaves cool. If they are not dry, reheat for 30 seconds and check again. Repeat as needed. Let cool. Do not overcook, or the herbs will lose their flavor.

Weights, Measures, and Equivalents

COMMON HOUSEHOLD MEASURES

3 teaspoons = 1 tablespoon
16 tablespoons = 1 cup
1 cup = 8 ounces
2 cups = 1 pint
2 pints = 1 quart
4 quarts = 1 gallon

METRIC CONVERSIONS

½ teaspoon = 2 mL
1 teaspoon = 5 mL
1 tablespoon = 15 mL
¼ cup = 60 mL
⅓ cup = 75 mL
½ cup = 125 mL
⅔ cup = 150 mL
¾ cup = 175 mL
1 cup = 250 mL
1 liter = 1.057 U.S. liquid quarts
1 U.S. liquid quart = 0.946 liter
1 U.S. liquid gallon = 3.78 liters
1 gram = 0.035 ounce
1 ounce = 28.349 grams
1 kilogram = 2.2 pounds
1 pound = 0.45 kilogram

TEMPERATURE CONVERSION

- **To convert Fahrenheit to Celsius, subtract 32 from the Fahrenheit number, multiply by 5, and divide by 9.**

VEGETABLE EQUIVALENTS

Asparagus: 1 pound = 3 cups chopped

Beans (string): 1 pound = 4 cups chopped

Beets: 1 pound (5 medium) = 2½ cups chopped

Broccoli: ½ pound = 6 cups chopped

Cabbage: 1 pound = 4½ cups shredded

Carrots: 1 pound = 3½ cups sliced or grated

Celery: 1 pound = 4 cups chopped

Cucumbers: 1 pound (2 medium) = 4 cups sliced

Eggplant: 1 pound = 4 cups chopped = 2 cups cooked

Garlic: 1 clove = 1 teaspoon chopped

Leeks: 1 pound = 4 cups chopped = 2 cups cooked

Mushrooms: 1 pound = 5 to 6 cups sliced = 2 cups cooked

Onions: 1 pound = 4 cups sliced = 2 cups cooked

Parsnips: 1 pound unpeeled = 1½ cups cooked, puréed

Peas: 1 pound whole = 1 to 1½ cups shelled

Potatoes: 1 pound (3 medium) sliced = 2 cups mashed

Pumpkin: 1 pound = 4 cups chopped = 2 cups cooked and drained

Spinach: 1 pound = ¾ to 1 cup cooked

Squashes (summer): 1 pound = 4 cups grated = 2 cups sliced and cooked

Squashes (winter): 2 pounds = 2½ cups cooked, puréed

Sweet potatoes: 1 pound = 4 cups grated = 1 cup cooked, puréed

Swiss chard: 1 pound = 5 to 6 cups packed leaves = 1 to 1½ cups cooked

Tomatoes: 1 pound (3 or 4 medium) = 1½ cups seeded pulp

Turnips: 1 pound = 4 cups chopped = 2 cups cooked, mashed

FRUIT EQUIVALENTS

Apples: 1 pound (3 or 4 medium) = 3 cups sliced

Bananas: 1 pound (3 or 4 medium) = 1¾ cups mashed

Berries: 1 quart = 3½ cups

Dates: 1 pound = 2½ cups pitted

Lemons: 1 whole = 1 to 3 tablespoons juice; 1 to 1½ teaspoons grated rind

Limes: 1 whole = 1½ to 2 tablespoons juice

Oranges: 1 medium = 6 to 8 tablespoons juice; 2 to 3 tablespoons grated rind

Peaches: 1 pound (4 medium) = 3 cups sliced

Pears: 1 pound (4 medium) = 2 cups sliced

Rhubarb: 1 pound = 2 cups cooked

Substitutions for Common Ingredients

ITEM	QUANTITY	SUBSTITUTION
Allspice	1 teaspoon	½ teaspoon cinnamon plus ⅛ teaspoon ground cloves
Arrowroot, as thickener	1½ teaspoons	1 tablespoon flour
Baking powder	1 teaspoon	¼ teaspoon baking soda plus ⅝ teaspoon cream of tartar
Bread crumbs, dry	¼ cup	1 slice bread
Bread crumbs, soft	½ cup	1 slice bread
Buttermilk	1 cup	1 cup plain yogurt
Chocolate, unsweetened	1 ounce	3 tablespoons cocoa plus 1 tablespoon butter or fat
Cracker crumbs	¾ cup	1 cup dry bread crumbs
Cream, heavy	1 cup	¾ cup milk plus ⅓ cup melted butter (this will not whip)
Cream, light	1 cup	⅞ cup milk plus 3 tablespoons melted butter
Cream, sour	1 cup	⅞ cup buttermilk or plain yogurt plus 3 tablespoons melted butter
Cream, whipping	1 cup	⅔ cup well-chilled evaporated milk, whipped; or 1 cup nonfat dry milk powder whipped with 1 cup ice water
Egg	1 whole	2 yolks
Flour, all-purpose	1 cup	1⅛ cups cake flour; or ⅝ cup potato flour; or 1¼ cups rye or coarsely ground whole grain flour; or 1 cup cornmeal
Flour, cake	1 cup	1 cup minus 2 tablespoons sifted all-purpose flour
Flour, self-rising	1 cup	1 cup all-purpose flour plus 1¼ teaspoons baking powder plus ¼ teaspoon salt
Garlic	1 small clove	⅛ teaspoon garlic powder; or ½ teaspoon instant minced garlic
Herbs, dried	½ to 1 teaspoon	1 tablespoon fresh, minced and packed
Honey	1 cup	1¼ cups sugar plus ½ cup liquid
Lemon	1	1 to 3 tablespoons juice plus 1 to 1½ teaspoons grated rind
Lemon juice	1 teaspoon	½ teaspoon vinegar
Lemon rind, grated	1 teaspoon	½ teaspoon lemon extract
Milk, skim	1 cup	⅓ cup instant nonfat dry milk plus about ¾ cup water
Milk, to sour	1 cup	Add 1 tablespoon vinegar or lemon juice to 1 cup milk minus 1 tablespoon. Stir and let stand 5 minutes.
Milk, whole	1 cup	½ cup evaporated milk plus ½ cup water; or 1 cup skim milk plus 2 teaspoons melted butter
Molasses	1 cup	1 cup honey
Mustard, prepared	1 tablespoon	1 teaspoon ground mustard
Onion, chopped	1 small	1 tablespoon instant minced onion; or 1 teaspoon onion powder; or ¼ cup frozen chopped onion
Sugar, granulated	1 cup	1 cup firmly packed brown sugar; or 1¾ cups confectioners' sugar (do not substitute in baking); or 2 cups corn syrup; or 1 cup superfine sugar
Tomatoes, canned	1 cup	½ cup tomato sauce plus ½ cup water; or 1⅓ cups chopped fresh tomatoes, simmered
Tomato juice	1 cup	½ cup tomato sauce plus ½ cup water plus dash each salt and sugar; or ¼ cup tomato paste plus ¾ cup water plus salt and sugar

ITEM	QUANTITY	SUBSTITUTION
Tomato ketchup	½ cup	½ cup tomato sauce plus 2 tablespoons sugar, 1 tablespoon vinegar, and ⅛ teaspoon ground cloves
Tomato purée	1 cup	½ cup tomato paste plus ½ cup water
Tomato soup	1 can (10¾ ounces)	1 cup tomato sauce plus ¼ cup water
Vanilla	1-inch bean	1 teaspoon vanilla extract
Yeast	1 cake (⅗ ounce)	1 package (¼ ounce) active dried yeast
Yogurt, plain	1 cup	1 cup buttermilk

Pan Sizes and Equivalents

One pan size can be substituted for another, but the cooking time may change. For example, if a recipe calls for using an 8-inch round cake pan and baking for 25 minutes, and a 9-inch pan is used, the cake may bake in only 20 minutes because the batter forms a thinner layer in the larger pan.

Also, specialty pans such as tube and Bundt pans distribute heat differently. Results may vary if a regular cake pan is substituted for a specialty one, even if the volume is the same. Here's a plan for those times when the correct-size pan is unavailable:

PAN SIZE	VOLUME	PAN SUBSTITUTE
9x1¼-inch pie pan	4 cups	8x1½-inch round cake pan
8½x4½x2½-inch loaf pan	6 cups	Four 5x2¼x2-inch loaf pans 11x7x2-inch cake pan
9x5x3-inch loaf pan	8 cups	8x8x2-inch cake pan 9x2-inch round cake pan
15½x10½x1-inch jelly-roll pan	10 cups	9x9x2-inch cake pan Two 8x2-inch round cake pans 9x2½-inch springform pan
10x3½-inch Bundt pan	12 cups	Two 8½x4½x2½-inch loaf pans 9x3-inch tube pan 9x3-inch springform pan
13x9x2-inch cake pan	14 to 15 cups	Two 9x2-inch round cake pans Two 8x8x2-inch cake pans

■ If the correct-size casserole is unavailable, substitute a baking pan. Again, think about the depth of the ingredients in the dish and lengthen or shorten the baking time accordingly.

CASSEROLE SIZE	VOLUME	PAN SUBSTITUTE
1½ quarts	6 cups	8½x4½x2½-inch loaf pan
2 quarts	8 cups	8x8x2-inch cake pan
2½ quarts	10 cups	9x9x2-inch cake pan
3 quarts	12 cups	13x9x2-inch cake pan
4 quarts	16 cups	14x10x2-inch cake pan

Sources

These are a sampling of mail-order companies that offer seeds, plants, and products to help you garden. For more choices, check local nurseries or online.

W. Atlee Burpee & Co.
300 Park Ave.
Warminster, PA 18974
800-333-5808
www.burpee.com

The Cook's Garden
P.O. Box C5030
Warminster, PA 18974
800-457-9703
www.cooksgarden.com

Dominion Seed House
P.O. Box 2500
Georgetown, ON L7G 5L6
800-784-3037
www.dominion-seed-house.com

Ferry-Morse Seed Company
601 Stephen Beale Dr.
Fulton, KY 42041
800-626-3392
www.ferry-morse.com

Gardener's Supply Company
128 Intervale Rd.
Burlington, VT 05401
888-833-1412
www.gardeners.com

Gardens Alive!
5100 Schenley Pl.
Lawrenceburg, IN 47025
513-354-1482
www.gardensalive.com

Henry Field's Seed and
    Nursery Co.
P.O. Box 397
Aurora, IN 47001
513-354-1494
www.henryfields.com

Johnny's Selected Seeds
955 Benton Ave.
Winslow, ME 04901
877-564-6697
www.johnnyseeds.com

J.W. Jung Seed Co.
335 S. High St.
Randolph, WI 53956
800-297-3123
www.jungseed.com

McFayden Seed Co.
1000 Parker Blvd.
Brandon, MB R7A 6N4
800-205-7111
www.mcfayden.com

Park Seed Company
1 Parkton Ave.
Greenwood, SC 29647
800-213-0076
www.parkseed.com

Raintree Nursery
391 Butts Rd.
Morton, WA 98356
800-391-8892
www.raintreenursery.com

Richters Herbs
357 Hwy. 47
Goodwood, ON L0C 1A0
905-640-6677
www.richters.com

Seed Savers Exchange
3094 North Winn Rd.
Decorah, IA 52101
563-382-5990
www.seedsavers.org

Seeds of Change
3209 Richards Ln.
Santa Fe, NM 87507
888-762-7333
www.seedsofchange.com

Southern Exposure Seed
    Exchange
P.O. Box 460
Mineral, VA 23117
540-894-9480
www.southernexposure.com

Stark Bro's Nurseries &
    Orchards Co.
P.O. Box 1800
Louisiana, MO 63353
800-325-4180
www.starkbros.com

Territorial Seed Company
P.O. Box 158
Cottage Grove, OR 97424
800-626-0866
www.territorialseed.com

Thompson & Morgan
    Seedsmen, Inc.
220 Faraday Ave.
Jackson, NJ 08527
800-274-7333
www.tmseeds.com

Tomato Growers Supply
    Company
P.O. Box 60015
Fort Myers, FL 33906
888-478-7333
www.tomatogrowers.com

Veseys Seeds
P.O. Box 9000
Charlottetown, PE C1A 8K6
also: P.O. Box 9000
Calais, ME 04619
800-363-7333
www.veseys.com

West Coast Seeds
3925 64th St., RR #1
Delta, BC V4K 3N2
888-804-8820
www.westcoastseeds.com

Index

A

Acorn squash
    Apple-Stuffed Acorn Squash, 133
    Rice-Stuffed Acorn Squash, 133
Almond Chutney, Cherry, 163
Almonds, Chicken With Avocado and, 174
Appetizers, 25–35
Applejack Fish Bake, 208
Apple(s)
    Apple and Beet Salad, 79
    Apple Artichoke Soup, 39
    Apple Carrot Tzimmes, 118
    Apple Cheese Bread, 245
    Apple Cranberry Pie, 280
    Apple Crepes à la Mode, 20
    Apple Curry Soup, 40
    Apple Fritters, 22
    Apple Mint Jelly, 170
    Apple Pepper Relish, 157
    Apple Pie With Cider Pecan Crust, 278
    Apple Pudding, 268
    Apple Spiced Cheesecake, 284
    Apple Squash Pie, 280
    Apple Stuffing, 190
    Apples and Pork, 198
    Apple-Stuffed Acorn Squash, 133
    Breakfast Muffins, 250
    Cheesy Apple Squares, 286
    Crab Apple Jelly, 170
    Harvest Jelly, 172
    Maple Apple Pork Chops With Apple Rice
      Pilaf, 197
    tips for, 162, 170, 197, 281
    types of, 281
    Watermelon Apple Chutney, 165
    Zesty Apple Chutney, 162
Applesauce
    Apples and Pork, 198
    Caraway Applesauce Cookies, 286
    Indian Summer Applesauce, 231

    Rice-Stuffed Acorn Squash, 133
Apricot(s)
    Apricot Jam, 168
    Bobotie, 192
    Curried Apricot-and-Peppercorn Chutney,
      161
    tips for, 168, 192
Artichoke(s)
    Apple Artichoke Soup, 39
    grilling of, 105
    tip for, 39
Arugula
    Arugula, Egg, and Lemon Soup, 42
    Shrimp, Arugula, and Chicory Salad, 70
    tip for, 42
Asparagus
    grilling of, 105
    Roasted Asparagus, 102
    Scandinavian Asparagus Soufflé With
      Creamy Butter Sauce, 10
    Shrimp and Asparagus Crepes, 17
    Spring Risotto, 228
    tips for, 10, 17, 102
Au Gratin, Buttermilk-Blue Potatoes, 128
Aubergine, 33. *See also* Eggplant
Autumn Garden Soup, 61
Avocado(s)
    Avocado and Bacon Spread, 32
    Chicken With Avocado and Almonds, 174
    tip for, 32

B

Baby Beet Greens Salad, 79
Bacon Cheddar Potato Kugelis, 130
Bacon Spread, Avocado and, 32
Baked Beans, Savory, 108
Baked Summer Squash, 134
Barbecue Marinade, Watermelon, 235
Barbecue Sauce, 235
Barbecued Beef, 193
Basic Crepes, 16

Basil
  Basil Rice, 223
  Basil Torta, 26
  Fruit Salsa With Thai Basil, 238
  Peach Basil Iced Tea, 303
  Spinach, Basil, and Walnut Soup, 63
  tips for, 27, 36
Basket (Watermelon) With Honey Lime
  Dressing, 21
Bean(s) (dried)
  Bean Salad With Lovage, 78
  Bean Salad With Summer Savory, 74
  Black Bean Dip, 35
  Black Bean Soup With Grapefruit, 45
  defined, 107
  drying, 108
  Frijoles Rio Grande, 107
  Hearty Kale, Bean, and Zucchini Soup, 51
  Lamb and Bean Soup, 44
  Layered Bean and Tomato Dip, 35
  measurement conversions, 44
  Plymouth Succotash, 106
  Portuguese Bean Soup, 50
  Savory Baked Beans, 108
  soaking, 44
  tips for, 103, 104, 107
  White Bean and Tuna Salad, 77
Bean(s) (green and wax)
  Bombay Beans, 104
  defined, 74 (wax), 75 (green), 155 (wax)
  Dilly Beans, 155
  Green Bean and Cauliflower Salad, 75
  Green Beans in Sour Cream, 103
  Green Beans Piccata, 73
  Green Beans With Mushrooms and Potatoes,
   103
  Lamb and Bean Soup, 44
  String Bean Pickles, 156
  Sweet-and-Sour Bean Salad, 74
  Sweet-and-Sour Wax Beans, 155
  tips for, 99, 104
  Yellow Beans With Fresh Dill, 80
Bean(s) (lima)
  butter beans vs., 155
  Lima Bean Salad, 80
  Lima Bean Timbales, 106
  tip for, 80

Béarnaise Sauce, 232, 233
Beef
  Barbecued Beef, 193
  Beef Provence Pie, 195
  Bobotie, 192
  Cranberry Beef, 192
  Cubaña Pie, 196
  Plymouth Succotash, 106
  Seven-Layer Dinner, 194
  Vegetable Beef Casserole, 194
  Winter Vegetable Beef Stew, 66
Beet(s)
  Apple and Beet Salad, 79
  Baby Beet Greens Salad, 79
  Beet, Egg, and Herring Salad, 82
  boiling, 82
  Harvard Beets, 109
  Harvard beets, defined, 109
  tips for, 88, 99
Berries in Grand Marnier Syrup, Fancy Crepes
  With, 19
Berry garden, 294–295
Berry Torte, Chocolate, 292
Best Fruit Muffins, The, 248
Beverages, 296–303
Biscuits, 254
Black Bean Dip, 35
Black Bean Soup With Grapefruit, 45
Blackberries, tip for, 295
Blanching, greens and, 122
Blueberry(ies)
  Blueberry Butter, 166
  Blueberry Conserve, 167
  Blueberry Pancakes, 23
  Blueberry Slog, 267
  Blueberry–Maple Walnut Bread, 246
  Chilled Blueberry Soup, 42
  Granny's Blueberry Muffins, 254
  Squash and Blueberry Muffins, 250
  tips for, 23, 294
Bobotie, 192
Bombay Beans, 104
Borage (Melon, Ginger, and) Drink, 300
Bourbon, Hot Potato Salad With, 95
Braised Chicken Breasts With Raspberry
  Sauce, 179
Bread(s), 245–260

Breakfast Muffins, 250
Broccoflower, fact about, 89
Broccoli
    broccoflower and, 89
    Broccoli Quiche, 16
    Broccoli Soup, 50
    Cheesy Stuffed Potato Skins With Broccoli, 27
    Royal Broccoli Casserole, 109
    tips for, 16, 50
Broiled Swordfish Kabobs, 206
Brown Rice Salad, Orange–, 226
Brown Rice Soup, Lentil and, 54
Brunswick Chicken Pie, 180
Brussels sprouts, tip for, 110
Brussels Sprouts With Sun-Dried Tomatoes, 110
Bubble and Squeak, 112
Burnet, salad, tip for, 93
Burnet (Salad), Coleslaw With, 93
Butter beans, lima beans vs., 155
Buttermilk-Blue Potatoes Au Gratin, 128
Butternut Squash Soup, Vermont, 47
Butters
    Blueberry Butter, 166
    Horseradish Butter, 241
    Pear Butter, 166
    Spiced Grape Butter, 166

C

Cabbage. *See also* Coleslaw(s); Sauerkraut
    Bubble and Squeak, 112
    Chinese Cabbage Soup, 48
    Farmer's Cabbage With White Sauce, 115
    Peel-a-Pound Cabbage Soup, 48
    tips for, 99, 112, 180
Cabbageworms, 50, 99, 180
Cacciatore, Turkey, 185
Cakes (dessert). *See also* Cheesecakes
    Chocolate Berry Torte, 292
    Fresh Tomato Cake With Cream Cheese Frosting, 290
    Hawaiian Carrot Cake With Coconut Frosting, 291
    Raspberry Honey Cake With Raspberry Sauce, 288
    tip for, 291

Cakes (savory)
    Dill and Potato Cakes, 131
    Parsnip Griddle Cakes, 24
Calendulas
    Confetti Salad With Calendula Petals, 91
    tips for, 91, 242
Calming Chamomile Tea, 303
Candied Flowers, 243
Canning and preserving, 143, 150–153
Cantaloupe and Cucumber Salad, 86
Cantaloupe and Peach Conserve, 168
Capers, Nasturtium, 159
Caponata With English Muffin Melbas, 33
Caraway
    Caraway and Tarragon Potatoes, 125
    Caraway Applesauce Cookies, 286
    Caraway Cheese Biscuits, 254
    Ruby Coleslaw With Caraway Dressing, 92
Carnations, tip for, 242
Carrot(s)
    Apple Carrot Tzimmes, 118
    Carrot Salad, 72
    Carrots Baked With Rice, 225
    Carrots Excelsior, 116
    Carrots With Grapes, 119
    Cinnamon Carrots, 118
    Curried Carrots, 118
    Hawaiian Carrot Cake With Coconut Frosting, 291
    Snow Pea and Carrot Salad, 73
    tips for, 66, 72, 99, 119
Cashews, Chicken Salad With, 183
Casseroles
    Cauliflower Casserole, 116
    Chile Cheese Casserole, 11
    German Potato Casserole, 131
    Royal Broccoli Casserole, 109
    Sweet Potato and Pineapple Casserole, 139
    Sweet Potato Casserole With Sausage, 198
    Vegetable Beef Casserole, 194
    Zucchini Casserole, 135
Cauliflower
    broccoflower and, 89
    Cauliflower Casserole, 116
    Green Bean and Cauliflower Salad, 75
    tip for, 50

Celery
  Celery Stuffing, 189
  Far East Celery, 114
  tip for, 55
Chamomile, tip for, 303
Chamomile Tea, Calming, 303
Chard, Swiss, tip for, 99
Chasseur, Chicken, 175
Cheddar (Bacon) Potato Kugelis, 130
Cheddar Eggplant, 120
Cheese. *See also* Cream cheese; Feta cheese
  Apple Cheese Bread, 245
  Bacon Cheddar Potato Kugelis, 130
  Buttermilk-Blue Potatoes Au Gratin, 128
  Caraway Cheese Biscuits, 254
  Cheddar Eggplant, 120
  Cheese Herb Biscuits, 254
  Cheese Soufflé in a Tomato, 140
  Cheesy Apple Squares, 286
  Cheesy Corn Creole, 114
  Cheesy Stuffed Potato Skins With Broccoli, 27
  Cherry Cheese Pie, 275
  Chile Cheese Casserole, 11
  Fennel and Parmesan Gratin, 120
  Shrimp in Prosciutto al Formaggio, 213
  tip for, 28
  Turkey With Cheese Sauce, 185
  Vegetable Cheese Bake, 142
Cheesecakes
  Apple Spiced Cheesecake, 284
  Cranberry-Crowned Pumpkin Cheesecake, 282
  Fresh Rhubarb Cheesecake, 283
Cherry(ies)
  Cherry Almond Chutney, 163
  Cherry Cheese Pie, 275
  Cherry-Raspberry Conserve, 164
  tip for, 163
Chervil, tip for, 49
Chervil Soup, Cucumber, 49
Chicken. *See also* Chicken salads
  Apple Curry Soup, 40
  Braised Chicken Breasts With Raspberry Sauce, 179
  Brunswick Chicken Pie, 180

Chicken Chasseur, 175
Chicken Oyster Pie, 214
Chicken Quiche, 14
Chicken With Avocado and Almonds, 174
Chicken With Rice, 178
Chicken-Stuffed Tomatoes, 181
Cock-a-leekie Pie, 182
East Indian Spaghetti, 221
Plymouth Succotash, 106
Poached Chicken With Niçoise Sauce, 179
poaching, 174
Roasted Lemon-Balm Chicken, 175
Rosemary Chicken With Spinach, 176
Skillet Chicken With Fresh Tomatoes, 181
Spinach and Chicken Soup, 64
Thai Chicken With Linguine, 218
Chicken salads
  Chicken Noodle Salad, 184
  Chicken Salad With Cashews, 183
  Marinated Chicken Salad, 183
Chickpeas, how to sprout, 29
Chicory
  Sautéed Chicory Greens, 123
  Shrimp, Arugula, and Chicory Salad, 70
  tip for, 70
Chiffon Pie, Pumpkin, 277
Chile Cheese Casserole, 11
Chili vs. chile, 260
Chilled Blueberry Soup, 42
Chiller, Mint, 302
Chinese Cabbage Soup, 48
Chive(s)
  Chive Mustard, 240
  Dill and Chive Biscuits, 254
  tips for, 36, 240
Chocolate Berry Torte, 292
Chocolate leaves, how to make, 293
Chowder, Potato, 59
Chowder, Turkey and Potato, 68
Chutneys, 161–165
Cider Pecan Crust, Apple Pie With, 278
Cilantro
  Cilantro and Mint Sauce, 241
  fact about, 12
  tip for, 36
Cinnamon Carrots, 118

Clams (Steamed) and Spanish Sausage, 211
Classic Gazpacho, 52
Clove Pinks, Fettuccine With Mushrooms and, 217
Clove pinks, tip for, 242
Cloves, defined, 96 (garlic), 223 (shallot)
Cock-a-leekie Pie, 182
Coconut, tip for, 221
Coconut Frosting, Hawaiian Carrot Cake With, 291
Cold Strawberry Soup, 41
Coleslaw(s)
    Coleslaw With Salad Burnet, 93
    Lobster Seaslaw Salad, 71
    Ruby Coleslaw With Caraway Dressing, 92
    Slaw With Shrimp and Creamy Horseradish Dressing, 94
Condiments. *See* Sauces and condiments
Confetti Rice Salad, 226
Confetti Salad With Calendula Petals, 91
Conserves, 164, 167, 168
Container gardening, 113
Cookies
    Caraway Applesauce Cookies, 286
    Cheesy Apple Squares, 286
    Cranberry Cookies, 285
    Pumpkin Cookies, 285
    tips for, 287
Coriander, tip for, 36
Corn
    Cheesy Corn Creole, 114
    Corn Bread With Pine Nuts and Rosemary, 256
    Corn Relish, 157
    grilling of, 105
    tips for, 114, 157
Crab Apple Jelly, 170
Crabmeat Omelet, 12
Cranberry(ies)
    Apple Cranberry Pie, 280
    Cranberry Beef, 192
    Cranberry Cookies, 285
    Cranberry Jelly, 231
    Cranberry Pears, 271
    Cranberry Sauce, 231
    Cranberry Soup, 41
    Cranberry-Crowned Pumpkin Cheesecake, 282

    facts about, 231
    Sour Cream Cranberry Rye Bread, 259
Cream, Sherried Shellfish With Leeks and, 212
Cream Cheese Frosting, Fresh Tomato Cake With, 290
Cream of Fiddleheads Soup, 51
Cream of Onion Soup, 57
Creamed Spinach, Scrambled Eggs With, 11
Creamy Butter Sauce, Scandinavian Asparagus Soufflé With, 10
Creamy Horseradish Dressing, Slaw With Shrimp and, 94
Creamy Spinach Feta Rice, Shrimp and, 210
Creole, Cheesy Corn, 114
Creole, Shrimp, 213
Crepes
    Apple Crepes à la Mode, 20
    Basic Crepes, 16
    Fancy Crepes With Berries in Grand Marnier Syrup, 19
    Shrimp and Asparagus Crepes, 17
Crostada, 13
Crunchy Pear Salad, 85
Crusts (pie). *See* Piecrusts
Cubaña Pie, 196
Cucumber(s)
    Cantaloupe and Cucumber Salad, 86
    Cucumber Chervil Soup, 49
    Cucumber Sauce, 232
    Cucumbers With Feta Cheese Dressing, 84
    Sweet Refrigerator Pickles, 154
    tips for, 84, 154
    Turkey-Stuffed Cucumbers, 187
Curry
    Apple Curry Soup, 40
    Curried Apricot-and-Peppercorn Chutney, 161
    Curried Carrots, 118
    Curried Pattypan Soup, 58
    Curry Mayonnaise, 240
    Curry powder, 40
Custard Pie, Pear, 277

D

Desserts, 261–293
Dill
    Dill and Chive Biscuits, 254
    Dill and Potato Cakes, 131

Dill Bread, 259
Dilly Beans, 155
Lemon Dill Rice, 224
Spinach Fettuccine With Smoked Salmon
    and Dill, 220
tips for, 36, 226, 234
Yellow Beans With Fresh Dill, 80
Dips, 29, 32–35
Dressings, 97. *See also* Salads; Vinaigrette
Cucumbers With Feta Cheese Dressing, 84
Ruby Coleslaw With Caraway Dressing, 92
Slaw With Shrimp and Creamy Horseradish
    Dressing, 94
Watermelon Basket With Honey Lime
    Dressing, 21
Drinks, 296–303
Drying beans, tip for, 108
Drying grapes, tip for, 290
Drying tomatoes, tips for, 141, 143
Duck With Turnips, 188

E

East Indian Spaghetti, 221
Easy Greens Pie, 122
Edible flowers. *See* Flowers, edible
Eggplant
Caponata With English Muffin Melbas, 33
Cheddar Eggplant, 120
Eggplant Dip, 34
Eggplant Stuffing, 189
fact about, 33
grilling of, 105
tip for, 187
Turkey-Stuffed Eggplant, 187
Egg(s). *See also* Crepes; Quiches; Soufflés
Arugula, Egg, and Lemon Soup, 42
Beet, Egg, and Herring Salad, 82
Crabmeat Omelet, 12
Pepper Eggs and Tortillas, 12
Scrambled Eggs With Creamed Spinach, 11
End-of-the-Garden Relish, 158
English Muffin Melbas, Caponata With, 33
Excelsior, Carrots, 116

F

Fancy Crepes With Berries in Grand Marnier
    Syrup, 19

Far East Celery, 114
Farmer's Cabbage With White Sauce, 115
Fennel
Fennel and Parmesan Gratin, 120
grilling of, 105
Peach Preserves With Fennel, 159
tips for, 120, 159
Feta cheese
Cucumbers With Feta Cheese Dressing, 84
Eggplant Dip, 34
Greek-Style Roast Lamb, 200
Kale With Feta and Olives, 123
Mediterranean Orzo, 217
Shrimp and Creamy Spinach Feta Rice, 210
Spinach Pie, 124
Watermelon Salad, 92
Fettuccine (Spinach) With Smoked Salmon and
Dill, 220
Fettuccine With Mushrooms and Clove Pinks,
217
Fiddleheads
Cream of Fiddleheads Soup, 51
Spring Fiddleheads, 121
tip for, 121
Filo dough. *See* Phyllo dough
Fish and seafood. *See also* Salmon; Shrimp
Applejack Fish Bake, 208
Beet, Egg, and Herring Salad, 82
Broiled Swordfish Kabobs, 206
Chicken Oyster Pie, 214
Crabmeat Omelet, 12
Flounder Fillets With Mushroom Sauce, 204
Flounder With Mint Lime Sauce, 205
Lobster Seaslaw Salad, 71
Mexican-Style Red Snapper, 206
Portuguese Skillet Haddock, 205
Sherried Shellfish With Leeks and Cream,
    212
Skillet Sea Scallops, 214
Steamed Clams and Spanish Sausage, 211
tips for, 205, 208
White Bean and Tuna Salad, 77
White Fish With Lemongrass Marinade,
    209
Flounder Fillets With Mushroom Sauce, 204
Flounder With Mint Lime Sauce, 205

Flowers, edible
    Candied Flowers, 243
    Confetti Salad With Calendula Petals, 91
    Fettuccine With Mushrooms and Clove
      Pinks, 217
    Fruit Salad With Pineapple Sage, 22
    garden, 242–243
    lavender, 255
    Lavender Scones, 255
    Nasturtium and Shrimp Salad Appetizer, 30
    Nasturtium Capers, 159
French Strawberry Pie, 274
Fresh Fruit Kabobs, Grilled, 269
Fresh Raspberry Muffins, 251
Fresh Rhubarb Cheesecake, 283
Fresh Tomato Cake With Cream Cheese
  Frosting, 290
Fresh Tomato Soup, 65
Fresh Tomatoes, Skillet Chicken With, 181
Frijoles Rio Grande, 107
Fritters, Apple, 22
Frost, 98, 99
Frosting (Coconut), Hawaiian Carrot Cake
  With, 291
Frosting (Cream Cheese), Fresh Tomato Cake
  With, 290
Fruit. *See also* Fruit salads; *specific fruit*
    The Best Fruit Muffins, 248
    canning, preserving and, 150–153
    choosing, 22
    Fruit Salsa With Thai Basil, 238
    Grilled Fresh Fruit Kabobs, 269
    juice from, 275, 299, 301
    Minted Fruit Mold, 265
    Mixed Fruit Jam, 169
    tip for, 284
    trees and, 268
Fruit salads
    Fruit Salad, 20
    Fruit Salad With Pineapple Sage, 22
    Watermelon Basket With Honey Lime
      Dressing, 21

G

Garden Dip, 34
Garden (End-of-the-) Relish, 158
Garden Relish, 156

Garden Soup, Autumn, 61
Gardens
    berry, 294–295
    container, 113
    edible flower, 242–243
    fruit trees and, 268
    herbs in a bag, 178
    herbs in a window box, 176
    kitchen herb, 36–37
    vegetable, 98–99
    water and, 130
Garlic
    Garlic Potato Soufflé, 127
    Roasted Garlic Bulbs, 29
    tips for, 96, 195
Gazpacho, Classic, 52
German Potato Casserole, 131
Ginger
    Ginger Lemonade, 299
    Ginger Peach Pie, 276
    Ginger Splash, 300
    Gingersnap Crust, 273
    Melon, Ginger, and Borage Drink, 300
    Pear Bread With Ginger, 246
    Red Potatoes With Lemon Ginger
      Vinaigrette, 125
    tip for, 300
Gingersnap Crust, 273
Glaze, Peachy, 236
Golden Onion Bake, 132
Graham Cracker Crust, 273
Grand Marnier Syrup, Fancy Crepes With
  Berries in, 19
Granny's Blueberry Muffins, 254
Granola With Sunflower Seeds, 9
Grapefruit, Black Bean Soup With, 45
Grape(s)
    Carrots With Grapes, 119
    Grape Jelly, 171
    Grape Pie, 275
    Harvest Jelly, 172
    Spiced Grape Butter, 166
    tips for, 171, 290
    Turkey and Grape Salad, 184
Greek Rice Salad, 227
Greek-Style Roast Lamb, 200

Green bean(s). *See also* Beans (green and wax)
    Green Bean and Cauliflower Salad, 75
    Green Beans in Sour Cream, 103
    Green Beans Piccata, 73
    Green Beans With Mushrooms and Potatoes, 103
Green Goddess Dressing, 97
Green-Pear Chutney, Spiced, 164
Green-Pepper Jelly, Sweet, 172
Greens. *See also* Salads; *specific greens*
    Baby Beet Greens Salad, 79
    blanching, 122
    Easy Greens Pie, 122
    mesclun, 91
    Sautéed Chicory Greens, 123
    tip for, 71
Griddle Cakes, Parsnip, 24
Grilled Fresh Fruit Kabobs, 269
Grilling, kabobs and. *See* Kabobs
Grilling, vegetables and, 105

H

Haddock, Portuguese Skillet, 205
Ham
    Black Bean Soup With Grapefruit, 45
    Cock-a-leekie Pie, 182
    East Indian Spaghetti, 221
    Frijoles Rio Grande, 107
    Lima Bean Salad, 80
    Portuguese Bean Soup, 50
Harvard beets
    defined, 109
    recipe for, 109
Harvest Jelly, 172
Hash, Vegetable, 148
Hawaiian Carrot Cake With Coconut Frosting, 291
Hearty Kale, Bean, and Zucchini Soup, 51
Herbs. *See also specific herbs*
    Cheese Herb Biscuits, 254
    fresh vs. dried, 37
    gardening and, 36–37
    Herb Marinade, 237
    Herbed Popovers, 256
    Sour Cream Herb Sauce, 234
    tips for, 49, 176, 178
Herring (Beet, Egg, and) Salad, 82

Honey Cake (Raspberry) With Raspberry Sauce, 288
Honey Lime Dressing, Watermelon Basket With, 21
Horseradish
    fact about, 94
    Horseradish Butter, 241
    Root Vegetable Salad, 88
    Slaw With Shrimp and Creamy Horseradish Dressing, 94
    tip for, 241
Hot Potato Salad With Bourbon, 95
Hot-Pepper Bread, Mexican, 260
Hummus, 29

I

Iced Tea, Peach Basil, 303
Indian Summer Applesauce, 231
Italian Vegetable Popover Pizza, 145
Italian Zucchini Crescent Pie, 136

J

Jams and jellies, 168–172, 231. *See also* Conserves; Marmalade

K

Kabobs, Broiled Swordfish, 206
Kabobs, Grilled Fresh Fruit, 269
Kale (Hearty), Bean, and Zucchini Soup, 51
Kale With Feta and Olives, 123
Kielbasa Squares, Regal, 202
Kitchen herb garden, 36–37
Kugelis, Bacon Cheddar Potato, 130

L

Lamb
    Greek-Style Roast Lamb, 200
    Lamb and Bean Soup, 44
    Lamb and Rice Salad With Fresh Mint, 228
    Lamb Shanks With Vegetables, 200
    Moussaka Soup, 56
Lasagna, Pesto, 220
Lasagna, Vegetable, 219
Lavender, tip for, 255
Lavender Scones, 255
Layered Bean and Tomato Dip, 35
Leaves, chocolate, how to make, 293

Leeks
  Cock-a-leekie Pie, 182
  grilling of, 105
  Sherried Shellfish With Leeks and Cream, 212
  tip for, 182
Lemon balm, tip for, 175
Lemon-Balm Chicken, Roasted, 175
Lemonade, Ginger, 299
Lemonade, Strawberry, 299
Lemon(s)
  Arugula, Egg, and Lemon Soup, 42
  Lemon Dill Rice, 224
  Lemon Marinade, 237
  Red Potatoes With Lemon Ginger
    Vinaigrette, 125
  tips for, 275, 299
Lemongrass Marinade, White Fish With, 209
Lentil and Brown Rice Soup, 54
Lentils, tip for, 54
Lettuce, tips for, 77, 99
Lima Bean Salad, 80
Lima Bean Timbales, 106
Lima beans. *See* Beans (lima)
Lime (Honey) Dressing, Watermelon Basket
  With, 21
Lime (Mint) Sauce, Flounder With, 205
Linguine, Thai Chicken With, 218
Lobster Seaslaw Salad, 71
Lovage, Bean Salad With, 78
Lovage, tip for, 78

M

Main Dish Minestrone, 55
Mango Smoothie, Mint, 302
Maple
  Blueberry–Maple Walnut Bread, 246
  Maple Apple Pork Chops With Apple Rice
    Pilaf, 197
  Maple Squash Soufflé, 134
  Maple syrup grades, 24
Marbled Rhubarb Orange Bread, 247
Marigolds, pot. *See* Calendulas
Marigolds, tip for, 98
Marinades
  Barbecue Sauce, 235
  Herb Marinade, 237
  Lemon Marinade, 237

Orange Marinade, 237
  Watermelon Barbecue Marinade, 235
  White Fish With Lemongrass Marinade,
    209
Marinated Chicken Salad, 183
Marinated Vegetables, 89
Marjoram Mushrooms, 28
Marmalade, Watermelon, 161
Martha Washington's Potato Rolls, 258
Mayonnaise, Curry, 240
Meats, 191–202. *See also* Fish and seafood;
  Pies (meat); Poultry; *specific meats*
Mediterranean Orzo, 217
Melbas (English Muffin), Caponata With, 33
Melons. *See also* Cantaloupe, Watermelon
  Melon, Ginger, and Borage Drink, 300
Mesclun, defined, 91
Mexican Hot-Pepper Bread, 260
Mexican Quiche, 14
Mexican Rice, 224
Mexican-Style Red Snapper, 206
Milk, tips for, 59, 258
Minestrone, Main Dish, 55
Mint
  Apple Mint Jelly, 170
  Cilantro and Mint Sauce, 241
  Flounder With Mint Lime Sauce, 205
  Lamb and Rice Salad With Fresh Mint, 228
  Mint Chiller, 302
  Mint Mango Smoothie, 302
  Mint Salad Dressing, 97
  Minted Fruit Mold, 265
  Peach Mint Sauce, 236
  tips for, 37, 265, 302
Mixed Fruit Jam, 169
Mold, Minted Fruit, 265
Mom's Flaky Pastry, 272
Moussaka Soup, 56
Mousse, Strawberry, 263
Muffins, 248–254
Mushroom(s)
  Fettuccine With Mushrooms and Clove
    Pinks, 217
  Flounder Fillets With Mushroom Sauce, 204
  Green Beans With Mushrooms and Potatoes,
    103

grilling of, 105
Marjoram Mushrooms, 28
Mushroom-Tomato-Spinach Spaghetti, 223
tips for, 28
Mustard, Chive, 240
Mustard (dry), tip for, 97

N

Nasturtiums
    Nasturtium and Shrimp Salad Appetizer, 30
    Nasturtium Capers, 159
    tips for, 30, 242
New Potato Salad, 94
Niçoise Sauce, Poached Chicken With, 179
Noodle Salad, Chicken, 184
Nuts. *See specific nuts*

O

Oatmeal Muffins, Zucchini, 253
Okra
    Brunswick Chicken Pie, 180
    Spicy Stewed Okra, 147
    tip for, 147
Olives, Kale With Feta and, 123
Omelet, Crabmeat, 12
Onion(s)
    Cream of Onion Soup, 57
    Golden Onion Bake, 132
    grilling of, 105
    Orange and Onion Salad, 84
    Sweet Onion Watermelon Salsa, 238
    tips for, 85, 132
    types of, 56–57
Orange(s)
    Marbled Rhubarb Orange Bread, 247
    Orange and Onion Salad, 84
    Orange Marinade, 237
    Orange–Brown Rice Salad, 226
    Orange-Glazed Sweet Potatoes, 137
    Watermelon Marmalade, 161
Oregano, tips for, 37, 193
Oregano Salsa, Salmon With, 210
Orzo, Mediterranean, 217
Oyster (Chicken) Pie, 214

P

Pakistani Rice, 225
Pancakes
    Blueberry Pancakes, 23
    Parsnip Griddle Cakes, 24
Pansies, tip for, 242
Papayas, tip for, 269
Parmesan Gratin, Fennel and, 120
Parsley, tips for, 13, 37
Parsnip Griddle Cakes, 24
Pasta
    Chicken Noodle Salad, 184
    East Indian Spaghetti, 221
    Fettuccine With Mushrooms and Clove Pinks, 217
    Mediterranean Orzo, 217
    Mushroom-Tomato-Spinach Spaghetti, 223
    Pesto Lasagna, 220
    Spaghetti Salad, 227
    Spinach Fettuccine With Smoked Salmon and Dill, 220
    Summertime Pasta, 218
    Thai Chicken With Linguine, 218
    tips for, 222
    Vegetable Lasagna, 219
Pastry, Mom's Flaky, 272
Pattypan Soup, Curried, 58
Pea (Snow) and Carrot Salad, 73
Peach(es)
    Cantaloupe and Peach Conserve, 168
    Ginger Peach Pie, 276
    Peach Basil Iced Tea, 303
    Peach Mint Sauce, 236
    Peach Preserves With Fennel, 159
    Peachy Glaze, 236
    Praline Peach Pie, 276
    Spiced Peach Shake, 297
    tip for, 236
Peanut Sauce, 234
Pear(s)
    Cranberry Pears, 271
    Crunchy Pear Salad, 85
    Pear Bread With Ginger, 246
    Pear Butter, 166
    Pear Custard Pie, 277
    Spiced Green-Pear Chutney, 164

Peas, tip for, 224
Pecan(s)
    Apple Pie With Cider Pecan Crust, 278
    Praline Peach Pie, 276
    Sweet Potato and Pecan Muffins, 253
    tip for, 278
Pectin, jams and jellies and, 169
Peel and seed a tomato, how to, 65
Peel-a-Pound Cabbage Soup, 48
Peppercorn Chutney, Curried Apricot-and-, 161
Peppers
    Apple Pepper Relish, 157
    Chile Cheese Casserole, 11
    chili vs. chile, 260
    grilling of, 105
    Mexican Hot-Pepper Bread, 260
    Pepper Eggs and Tortillas, 12
    roasting, 146
    Scoville heat units of, 52
    Sweet Green-Pepper Jelly, 172
    tips for, 52, 99, 142
Perfect Pumpkin Soup, 58
Pesto Lasagna, 220
Phyllo dough
    Regal Kielbasa Squares, 202
    Spinach Pie, 124
    tip for, 124
Piccata, Green Beans, 73
Pickles
    String Bean Pickles, 156
    Sweet Refrigerator Pickles, 154
    tips for, 153, 154
Piecrusts
    Apple Pie With Cider Pecan Crust, 278
    Gingersnap Crust, 273
    Graham Cracker Crust, 273
    Mom's Flaky Pastry, 272
Pies (dessert)
    Apple Cranberry Pie, 280
    Apple Pie With Cider Pecan Crust, 278
    Apple Squash Pie, 280
    Cherry Cheese Pie, 275
    French Strawberry Pie, 274
    Ginger Peach Pie, 276
    Grape Pie, 275
    Pear Custard Pie, 277

    Praline Peach Pie, 276
    Pumpkin Chiffon Pie, 277
    Rhubarb Pie, 274
Pies (meat)
    Beef Provence Pie, 195
    Brunswick Chicken Pie, 180
    Chicken Oyster Pie, 214
    Cock-a-leekie Pie, 182
    Crostada, 13
    Cubaña Pie, 196
    Shepherd's Pie, 201
Pies (seafood)
    Chicken Oyster Pie, 214
Pies (vegetable)
    Easy Greens Pie, 122
    Italian Zucchini Crescent Pie, 136
    Ratatouille Pie, 146
    Spinach Pie, 124
Pine Nuts and Rosemary, Corn Bread With, 256
Pineapple
    Mixed Fruit Jam, 169
    Sweet Potato and Pineapple Casserole, 139
Pineapple Sage, Fruit Salad With, 22
Pineapple sage, tip for, 243
Pizza, Italian Vegetable Popover, 145
Pizza Salad, 96
Plymouth Succotash, 106
Poached Chicken With Niçoise Sauce, 179
Popover Pizza, Italian Vegetable, 145
Popovers, Herbed, 256
Pork
    Apples and Pork, 198
    Bobotie, 192
    Chinese Cabbage Soup, 48
    Frijoles Rio Grande, 107
    Maple Apple Pork Chops With Apple Rice Pilaf, 197
    Savory Baked Beans, 108
    Sweet-and-Sour Pork, 196
Portuguese Bean Soup, 50
Portuguese Skillet Haddock, 205
Pot marigolds. *See* Calendulas
Potato salads
    Hot Potato Salad With Bourbon, 95
    New Potato Salad, 94

Potato(es). *See also* Potato salads; Sweet
  potato(es)
    Bacon Cheddar Potato Kugelis, 130
    Bubble and Squeak, 112
    Buttermilk-Blue Potatoes Au Gratin, 128
    Caraway and Tarragon Potatoes, 125
    Cheesy Stuffed Potato Skins With Broccoli, 27
    Dill and Potato Cakes, 131
    Garlic Potato Soufflé, 127
    German Potato Casserole, 131
    Green Beans With Mushrooms and Potatoes,
      103
    Martha Washington's Potato Rolls, 258
    Potato Chowder, 59
    Potato Walnut Stuffing, 190
    Red Potatoes With Lemon Ginger
      Vinaigrette, 125
    Shepherd's Pie, 201
    tips for, 59, 95
    Turkey and Potato Chowder, 68
    types of, 126–27, 130
    Vichyssoise (Potato Soup), 67
    Zucchini Potato Soup, 68
Poultry, 173–190. *See also* Chicken; Duck;
  Turkey
Praline Peach Pie, 276
Preserves (Peach) With Fennel, 159
Preserving. *See* Canning and preserving
Prosciutto al Formaggio, Shrimp in, 213
Provençal, Zucchini, 136
Puddings
    Apple Pudding, 268
    Blueberry Slog, 267
    Minted Fruit Mold, 265
    Strawberry Mousse, 263
    Summer Pudding, 266
Pumpkin
    Cranberry-Crowned Pumpkin Cheesecake,
      282
    Perfect Pumpkin Soup, 58
    Pumpkin Chiffon Pie, 277
    Pumpkin Conserve, 167
    Pumpkin Cookies, 285
    Spicy Pumpkin Muffins, 252
    tips for, 252
Punch, Watermelon, 301

Q
Quiches, 14, 16

R
Radishes, tips for, 72, 99
Raspberry(ies)
    Braised Chicken Breasts With Raspberry
      Sauce, 179
    Cherry-Raspberry Conserve, 164
    Fresh Raspberry Muffins, 251
    Raspberry Honey Cake With Raspberry
      Sauce, 288
    Raspberry Shrub, 297
    tips for, 251, 294–295
Ratatouille Pie, 146
Red Potatoes With Lemon Ginger Vinaigrette,
  125
Red Snapper, Mexican-Style, 206
Regal Kielbasa Squares, 202
Relishes, 156–158
Remoulade Sauce, 233
Rhubarb
    Fresh Rhubarb Cheesecake, 283
    Marbled Rhubarb Orange Bread, 247
    Mixed Fruit Jam, 169
    Rhubarb Pie, 274
    tips for, 247, 283
Rice
    Basil Rice, 223
    Carrots Baked With Rice, 225
    Chicken With Rice, 178
    Confetti Rice Salad, 226
    Cubaña Pie, 196
    Greek Rice Salad, 227
    Lamb and Rice Salad With Fresh Mint, 228
    Lemon Dill Rice, 224
    Lentil and Brown Rice Soup, 54
    Maple Apple Pork Chops With Apple Rice
      Pilaf, 197
    Mexican Rice, 224
    Orange–Brown Rice Salad, 226
    Pakistani Rice, 225
    Pizza Salad, 96
    Rice-Stuffed Acorn Squash, 133
    Shrimp and Creamy Spinach Feta Rice, 210
    Spring Risotto, 228

Risotto, Spring, 228
Roast Lamb, Greek-Style, 200
Roasted Asparagus, 102
Roasted Garlic Bulbs, 29
Roasted Lemon-Balm Chicken, 175
Rolls (Potato), Martha Washington's, 258
Root Soup, 62
Root Vegetable Salad, 88
Rosemary
    Corn Bread With Pine Nuts and Rosemary,
      256
    fact about, 61
    Rosemary Chicken With Spinach, 176
    Sorrel Soup With Rosemary, 64
    tip for, 37
Roses, tip for, 243
Royal Broccoli Casserole, 109
Ruby Coleslaw With Caraway Dressing, 92
Rye Bread, Sour Cream Cranberry, 259

S

Sage, tip for, 37
Salad Burnet, Coleslaw With, 93
Salad burnet, tip for, 93
Salads. *See also* Chicken salads; Coleslaws;
  Dressings; Fruit salads; Potato salads
    Apple and Beet Salad, 79
    Baby Beet Greens Salad, 79
    Bean Salad With Lovage, 78
    Bean Salad With Summer Savory, 74
    Beet, Egg, and Herring Salad, 82
    Cantaloupe and Cucumber Salad, 86
    Carrot Salad, 72
    Chicken Noodle Salad, 184
    Confetti Rice Salad, 226
    Confetti Salad With Calendula Petals, 91
    Crunchy Pear Salad, 85
    Cucumbers With Feta Cheese Dressing, 84
    Greek Rice Salad, 227
    Green Bean and Cauliflower Salad, 75
    Green Beans Piccata, 73
    Lamb and Rice Salad With Fresh Mint, 228
    Lima Bean Salad, 80
    Marinated Vegetables, 89
    Nasturtium and Shrimp Salad Appetizer, 30
    Orange and Onion Salad, 84
    Orange–Brown Rice Salad, 226
    Pizza Salad, 96
    Root Vegetable Salad, 88
    Shrimp, Arugula, and Chicory Salad, 70
    Snow Pea and Carrot Salad, 73
    Sorrel Salad, 81
    Spaghetti Salad, 227
    Strawberry Spinach Salad, 86
    Sweet-and-Sour Bean Salad, 74
    Tabbouli Salad, 87
    Turkey and Grape Salad, 184
    Watermelon Salad, 92
    White Bean and Tuna Salad, 77
    Yellow Beans With Fresh Dill, 80
Salmon
    Salmon With Oregano Salsa, 210
    Saucy Salmon Loaf, 209
    Spinach Fettuccine With Smoked Salmon
      and Dill, 220
Salsa
    Fruit Salsa With Thai Basil, 238
    Salmon With Oregano Salsa, 210
    Salsa Verde, 239
    Sweet Onion Watermelon Salsa, 238
Sauces and condiments, 230–241. *See also*
  Applesauce; Butters; Dressings; Marinades;
  Salsa
    Braised Chicken Breasts With Raspberry
      Sauce, 179
    Farmer's Cabbage With White Sauce, 115
    Flounder Fillets With Mushroom Sauce, 204
    Flounder With Mint Lime Sauce, 205
    Poached Chicken With Niçoise Sauce, 179
    Raspberry Honey Cake With Raspberry
      Sauce, 288
    Saucy Salmon Loaf, 209
    Scandinavian Asparagus Soufflé With
      Creamy Butter Sauce, 10
    tomato sauce, 143
    Turkey With Cheese Sauce, 185
Saucy Salmon Loaf, 209
Sauerkraut
    how to make, 202
    Regal Kielbasa Squares, 202
    Sauerkraut Stuffing, 190
Sausage. *See also* Kielbasa
    Greek-Style Roast Lamb, 200

Main Dish Minestrone, 55
Portuguese Bean Soup, 50
Steamed Clams and Spanish Sausage, 211
Sweet Potato Casserole With Sausage, 198
Sautéed Chicory Greens, 123
Savory, summer. *See* Summer savory
Savory Baked Beans, 108
Scalding, milk and, 258
Scallions, tips for, 57, 132
Scallops, Skillet Sea, 214
Scandinavian Asparagus Soufflé With Creamy
 Butter Sauce, 10
Scones, Lavender, 255
Scrambled Eggs With Creamed Spinach, 11
Seafood. *See* Fish and seafood; Salmon;
 Shrimp
Seven-Layer Dinner, 194
Shake, Spiced Peach, 297
Shallots, tips for, 57, 223
Shellfish. *See* Fish and seafood; Shrimp
Shepherd's Pie, 201
Sherried Shellfish With Leeks and Cream, 212
Shrimp
 Nasturtium and Shrimp Salad Appetizer, 30
 Shrimp, Arugula, and Chicory Salad, 70
 Shrimp and Asparagus Crepes, 17
 Shrimp and Creamy Spinach Feta Rice, 210
 Shrimp Creole, 213
 Shrimp in Prosciutto al Formaggio, 213
 Slaw With Shrimp and Creamy Horseradish
  Dressing, 94
 tip for, 213
Shrub, Raspberry, 297
Simple syrup, how to make, 303
Skillet Chicken With Fresh Tomatoes, 181
Skillet Haddock, Portuguese, 205
Skillet Sea Scallops, 214
Slaws. *See* Coleslaw(s)
Slog, Blueberry, 267
Smoked Salmon and Dill, Spinach Fettuccine
 With, 220
Smoothie, Mint Mango, 302
Snapper, Mexican-Style Red, 206
Snow Pea and Carrot Salad, 73
Sorrel
 fact about, 81

Sorrel Salad, 81
Sorrel Soup With Rosemary, 64
 tip for, 64
Soufflés
 Cheese Soufflé in a Tomato, 140
 Garlic Potato Soufflé, 127
 Maple Squash Soufflé, 134
 Scandinavian Asparagus Soufflé With
  Creamy Butter Sauce, 10
Soups, 38–68
Sour cream
 Green Beans in Sour Cream, 103
 Sour Cream Cranberry Rye Bread, 259
 Sour Cream Herb Sauce, 234
Spaghetti
 East Indian Spaghetti, 221
 Mushroom-Tomato-Spinach Spaghetti, 223
 Spaghetti Salad, 227
Spanish Sausage, Steamed Clams and, 211
Spiced (Apple) Cheesecake, 284
Spiced Grape Butter, 166
Spiced Green-Pear Chutney, 164
Spiced Peach Shake, 297
Spicy Pumpkin Muffins, 252
Spicy Stewed Okra, 147
Spinach
 Mushroom-Tomato-Spinach Spaghetti,
  223
 Rosemary Chicken With Spinach, 176
 Scrambled Eggs With Creamed Spinach, 11
 Shepherd's Pie, 201
 Shrimp and Creamy Spinach Feta Rice,
  210
 Spinach, Basil, and Walnut Soup, 63
 Spinach and Chicken Soup, 64
 Spinach Fettuccine With Smoked Salmon
  and Dill, 220
 Spinach Pie, 124
 Strawberry Spinach Salad, 86
 tips for, 11, 63, 210
Splash, Ginger, 300
Spread, Avocado and Bacon, 32
Spring Fiddleheads, 121
Spring Risotto, 228
Squares, Cheesy Apple, 286
Squares, Regal Kielbasa, 202

Squashes. *See also* Acorn squash; Summer
    squash; Zucchini
        Apple Squash Pie, 280
        Curried Pattypan Soup, 58
        Maple Squash Soufflé, 134
        Squash and Blueberry Muffins, 250
        tips for, 47, 133, 134, 252
        Vermont Butternut Squash Soup, 47
Steamed Clams and Spanish Sausage, 211
Stew, Winter Vegetable Beef, 66
Stewed Okra, Spicy, 147
Strawberry(ies)
        Cold Strawberry Soup, 41
        fact about, 41
        French Strawberry Pie, 274
        Mixed Fruit Jam, 169
        Strawberry Crunch Muffins, 248
        Strawberry Lemonade, 299
        Strawberry Mousse, 263
        Strawberry Spinach Salad, 86
        tips for, 248, 295
String Bean Pickles, 156
Stuffed vegetables
        Apple-Stuffed Acorn Squash, 133
        Chicken-Stuffed Tomatoes, 181
        Cheesy Stuffed Potato Skins With Broccoli, 27
        Rice-Stuffed Acorn Squash, 133
        Turkey-Stuffed Cucumbers, 187
        Turkey-Stuffed Eggplant, 187
Stuffings, 189–190
Succotash, Plymouth, 106
Sugar, tips for, 152, 280
Summer (Indian) Applesauce, 231
Summer Pudding, 266
Summer savory
        Bean Salad With Summer Savory, 74
        Carrots Baked With Rice, 225
        Sweet-and-Sour Wax Beans, 155
        tip for, 225
Summer squash
        Baked Summer Squash, 134
        grilling of, 105
        tips for, 68, 99
Summertime Pasta, 218
Sun-Dried Tomatoes, Brussels Sprouts With,
    110

Sunflower Seeds, Granola With, 9
Sunflower seeds, tip for, 9
Sweet-and-Sour Bean Salad, 74
Sweet-and-Sour Pork, 196
Sweet-and-Sour Wax Beans, 155
Sweet Green-Pepper Jelly, 172
Sweet Onion Watermelon Salsa, 238
Sweet potato(es)
        defined, 62
        Orange-Glazed Sweet Potatoes, 137
        Root Soup, 62
        Sweet Potato and Pecan Muffins, 253
        Sweet Potato and Pineapple Casserole, 139
        Sweet Potato Casserole With Sausage, 198
        tips for, 137, 139
Sweet Refrigerator Pickles, 154
Sweet violets, tip for, 243
Swiss chard, tip for, 99
Swordfish Kabobs, Broiled, 206
Syrup(s)
        Fancy Crepes With Berries in Grand Marnier
            Syrup, 19
        maple syrup grades, 24
        simple syrup, how to make, 303

T

Tabbouli Salad, 87
Tarragon, tip for, 233
Tarragon Potatoes, Caraway and, 125
Teas
        Calming Chamomile Tea, 303
        Peach Basil Iced Tea, 303
Thai Basil, Fruit Salsa With, 238
Thai Chicken With Linguine, 218
Thyme, tips for, 37, 180
Timbales, Lima Bean, 106
Tomatillos, recipe using, 239
Tomatillos, tip for, 239
Tomato(es)
        Brussels Sprouts With Sun-Dried Tomatoes,
            110
        Cheese Soufflé in a Tomato, 140
        Chicken-Stuffed Tomatoes, 181
        drying, 141, 143
        freezing, 143
        Fresh Tomato Cake With Cream Cheese
            Frosting, 290

Fresh Tomato Soup, 65
Harvest Jelly, 172
Layered Bean and Tomato Dip, 35
Mushroom-Tomato-Spinach Spaghetti, 223
peeling and seeding, 65
sauce, 143
Skillet Chicken With Fresh Tomatoes, 181
tips for, 34, 99, 140, 142, 206
Torta, Basil, 26
Torta, defined, 26
Torte, Chocolate Berry, 292
Tortillas, Pepper Eggs and, 12
Toxins, 80, 121
Trussing, 188
Tuna Salad, White Bean and, 77
Turkey
    Peel-a-Pound Cabbage Soup, 48
    Turkey and Grape Salad, 184
    Turkey and Potato Chowder, 68
    Turkey Cacciatore, 185
    Turkey With Cheese Sauce, 185
    Turkey-Stuffed Cucumbers, 187
    Turkey-Stuffed Eggplant, 187
Turnip(s)
    Duck With Turnips, 188
    White Turnip Soup, 67
Tzimmes, Apple Carrot, 118

V

Veal (ground), recipe using, 201
Vegetable(s)
    canning, preserving, and 150–153
    dishes, 100–148
    garden, beginner's, 98–99
    grilling and, 105
    Italian Vegetable Popover Pizza, 145
    Lamb Shanks With Vegetables, 200
    Marinated Vegetables, 89
    Root Vegetable Salad, 88
    steaming vs. boiling, 115
    Vegetable Beef Casserole, 194
    Vegetable Cheese Bake, 142
    Vegetable Hash, 148
    Vegetable Lasagna, 219
    Winter Vegetable Beef Stew, 66
Vermont Butternut Squash Soup, 47
Vichyssoise (Potato Soup), 67

Vinaigrette, Red Potatoes With Lemon Ginger, 125
Vinegar, canning, preserving and, 152
Violets (sweet), tip for, 243
Vitamin C, tip for, 95

W

Walnut(s)
    Blueberry–Maple Walnut Bread, 246
    Potato Walnut Stuffing, 190
    Spinach, Basil, and Walnut Soup, 63
Watermelon(s)
    fact about, 21
    Sweet Onion Watermelon Salsa, 238
    tips for, 21, 165
    Watermelon Apple Chutney, 165
    Watermelon Barbecue Marinade, 235
    Watermelon Basket With Honey Lime
        Dressing, 21
    Watermelon juice, how to make, 301
    Watermelon Marmalade, 161
    Watermelon Punch, 301
    Watermelon Salad, 92
Wax beans. See Beans (green and wax)
Wax Beans, Sweet-and-Sour, 155
White Bean and Tuna Salad, 77
White Fish With Lemongrass Marinade, 209
White Sauce, Farmer's Cabbage With, 115
White Turnip Soup, 67
Winter Vegetable Beef Stew, 66
Worms, tips for, 50, 99, 180

Y

Yam, defined, 62
Yellow Beans With Fresh Dill, 80

Z

Zesty Apple Chutney, 162
Zucchini
    grilling of, 105
    Hearty Kale, Bean, and Zucchini Soup, 51
    Italian Zucchini Crescent Pie, 136
    tips for, 68, 135
    Zucchini Casserole, 135
    Zucchini Oatmeal Muffins, 253
    Zucchini Potato Soup, 68
    Zucchini Provençal, 136